THE BLACK BRUINS

The Black Bruins

THE REMARKABLE LIVES OF UCLA'S JACKIE ROBINSON, WOODY STRODE, TOM BRADLEY, KENNY WASHINGTON, AND RAY BARTLETT

JAMES W. JOHNSON

UNIVERSITY OF NEBRASKA PRESS · LINCOLN & LONDON

Library of Congress Cataloging-in-Publication Data
Names: Johnson, James W., 1938– author.
Title: The Black Bruins: The Remarkable Lives of UCLA's
Jackie Robinson, Woody Strode, Tom Bradley, Kenny
Washington, and Ray Bartlett / James W. Johnson.
Description: Lincoln: University of Nebraska Press, [2017]
| Includes bibliographical references and index.
Identifiers: LCCN 2017038821
ISBN 9781496201836 (hardback: alk. paper)
ISBN 9781496204554 (epub)
ISBN 9781496204561 (mobi)
Subjects: LCSH: African American athletes—
United States—California—Biography. | University
of California, Los Angeles—Sports—History—20th
century. | Discrimination in sports—United States—
History—20th century. | Racism in sports—United
States—History—20th century. | BISAC: SPORTS &
RECREATION / History. | SOCIAL SCIENCE / Eth-
nic Studies / African American Studies. | HISTORY /
United States / State & Local / West (AK, CA, CO, HI,
ID, MT, NV, UT, WY).
Classification: LCC GV697.A1 J65 2017 | DDC 796.0922
[B]—dc23 LC record available at https://lccn.loc.
gov/2017038821

Set in Lyon Text by Mikala R Kolander.

To my son, Thayer, of whom I am so proud.
To the many mentors whose patience is reflected in this book.

Come listen all you galls and boys
I'm going to sing a little song,
My name is Jim Crow
Weel about and turn about and do jis so,
Eb'ry time I weel about I jump Jim Crow

—From the song "Jim Crow"

CONTENTS

ACKNOWLEDGMENTS

If you are a writer, especially of long-ago sports heroes, two sources are invaluable—the Internet and the libraries. They make the writer's job so much easier. The material I gathered for this book came from a bounty of information from those two sources. While the Internet can be surfed at home, libraries have to be visited to cull out the books that pay tribute to the young stalwarts.

The Internet is invaluable because so much has been written about the subjects of this book as individuals, but the athletes have had little written about their times together. So piecemeal one puts together biographies and melds them into one story. And one looks at multiple numbers of articles and essays that can be compared against each other to arrive at an accurate picture. So Great Google in the Sky, thanks for all you contributed to this effort.

The librarians, ah, what a pleasure it is to work with them. Sure, that's their job, but when one pestered them as much as I did and they were still smiling, one can't help but feel gratitude. The librarians at the University of Arizona went out of their way to accommodate this helpless author. The photo librarians were no different. Thanks to Simon Elliott and Amy Wong at the UCLA library, Don Liebig at the school's photography department, Anuja Navare at the Pasadena Museum of History, and John Horne at the Baseball Hall of Fame, who were cooperative to a fault.

I'd be remiss if I didn't credit at least the following authors for their books, which were invaluable in my research: Arnold Rampersad (*Jackie Robinson*), Woody Strode (*Goal Dust*), and Gregory J. Payne and Scott C. Ratzan (*Tom Bradley: The Impossible Dream*).

I'm indebted as always to Rob Taylor, the sports editor at the University of Nebraska Press, who once again took a chance on one of my manuscripts. This will be the fourth book Rob has overseen, and his suggestions have been right on the nose when it came to making each book better. He is a most patient editor, given my rambling prose. Courtney Ochsner, associate acquisitions editor, kept me on task and was patient with my efforts to fathom the mysteries of the photography and who owns the rights thereto. She no doubt saved me from big trouble by assuring that the owners of picture rights gave me permission to use them. Anyone who thinks the work is over when a manuscript is submitted better think again. The work has just started. Courtney's tolerance showed even when I threw up my hands—via email—and said I had had enough. She waited that out, and we again got down to business. Bojana Ristich was a superb copy editor who sharpened the words and corrected grievous errors.

Numerous friends also supported me in this effort, particularly Jerry Guibor, a copy editor par excellence who kept me from making some serious mistakes in both grammar and facts. Jim Price also found typos that had escaped me, while Don Carson, Mark Woodhams, Ron Navarette, Mark Walker, and particularly my wife, Marilyn (who had to listen far too much and too often about the manuscript until it was sent off to Rob Taylor) expressed their enthusiasm and support for the project.

So thank you all. It's trite to say I couldn't have done it without you, but what's one trite saying (I hope!) in the whole book?

INTRODUCTION

Expectations were high at the University of California, Los Angeles, in the fall of 1939, when sixty football players turned out for practice for the coming season. The Bruins' new coach, Edwin C. "Babe" Horrell, gathered the players on a beautiful fall day on the practice field perched on a hill above Los Angeles. If the wind blew in the right direction, the sweet salty smell of the Pacific Ocean, seven miles away, wafted across the field.

UCLA's expectations were heightened not only by a new coach, but also by the return of two stars for their senior season. In addition, the Bruins welcomed two junior college All-Americans from nearby Pasadena Junior College.

The upcoming season also had an important subplot: the two seniors and two All-Americans on the sixty-player roster were African Americans. That was an unprecedented number on one team at a time when perhaps no more than thirty-eight African American players were on traditionally white football teams across the country, virtually none of whom received much playing time. Three of the black players were starters; the fourth earned plenty of playing time. "Three African American players out of eleven in the starting lineup was highly unusual for the time," says Kent Stephens, curator and historian for the College Football Hall of Fame in South Bend, Indiana. Twenty-two years later, it still wasn't common to see even two African American starters on most college football teams, Stephens notes.

The black players on the UCLA team made it the most racially integrated squad in college football history at the time. "We have yet to find another single coach in the history of football that has had the guts to play three of our race at one time and have [four] on the squad," a reporter for the *Chicago Defender*, a newspaper for black readers, wrote later in the year. Moreover, the season had started with five players; Johnny Wynne left the team but it is unclear when. The four players were Jackie Robinson, Woody Strode, Kenny Washington, and Ray Bartlett. A sixth African American, Tom Bradley, who was an all-city football player in Los Angeles, could have joined them; instead he chose to focus on track, his first love, and academics at UCLA.

The four black football players participated in multiple sports: Robinson and Bartlett played football, basketball, baseball, and track; Washington played football, baseball, and track; and Strode played football and track. "We were a tough group of dead-end kids," Strode said.

The four had a lot more in common than just the fact that they were black athletes. They were movie-star handsome and dignified. Three of them appeared in motion pictures during their careers. All of them, except Robinson, took racism against them in stride, although they didn't like it. It was what Negroes—that's what they were called then—did. Just go along to get along.

How did it come to be that these athletes chose UCLA? Mainly UCLA was trying to make its mark in athletics. Since its inception in 1919, the university had few athletic accomplishments. Just a few years earlier UCLA was playing such schools as Pomona, Occidental, and Whittier Colleges, whose teams were considered less than top-notch. Other schools, such as the University of Southern California (USC), rejected African American players. If the USC Trojans did recruit one, he often sat on the bench no matter how talented he was. As Edwin Bancroft Henderson wrote in his 1939 book *The Negro in Sports*, "Where scholarships are the means by which many a poor boy gets to and stays in college for athletics, some of the bigger scouting colleges make it a policy not to subsidize college life for more than one good colored athlete per team."

UCLA sought the best players regardless of color. "[UCLA] wanted to compete with USC for the local football dollar," Strode said. "I don't think UCLA made a conscious effort to bring some black kids into the program; the effort was to bring in some top-notch athletes." That was one reason the four young athletes chose UCLA. They also selected it because they grew up in Los Angeles. They lived at home. They wanted to play before the hometown crowd. Most colleges didn't recruit nationwide as they do today.

The USC Trojans didn't want them. In Kenny Washington's case, "they were interested in sitting him on the bench so none of the other schools could have him," Strode said. If they played elsewhere, they might have had to travel to schools in the Jim Crow South. Texas Christian University, the University of Missouri, and Southern Methodist University played UCLA in the Los Angeles Coliseum, but for the most part the Bruins played schools on the West Coast. Said teammate Don McPherson: "We couldn't play in Texas because we had black guys on our team. They couldn't stay in the hotels or eat in the restaurants, so we didn't travel there."

UCLA had a more tolerant atmosphere for African Americans. "Whatever racial pressure was coming down in the City of Los Angeles, the pressure was not on me in Westwood," Strode said. "We had the whole melting pot, and it was an education for all of us.... I was just like any other athlete. And I worked hard because there was always the overriding feeling [that] UCLA really wanted me." Said the Bruins' graduate manager Bill Ackerman: "Perhaps the whole tradition of newness here in the West has been instrumental in keeping our attitudes toward racial differences genuinely healthy and providing our student body with a bold, non-discriminatory outlook."

They received lucrative benefits. "UCLA ended up taking care of me and my whole family while I was in school," Strode said—including twenty dollars under the table. It's no stretch that Washington probably did even better.

What made their appearance on the UCLA campus extraordinary was more than their athletic prowess. All, with the exception of Wynne, whose career is unknown, became highly successful after leaving the campus.

They weren't the first. Ralph Bunche, a basketball player who graduated in 1927, went on to earn a doctorate at Harvard and won the Nobel Peace Prize for helping to write the United Nations charter and his efforts to bring peace to the Middle East. UCLA graduate James LuValle won a bronze medal in the 400 meters in the 1936 Olympics in Nazi Germany. He went on to earn a doctorate from the California Institute of Technology and retired as the laboratory administrator for the chemistry department at Stanford University.

Jackie Robinson was best known for breaking the color barrier in Major League Baseball. Less known is that Washington and Strode integrated the National Football League a year before Robinson's feat in 1947. Strode became a ground-breaking movie star. Bradley was elected the first black mayor of Los Angeles and the first in a major city in which the population held a white majority. Bartlett was a respected civic leader throughout southern California. If there was any other group of athletes at one school and at one time that so profoundly affected the social, athletic, and political climate in the nation, it doesn't come to mind.

Perhaps none of these athletes would have had a chance if it hadn't been for the black press, civil rights groups, the Communist Party, progressive white activists, and "radical" politicians who mounted campaigns to integrate sports as part of a larger movement to improve conditions across America for African Americans.

It was never easy for the African American athletes, either at UCLA or later in their professional careers. They had to overcome the overwhelming presence of racial prejudice to succeed. And did they ever!

THE BLACK BRUINS

Prologue

The Negroes who migrated came out here to escape the
hate down South. To them, the Far West was just like the
Promised Land. That's why my parents moved out here.

—Woody Strode

Of the five superb black athletes who would be enrolled at UCLA,
three were born in the Southern California area and two had migrated
from the South. Those two—Jackie Robinson and Tom Bradley—
and their families were trying to escape from Jim Crow, only to dis-
cover that racial discrimination existed in Los Angeles as well, with
the distinction that it was more subtle but at the same time equally
oppressive.

With African Americans leaving the discrimination of the South
during the Great Migration, many of them headed for the land of
milk and honey called Los Angeles. Undoubtedly they bought into
the belief that they were heading for a racial paradise, a notion that
was propagated by the praise heaped upon the City of Angels by
W. E. B. Du Bois, one of the co-founders of the National Association for the Advancement of Colored People (NAACP) in 1913. He
called Los Angeles "wonderful," noting that "nowhere in the United
States is the Negro so well and beautifully housed, nor the average efficiency and intelligence in the colored population so high."

Such praise was coupled with comments by Jefferson L. Edmonds,
editor of the *Liberator*, the African American newspaper in Los Ange-

les. He wrote that Southern California was "ripe for advancing the race" and noted that African Americans had a good opportunity to own businesses and homes. Edmonds saw home ownership as vital to their quest for full citizenship. In 1910 almost 36 percent of African Americans in Los Angeles County owned their own homes—a remarkable number that almost matched that of white homeowners. Few cities in the North and Midwest had black home ownership of even 10 percent. "Only a few years ago, the bulk of our present colored population came here from the South without any money, in search of better things and [they] were not disappointed," Edmonds wrote in 1912. "The hospitable white people received them kindly, employed them at good wages, treated them as men and women, [and] furnished their children with the best educational advantages offered anywhere."

As George Beavers Jr. put it in 1902 after migrating from Atlanta, Georgia, "When people were ready to move from the South to come out West, we were getting the best of the lot, because it took a certain amount of income and vision to be able to do that, to be able to move so far West and start over again."

Whether those views were realistic is questionable. Certainly by the 1930s and the Great Depression, such expectations fell short. While African Americans improved their lot in life by migrating to Southern California, their standards of living never matched those of the white population. "The boomtown atmosphere of Los Angeles provided important economic opportunities for the early Black community," historian Raphael J. Sonenshein wrote. "But the puritanical conservatism of the city's leadership severely constrained the long-term prospects for all minorities."

In 1900 the black population made up 2.1 percent of Los Angeles's 102,489 residents. By 1910 the black share of the population rose to 2.4 percent; by 1920, to 2.7 percent; and by 1940, to 4.2 percent of the 1.5 million residents.

Of the fifty thousand African Americans in Los Angeles in the late 1930s, thirty thousand lived in a long narrow strip of a community extending from Seventh Street to Slauson Avenue, a few blocks each side of Central Avenue. They also found a culture with a strong

Mexican influence, attributed to the more than ninety-seven thousand residents of Mexican heritage. They were joined by more than twenty-one thousand Japanese, three thousand Chinese, and three thousand Filipinos. Los Angeles had the largest African American population in the West and all other cities in the country with the exception of Chicago and New York. And the African American population was growing at a rate faster than that of the white race. The largest numbers came from Texas, Louisiana, and Mississippi.

As a writer for the Works Progress Administration put it about Los Angeles in the 1930s, "To many a newcomer, it is a modern Promised Land. It amazes and delights him, and thaws him out physically and spiritually. There is a heady fragrance in the air, and a spaciousness of sky and land and sea that give him a new sense of freedom and tempt him to taste new pleasures, new habits of living, new religions."

White Southerners also were moving to Los Angeles, and they brought Jim Crow with them, especially in the 1930s. As historian Douglas Flamming has pointed out, the white Southerners "complained that blacks were too free in Los Angeles, that the city should adopt the South's model of segregation." If attaining a good job in the early 1900s was not hard enough, by 1934, at the height of the Great Depression, 50 percent of African Americans were out of work. If black men found jobs, these were mostly as waiters, porters, or janitors who earned about fifty dollars a month. Their wives often had to work as domestic servants to supplement their incomes. Eighty-seven percent of black women and 40 percent of black men worked as domestic servants. One bright spot was that Los Angeles hired more African Americans as police officers and firefighters than most other American cities.

African Americans did find better schools that were not segregated, better housing that was affordable and had no covenants prohibiting blacks, and better jobs that freed them from a lowly sharecropper existence in the South. Many, though, lived at poverty levels or just above. As noted, they also found an abundance of racial discrimination, despite their perceptions before they arrived that Jim Crow would be left behind.

The growing African American population was a perceived threat to the white population. Southern whites in the West were hostile toward African Americans, and white Protestants wanted to keep the small-town feeling. As the black population grew, covenants prohibiting the sale of houses to African Americans began cropping up. Jackie Robinson's widow, Rachel, who met her husband while they were attending UCLA, noted that her "anxiety had a lot to do with knowing about the Northern-style bigotry so common in Los Angeles; unlike the South, incidents of discrimination were often unexpected and inexplicable—you never knew when they would happen."

Jobs went to whites first, and the rule of "last hired, first fired" prevailed. Beaches were segregated. African Americans' use of public facilities like swimming pools was restricted to times when whites weren't using them. The Pasadena pool was open just one day a week for them. During hot spells black kids stood outside the picket fence and watched the white kids splashing in the pool. "I honestly thought the officials didn't think Negroes got as warm and uncomfortable as white people during the Pasadena heat," Jackie Robinson said. Although forbidden to do so by state law, many hotels and restaurants refused service to African Americans. They found ways around the law by telling African Americans who were trying to go to the movies that the theater was sold out or that they might be ejected from a restaurant on trumped-up allegations of disorderly conduct.

Woody Strode called the racism "very subtle." "We knew where we weren't wanted, and we didn't go to those places. Why would I want to go somewhere and have the door slammed in my face?" If African Americans did try to go to a restricted club, the owners set entrance prices so high that they couldn't afford a ticket. Strode recalled that the Communists were trying to spread their influence by seeking support from minorities in the early 1930s. "That's when our life was most vulnerable," he said. He noted that the Communists would hold mixed dances for blacks with white girls. Strode said they would say, "'See what we've done for you; you're free.' I saw through that even as a teenager."

The white population in Los Angeles began putting up resistance to minorities moving into white neighborhoods. They used restrictive covenants and block agreements to keep them out. The covenants prohibit homeowners from selling to minorities. Block agreements were just what they sounded like: agreements by blocks of white owners to restrict blacks from moving in. With such restrictions, African Americans were forced into fast-growing ghettos like the community that eventually became Watts.

Communities like Inglewood posted signs forbidding Jews and "coloreds." Strode remembered the signs saying that these groups weren't welcome in Inglewood. Pasadena, home to the wealthy, also was highly prejudiced toward African Americans. "Housing discrimination was a devastating blow to Black economic prospects in Los Angeles," historian Sonenshein wrote. And the Ku Klux Klan operated in the mid-1920s, although certainly not with the political or violent force that it exhibited in the deep South. Strode remembers when Mayor Frank Shaw was running for reelection. "He used to walk through [Strode's neighborhood], knock on doors and say, 'Don't vote for so-and-so because he belongs to the Ku Klux Klan.' They tried to scare us, but we didn't believe it," Strode said. "We had just left that in the South." Strode called the Klan passive. "They read books, talked and all that but they never put on the hoods or got involved with any terrorism. They did no parading because we weren't afraid of them."

Such was the world in which the five future UCLA athletes found themselves growing up. The families of Kenny Washington, Woody Strode, and Ray Bartlett were longtime residents of Los Angeles. Jackie Robinson and Tom Bradley moved from the South to Southern California with their families in search of the elusive Promised Land.

1

No Bed of Roses in Pasadena

"If you poor Georgians want to get a little closer
to heaven, come on out to California."
—Burton Thomas, Jackie Robinson's uncle

Mallie Robinson had had enough. Her husband, Jerry, had left her for another woman and she was strapped with five children, the youngest of whom, Jack Roosevelt Robinson, was just over a year old. (He was known as Jack until sportswriters began calling him Jackie when he played football at UCLA.) Years later Robinson said that when he became of aware of how much his mother had to endure, "I could only think of [my father] in bitterness. He, too, may have been a victim of oppression, but he had no right to desert my mother and five children." When Robinson became famous, his father tried to pay a visit, but Jackie turned his back on him.

The Robinsons were living as sharecroppers on a plantation in Cairo (pronounced KAYrow), Georgia, in the heart of the Black Belt, the fertile land in the middle of the state where the densest population of African Americans in the United States lived. Cairo was just "a day's hike" from the Florida state line. Robinson would later call living as a sharecropper in Cairo "a newer, more sophisticated form of slavery." Mallie and her husband were making a decent living by sharecropping but only after she had stood up to the tough plantation owner for a greater share of the profits earned from their labor. They were what were called "half-croppers" because they had to give half of their crops to the white landowner. But when Jerry left, the owner would not allow Mallie's brother to help her bring in the crops. "You might as well go," he told Mallie. "I ain't gonna give you nothing." He kicked her out of their house, which he owned, one that was barely inhabitable. She saw only a bleak future, one of poverty and living under the humiliation of Jim Crow laws.

Then Mallie's half-brother Burton Thomas, well-dressed and exuding prosperity, paid a visit to Cairo and the Robinson family. He espoused the wonders of where he was living—Southern California. Mallie, her sister, and brother agreed to pack up their meager belongings and head to the Promised Land. The family entourage of thirteen (including children) boarded a midnight train from Cairo on May 21, 1921. Mallie remarked, "I hear that freedom train awhistling 'round that bend out yonder!"

A family friend, a young Charles Copeland, remembered the commotion at the train station. "I had never seen anything like it," he said. "It was a big thing for us, everyone was so excited."

When Mallie and the others passed through the San Gabriel Mountains, she was stunned by the beauty of Los Angeles. She called it "the most beautiful sight of my whole life." The train stopped at Pasadena, where the entourage got off. They were going to live in what was called the "the richest city per capita in America." "What my mother didn't know when she brought us here, what none of us knew, was that Pasadena was as prejudiced as any town in the South," said Jack's brother Mack years later. "They let us in all right, but they wouldn't let us live."

Mallie and her children—Edgar (ten), Frank (nine), Mack (six), Willa Mae (four), and Jack (sixteen months)—found a tiny three-room apartment near the train station. Thirteen people lived in that apartment, which had no hot water and no kitchen sink, and dishes were washed in a tub that also served as a bathtub. Mallie then set out to look for a job as she had but three dollars in her purse. A white Pasadena family agreed to hire her as a maid, a job she held for twenty years. After two years in Pasadena, Mallie and her sister's family bought a house at 121 Pepper Street in a white working-class section of Pasadena. Two more years passed before her sister and husband bought a house of their own, leaving Mallie the sole owner of the property where Jack would live until he left home seventeen years later.

The Robinsons were among eleven hundred African Americans who lived in Pasadena. They quickly learned that Jim Crow also resided in their new home. Blacks could find only menial jobs, and they were barred from many public places, such as the Brookside Plunge, which they were allowed to use only one day a week, after which the pool was drained. "Pasadena regarded us as intruders," Robinson would say. "My brothers and I were in many a fight that started with a racial slur on the very street we lived on. We saw movies from segregated balconies, swam in the municipal pool only on Tuesdays, and were permitted in the YMCA only one night a week."

Pasadena residents also were concerned that African Americans living in their neighborhoods were driving down property values, and they wanted to emulate such nearby cities as Glendale, Eagle Rock, and San Marino, which refused to hire African Americans and had nary any within their limits. By 1940 Pasadena had hired no blacks as police officers, firefighters, or teachers. Some worked as laborers in the streets, parks, and refuse departments. The African American newspaper, the *California Eagle*, noted, "The condition of affairs surrounding the racial issues in Pasadena is nothing less that nauseating."

Even though the Robinsons lived in a comfortable two-story house with two bathrooms, a garden, and fruit trees in the backyard, they still were poor and often went without a meal. "Sometimes there were only two meals a day, and some days we wouldn't have eaten at all if it hadn't been for the leftovers my mother was able to bring home from her job," Robinson remembered. Sometimes they ate just bread and a concoction of sugar and water Robinson called "sweet water." Years later his wife Rachel had to remind him to eat his vegetables. "I never developed a taste for them because I never ate them as a youngster," he said. His sister Willa Mae denied that the family went without meals, but Robinson remembered differently. He recalled that he could "never get my belt tight enough to keep that hurt in my stomach away." He added that if they went hungry, "you can bet money that my mother was twice as hungry." As noted, at times the people Mallie worked for let her fill her apron with leftover food to bring home. "We'd wait up, hoping she'd come home with a cake or pie," Robinson said.

Mallie found time in her busy work schedule to teach her children to respect themselves and to demand respect from others. "That's why I refused to back down in later life," Robinson wrote years later, "and won't back down now." Brother Mack said Jackie got his strength from his mother. "She instilled pride in him," he said. "She wouldn't take anything from anybody. She was a real strong woman. It took a lot of guts to come out to California with five small kids. . . . Jackie inherited a lot from her; we all did."

There was little doubt of racism in their neighborhood and beyond. "We went through a sort of slavery with the whites slowly, very slowly, getting used to us," Willa Mae said. Neighbors tried unsuccessfully to buy the Robinsons out of their home. A cross was burned on the front lawn. Police often were called to keep the black children off the streets. When Jack was about eight years old, he was sweeping the sidewalk in front of his house when a little white girl began chanting, "Nigger! Nigger! Nigger!" Jack responded by calling her "a cracker," a slur that his brother Mack told him was the worst thing you could call a white person. The girl's father ran out of the house after Jack. They began throwing rocks at each other until the man's wife coaxed him back into the house.

Once Jack's brother Edgar rode his skates to the grocery store to buy bread. A neighbor complained to police about the noise. "I'm sorry they're so touchy that the noise of skates disturbs them," Mallie told police. "But there's no law against skating on the sidewalk, is there?" The policeman replied, "No, but the man who called us told us that his wife is afraid of colored people." Mallie told the officer she would tell Edgar to go around the block and avoid the neighbor's house.

While Mallie was working, Willa Mae cared for Jack, bathing, dressing, and feeding him. She even took him to school with her when Jack wasn't old enough to attend. He would play in the sandbox on the school grounds while he waited for her. When it rained, Willa Mae's teacher brought him inside.

When it was time for Jack to attend school, he was enrolled in Cleveland Elementary School for two years before transferring to Washington Elementary. "In those days he would come home from school, gulp down a glass of milk, put his books on that old dresser, and be out the door playing ball with the kids," Willa Mae said. All he was interested in was playing sports. "He wasn't a great student," Willa Mae said, "but that was only because somewhere along the line he decided sports would be his life." He was a C student in high school. When one of his grades would slip, he would work harder on another subject to keep the average necessary to play sports. "To do more would have meant giving up at least one sport, and I couldn't," he recalled.

When he was eight, Jack discovered that at least in sports he was allowed to compete with whites. "Sports were the big breach in the wall of segregation about me," Robinson said. "In primary and high school white boys treated me as an equal." Robinson's classmates would share their lunches with him if he played on their team. "He was a special little boy, and ever since I can remember he always had a ball in his hand," Willa Mae said.

At twelve Jack moved on to Washington Junior High, where he earned C's and B's. His school transcript carried a remark from a school official stating that he probably would wind up as a gardener. In his free time Robinson delivered newspapers, ran errands, sold hot dogs at the nearby Rose Bowl, and cut grass to help out the family. During those years several more black families moved into the neighborhood, as did Mexicans, Asians, and poor whites. Their commonality was that they were poor. The boys formed the Pepper Street Gang, where they all—blacks, Latinos, Asians, and even a few whites—hung out together, at times getting into minor mischief. Robinson's widow said the gang was more like the "Little Rascals" than the gangs of today. They threw dirt clods at cars, found lost golf balls on the golf course and sold them back to golfers, and stole items from stores, mostly food. "People used to ask me how Jack got so good throwing a baseball and a football," Willa

Mae remarked, "and I said it was from throwing rocks at the other kids who threw rocks at him."

As his competitive nature started to show, Robinson once confronted a quarterback from a rival school before a game. He didn't introduce himself. He simply said, "I heard you were lucky in your last game. How are you gonna go ninety-eight yards for a touchdown against us?" Then he turned and walked away. Early day trash talk.

During this time he became more and more aware of "a growing resentment at being deprived of some of the advantages the white kids had." Because he and his friends had little access to the municipal pool, they would swim in a nearby reservoir. One day they heard a booming voice say, "Looka there—niggers swimming in my drinking water." They were escorted to jail at gunpoint before they were sent home.

Robinson, Ray Bartlett, and their friends would go to the movie theaters, "but we could only sit in certain places," said Bartlett, who had known Robinson since they were seven years old. "I never thought much about it . . . , but Jackie knew how the world really worked back then. What he saw bothered him. It bothered him much more than the rest of us."

"They weren't out to do trouble," Willa Mae said. "They just were a bunch of kids who enjoyed being together and mostly playing ball games." Bartlett and Robinson became lifelong friends who went through grade school, high school, and college together and stayed in touch over the years.

Bartlett was born in Pasadena and lived most of his life there. His father, Vincent, sold real estate, and his mother, Fay, was a nurse. When his mother told him the racism he faced would "all change one day," he didn't believe her, Bartlett recalled. "But I felt that things could be changed through the system. That's what I worked for."

Robinson said his mother always maintained her composure. "She didn't allow us to go out of our way to antagonize the whites, and she still made it perfectly clear to us and to them that she was not at all afraid of them and that she had no intention of allowing them to mistreat us."

Eventually the white neighbors began to accept the Robinsons, mostly out of respect for Mallie, who worked so hard to nurture her family despite daunting odds. Said Bartlett: "I can't think of any way that growing up [in Pasadena] helped Jackie. I really can't." Robinson wrote later in life that when he left UCLA, he "didn't want anything to do with Pasadena."

Robinson could have become a juvenile delinquent had it not been for two men who shared his mother's values. One was a mechanic, Carl Anderson, who took him aside to tell him that following the crowd didn't take guts but that he had to show courage and intelligence to walk away. That was a lesson that proved extremely valuable to Robinson when he broke the color barrier in baseball many years later. The other man was the Reverend Karl Downs, a young minister where Mallie attended church. Robinson grew to trust Downs, often going to him for advice. "He helped ease some of my tensions." Over a period of ten years, Downs offered Robinson advice that he found useful while attending junior high, high school, and UCLA. "I'm not sure what would have happened to Jack if he had never met Reverend Downs," Bartlett said years later.

Downs watched Robinson play football on Saturdays and then made sure that Robinson taught a Sunday school class the following morning. Robinson agreed to teach the class because he respected Downs so much. He would rather have slept in after a grueling football game on Saturday night, "but no matter how terrible I felt, I had to get up. It was impossible to shirk duty when Karl Downs was involved." Years later Rachel Robinson recalled how Downs helped Robinson change his life. "The religious beliefs that Karl helped stimulate in him would strengthen his ability to cope with all the challenges he would face in his life," she said.

Across town thirteen-year-old Woodrow Wilson Woolwine Strode was starting at McKinley Junior High School, where his athletic ability began to develop. Because he was five years older than Robinson and lived in a section of Los Angeles called the East Side, Strode and Robinson most likely never crossed paths until they arrived at UCLA.

Strode was born in Los Angeles on July 25, 1914, to parents who had emigrated from New Orleans, Louisiana, in 1900. They too were looking for the Promised Land. He had a brother, Baylous Strode Jr., who was two years older. (In his autobiography, *Goal Dust*, Strode does not give the first names of his parents. It is likely his father's first name was Baylous.) His father was a brick mason and his mother a homemaker. His father earned his high school diploma at night.

Strode's three given names came from President Woodrow Wilson and Los Angeles district attorney Tom Woolwine. "Well, I had to get rid of that title," he said. "'And now, ladies and gentlemen, Woodrow Wilson Woolwine Strode!' It was like a goddamned announcement. So I cut it down to Woody Strode," he wrote in his autobiography. His lineage was a mix of African American and Native American, a heritage that gave him a distinct look that would pay huge dividends in his adult years. His great-grandfather married a Creek Indian, and his grandfather, a Blackfoot. His mother's mother was a slave who was part Cherokee. "That's how close the Indians and the slaves were in those days. They were both downtrodden in America," Strode wrote.

Strode was born four years after his parents moved from New Orleans. His parents raised Strode to be color-blind. They never talked about race. "He saw the white people out here were different from the white people where he came from," Strode wrote about his father. "He wanted me to fall into their path. That's why he never talked about race." It was this upbringing that separated Jackie Robinson from Strode in their attitude toward race relations in the 1930s and beyond. Their attitudes also differed because of where they lived. Strode lived in a predominately black area, with some Germans, Italians, and Mexicans mixed in, while Robinson resided in a poor neighborhood that was surrounded and dominated by a wealthy white enclave. "I think that's why Jack had a little more hate going than the rest of us," Strode said.

Strode attended the Holmes Avenue Grammar School across the street from his house on the East Side, later to be known as South-Central, and not far from the Los Angeles Coliseum. Today the East Side is more than 90 percent Latino. The school was run by a black principal, Bessie Burke, the first black teacher in the Los Angeles schools.

Strode remembers playing in the Los Angeles River and catching crawdads in the unfortunately named Nigger Slough (now named Dominguez Slough). But he spent most of his time on the playgrounds where city workers taught youngsters basketball, football, and baseball, along with other sports. He played baseball and basketball, but his first love was football. "I was one of the gorillas (linemen). My athletic ability didn't begin to show up until I hit McKinley Junior High School." While attending McKinley, he would play sports at lunchtime and recess. It was that love of sports and his athletic ability that brought him together with Robinson and another talented athlete, Kenny Washington, who would become his best friend.

2

The Kingfish and Woody

"The two finest football players as backs that I ever
had the pleasure of playing with were Kenny
Washington and Whizzer White."

—Former UCLA quarterback Ned Mathews

Kenny Washington grew up in white, middle-class Lincoln Heights—
the "Heights" as it was called—an Italian community with a few
Irish here and there. The Heights sat on the hills of the East Side,
across the Los Angeles River from downtown. The Washington
family may have been the only African Americans in the community. Today Lincoln Heights is more than 70 percent Latino. When
Woody Strode met Kenny for the first time, he thought he was Italian; he had an accent that was half Italian, and his English wasn't
too good. "I used to make fun of him because I couldn't understand
him," Strode said. But, he added, Washington was a good student.
Los Angeles Times sports columnist Jim Murray wrote in 1961 that
because he was raised among Italians, Washington "logged more
lasagna than a regiment of Mussolinis."

Many of the men who lived in Lincoln Heights worked for the
railroad as engineers, firemen, brakemen, or switchmen. Those jobs
weren't available to African Americans, so Washington's grandfather worked as a cook for the railroad. His grandmother Susie
raised him and was a janitor at a nearby grammar school. Washington's grandparents had three sons: Julius, Roscoe (better known as

Rocky), and Edgar. Edgar married Kenny's mother, Marion, when he was eighteen and she was sixteen. The marriage crumbled when Edgar began seeing another woman. That's when Kenny moved in with his grandparents.

Edgar, who was known as Blue, lived the high life, chasing after girls and following the bright lights. From 1919 to 1961 he appeared in eighty-seven films, mostly bit parts, including cowboy movies with Ken Maynard and Tom Mix, and he had a small role in *Gone with the Wind*. "[As an] African American character actor [he] typified Hollywood's racist treatment—and views—of blacks in the 1930s as an easily frightened, wide-eyed, menial type. His career declined as the image of the black male became more [respectable] in an increasingly race-conscious age," notes the Internet Movie Database website. Blue also appeared in *The Birth of a Nation* and the original *King Kong*. One of his best friends was Frank Capra, the film director, producer, and writer.

Blue was making seventy-five dollars a day acting when other African Americans were making ten to fifteen dollars a week. He would disappear for days at a time, spending money and having a good time, and then coming home broke. He also earned a living boxing and playing baseball. He fought in open-air boxing arenas in Southern California and played as a pitcher and fielder for such black baseball teams as the Kansas City Monarchs, the Chicago American Giants, and the Los Angeles White Sox.

Kenny Washington derived his considerable talent from his father, who stood 6 feet 5 inches tall and weighed more than two hundred pounds. Blue was described as a "ruggedly charismatic character, whether knocking heads, bruising baseballs or performing his own movie stunts." Said Strode: "Athletically, Blue had the ability to do just about any damn thing he wanted. He was a hell of a baseball player, a big powerful man, playing outfield, [pitching] and first base." As a pitcher he had a deceptive underhand delivery. But liquor led to Blue's downfall. For example, he was released from the Chicago American Giants because he had "too much King Alcohol under his belt. No place on a ball team for those who want to get soused. . . ." Blue Washington faced his share of racism while playing baseball.

The Oregonian newspaper in Portland, Oregon, reported that "a big, black-skinned gem'm'm named Washington was having the time of his shoe-shining life out there in the box for the Negroes."

If grandmother Susie Washington was the woman who raised him, Kenny Washington's "father" was his uncle Rocky, a Los Angeles police officer, one of only a handful of African Americans on the force. He also became the first African American lieutenant, despite rampant racism in the department. Rocky provided the discipline that Susie needed when Kenny ran afoul of the rules. "If Kenny got in trouble, Rocky would carry out the orders. . . . He'd whip Kenny's butt," Strode stated. Rocky was always there for Kenny, offering advice throughout his career. "Rocky was level-headed, the kind of guy that always had his feet on the ground," Strode said. "Rocky got a lot of praise for the way he brought up Kenny." (Rocky's wife, Hazel, was a business partner with the actress Rosalind Russell and was one of the first licensed black hairdressers in Hollywood.)

The Washingtons lived two blocks from the Downey Avenue Playground, where Kenny played all sports, including boxing, but football and baseball were his two main loves. He had one setback when he was ten years old: he broke both knees in a bicycle accident, and those knees would bother him throughout his athletic career. When he played with the Rams, Tom Harmon, a teammate and the 1940 Heisman Trophy winner, described Washington's running: "He had a crazy gait, like he had two broken legs. He'd be coming at you straight, and it would look like he was going sideways."

Strode called Kenny the original "Crazylegs," a name that had been stuck on Rams' receiver Elroy Hirsch when he played at Wisconsin in 1942. The *Los Angeles Times* described him this way: "As a broken-field runner he had a straight arm that felled giants and a de-step that looked like an adagio dance. Speedy and a good blocker, he also had a slingshot pass that for accuracy and distance surpassed anything Jim Thorpe ever threw."

Not far from where Woody Strode grew up, another black youngster was gaining attention for his athletic skills in football and track: Tom Bradley, the future mayor of Los Angeles. Unlike Strode and

Washington, Bradley was not a California native. The grandson of slaves, he was born in Calvert, Texas, on December 27, 1917, the son of Lee and Crenner Bradley, whose families had moved there in the 1880s. Calvert, which lies between Waco and Houston, was the state's fourth largest city at the end of the nineteenth century because it boasted the world's largest cotton gin. For cotton was king and held the promise of sharecropping to earn a living.

The Bradleys worked grueling eighteen-hour days picking cotton in one-hundred-degree temperatures, climate changes including droughts and drenching storms, and a widely varying price for cotton. When Bradley ran for governor of California in the 1980s, he looked out a car window at a cotton field as he drove through the Central Valley of California. He turned to a fellow passenger and remarked, "That was enough." I never did fill that twenty-pound sack." His parents lost five children in infancy during those times, leaving only an older brother and younger sister as Tom Bradley's siblings. They all worked in the fields to help out.

In 1921 the Bradleys gave up and left Calvert for Dallas, where Lee Bradley took any job he could find and Crenner worked as a maid, but still they couldn't make ends meet after two years. Finding a good job was difficult. Lee was limited by his fifth-grade education, and Crenner had finished only the third grade. Then came the lure of California. They piled into their old car and began the trip west, sleeping in their car because no motel would take in blacks, and they were turned away at restaurants. They ate bologna and mashed potato sandwiches as they made their way to Somerton, Arizona, not far from the California border, where they moved in with relatives. Lee Bradley went on to California to find work. At the age of six, Tom Bradley began school.

In Somerton, Bradley developed a love of reading. While other children were out playing ball, he could be found reading a book. His parents taught him the value of a good education. "Seeing me read all the time, my parents, especially my mother, nurtured this desire to work hard, to study hard," Bradley said.

His mother told him the family was "going to a place where it didn't matter what your name was or where you lived," he recalled.

"She told me California was a special place where people judge you on what you did, and nothing else." Within a year the Bradley family joined Lee in Los Angeles, even though he had been unable to find work. Eventually he found a job as a porter on the Santa Fe Railroad and later as a crew member on ocean liners that plied the coast from Seattle to Los Angeles. He was gone from home for long periods of time.

The family settled in Los Angeles's East Side but moved as many as four times in one year, probably because they could not afford the rents. And two more children joined the family. Bradley's mother found work as a maid. "She made so many sacrifices to keep the family provided for," Bradley remembered.

When Bradley was ten years old, his father deserted the family, a major trauma in Bradley's life. Coupled with the moves to four different homes and four different schools, it is unlikely Bradley felt very secure in his childhood and adolescence. "Many black men in America leave their families, either of despair or desperation," James Lee Robinson Jr. wrote in his doctoral thesis about Bradley at UCLA in 1976. "They cannot stand to see their families do without, so they simply leave."

Bradley's father helped out the family when he could, but Crenner still was having a hard time making ends meet. "We were so poor that when our shoes wore out we'd shove cardboard in the bottoms, and by third period by running over the school grounds the cardboard would wear out and my socks would come slipping out," Bradley remembered. (As an adult, when Bradley saw a sale on socks, he'd stock up on them until one day he realized he had about two hundred pairs.) The Bradleys desperately needed help at one point. "Public assistance during the Depression was not an unusual thing," Bradley recalled years later, "and it just seemed that everybody we knew in one way or another received some kind of help."

Although Bradley was close to his mother, she was virtually an absentee mom. She worked day and night to feed her family. Bradley took over the role of father and mother, keeping his siblings in line. This "desertion" also took its toll. "She left home every morning to attend to somebody else's children, to take care of somebody else's home, and left us there to struggle alone. . . . That was the only way we could make it."

When Bradley was about ten years old, he experienced racial prejudice in the West Temple area, an integrated neighborhood on the East Side. One day his friend Billy, a white boy, told Bradley his parents forbade him from playing with the other "colored children" on the block. The experience shocked him. "I remember feeling hurt and thinking how terribly wrong it was," he said. "And I think he was hurt by it, too. . . . I think as young as I was, that I decided then and there that I never wanted racial feelings on my part to color my own reaction to other human beings."

To his good fortune, Bradley fell under the mentorship of a teacher, Pearl Briley, who pushed him to excel in school. That changed when he attended Lafayette Junior High School, where minorities were discouraged from pursuing their dreams. A counselor tried to steer him into vocational courses instead of preparing him for college. He refused. It was "one of my most depressing memories," Bradley recalled. But he never faltered and refused to give in to racial prejudice. Bradley continued to show a love of reading that singled him out as the most studious of the children, the one his family pushed to get a college education. "They stressed the importance of education on me from as early as I can remember."

To help with bills Bradley delivered newspapers, at two cents a copy. When he wasn't working or going to school, he spent a lot of time alone. "I was pretty much a loner during my leisure hours and spent much of my time reading or working on homework," Bradley recalled. A friend, Alfred Goodlowe, said, "He never hung around with us." Another friend, Bill Elkins, said, "I never saw Tom have a fight with another boy."

In the junior high years Bradley's athleticism began to develop. He would play sports at the Central Recreation Center, urged on by a well-meaning coach who recognized that the tall, lanky Bradley had more talent than other boys his age. "Perhaps it was these centers, whose role is so often overlooked as an important force in youngsters' lives," Bradley recalled, "where the program play-yard director influenced me to begin working toward all my goals in life."

He called it a "critical turning point in my life." It was in these centers that Bradley realized he could attend college if he could earn an athletic scholarship. "So I quit my job as a paperboy to concentrate on athletics." That would prove to be a good decision; his athletic career put college within reach.

3

The High School Years

"Yeah, he's good enough."

—UCLA football coach Bill Spaulding on whether
to offer a scholarship to Kenny Washington

In 1935 Jackie Robinson enrolled at the John Muir Technical High School. His brother Mack and sister Willa Mae also were students at Muir Tech, which had once been a vocational school but had long since become a traditional high school. It was one of two Pasadena high schools, both of which had a predominantly white student body.

In the spring Robinson, all of 135 pounds, had such great eye-to-hand coordination that he manned the shortstop position as a freshman for the Muir Tech Terriers. He also participated (with Mack) in the broad jump, later to be renamed the long jump, and the high jump. His baseball team made it to the finals of a regional tournament in Pomona, and he showed great promise in the broad jump.

The following fall Robinson turned out for football on a team that went undefeated. He played behind brothers Bill and George Sangster, two of the best athletes in Pasadena history. He played a little at quarterback in the single wing, an offense that was fashionable at that time. As soon as the football season ended, Jack turned out for basketball, where his quickness, ball handling, and team play showed his athletic versatility. His team fell short of the league championship on the last game of the season.

In 1936 in the conference championship football game against

Glendale, Robinson was deliberately kneed as he rose from being tackled on the opening kickoff after the whistle blew. The kick took the wind out of him and broke two ribs, forcing him out of the game that Muir eventually lost. "It was a bigot's reminder that he intended to drive me off the gridiron, singlehandedly," he said. His substitute wound up throwing three interceptions, and Glendale won 19–7.

Robinson was winning people over to his side with his athletic prowess despite his race. The *Pasadena Star-News* begrudgingly finally conceded that Jack Robinson "for two years has been the outstanding athlete at Muir, starring in football, basketball, track, baseball, and tennis." At the same time, Robinson was getting a reputation as cocky, too aggressive, arrogant, and uppity. Because he was a terrific athlete, opponents often resorted to derogatory remarks about his race, his ancestry, and his economic status to get under his skin, but such remarks only spurred his competiveness.

Robinson graduated at midyear and didn't play baseball in the spring. Because he had turned five years old on January 30, 1919, he was allowed to enter grade school and high school in midyear. It meant he graduated in midyear 1937. A day after his eighteenth birthday, he enrolled in Pasadena Junior College.

Jack's childhood friend Ray Bartlett recalled that Robinson saw sports as his way out of poverty, although sports hadn't help his brother Mack. "Jack was an extremely competitive person and a very determined athlete," Bartlett said. "He fought the racism in the community very bitterly. . . . We took a lot of name-calling in those days. . . . Jack was dedicated to being the best athlete he could possibly be because he saw that as an escape." In addition, Bartlett said, "Every time we played anybody, I don't care what it was, whether it was a pickup game, win was all Jack knew, and I remember when we thought things were sort of down, he was the guy that kept us going, really."

Across town four and a half years before Robinson started high school, Woody Strode enrolled at age sixteen in Jefferson High School, standing 6 feet 1 inch and weighing 130 pounds. String bean that he was, he nonetheless went out for football. "I was so skinny the only thing that stayed on me good was the helmet," he said. Strode played end because he was too light to play on the interior line and too slow for the backfield. End would be his position for the rest of his football career, a position he grew into.

Strode sat on the bench for two or three games until the first-team end suffered an injury. The coach put him in, and Strode commented, "I was like a wild man." He remained first team for the rest of his high school days. In those days players were on the field for defense and offense, and Strode wound up playing as many as fifty-five minutes of a sixty-minute game. The *Los Angeles Examiner* reporters raved about Strode's talents. "He haunts his end like a departed spirit, taking out four men on one play if needed be," one wrote.

In the offseason Strode used track to keep himself in shape for football season. He participated in the shot put, high jump, and high and low hurdles. He consistently won shot-put and high-jump events throughout the city. He also was named all-state in the low hurdles. "By the time I was a senior I was all-state in everything," he recalled. By that time he had grown to 6 feet 3 inches and weighed 175 pounds and had greater speed, strength, and coordination.

Strode was named to the all-city football team and then team captain. He received five university scholarship offers: UC Berkeley, the University of Washington, the University of Oregon, Loyola, and UCLA. But most African Americans weren't offered a high school education that prepared them for college. They were taught trades such as shop, printing, and industrial math that would get them ready for a job.

In his autobiography Strode made no mention of any discrimination in high school. That may be primarily because he attended a school whose enrollment was mainly African American. But nor did he mention any discrimination by other teams against which he played in Los Angeles.

Strode caught the attention of UCLA football coaches, who he said were not recruiting African Americans but rather the best athletes. Strode recalled that he barely knew that UCLA's new campus in Westwood existed when he was in high school. One of UCLA's biggest boosters was the actor Joe E. Brown, who actively recruited Strode. But Strode would have to clear one big hurdle before he could enroll: he would have to make up several classes to qualify for UCLA.

When Kenny Washington entered Lincoln High School, he was tall, lanky, and somewhat awkward. Lacking strength, Washington stayed off the football field until his junior year. Instead he excelled at baseball in all four of his high school years. Then his weight blossomed to 175 pounds. Once he stepped on the gridiron, there was no stopping him.

In his junior year Washington uncorked a pass in one game that traveled 60 yards before the receiver caught it. He also returned an interception 95 yards and scampered 70 yards on offense, both for touchdowns.

The next year Washington's team, the Tigers, went undefeated and won the city championship. His teammates were well aware of Washington's value to the team. "The kids on the team loved him, and they took care of him," Strode noted. "If Kenny pulled a muscle, hurt his knee or something, the whole football team [mostly white] would come over to his house, put hot packs on him, rub him down and make sure he was all right."

In one game during the championship season, Washington led Lincoln to a 27–0 victory over Garfield; in that game the *Los Angeles Times* described him as "tall, gaunt and oh, so colored." In another game Fairfax had stopped Washington cold in the first half, but in the second half he engineered five touchdowns that "left the Colonials and the customers stunned."

Before the championship game the *Los Angeles Times* called Washington "perhaps the greatest and most unorthodox back that has ever performed for a Los Angeles high school." Against Fremont High, "Hustlin' shufflin'" Washington accounted for all but 4 yards of offense for Lincoln. The "Black Beauty" gained 173 yards from scrimmage.

In the spring Washington helped the Tigers to the city championship in baseball while leading the league in batting and hitting a home run in the championship game. He was named all-city in both sports for his junior and senior years. To this day he is still considered to be one of the greatest high school football players in Southern California history. He also found time for the shot put, finishing second in the all-city track championships in 1936.

Washington knew he was a good football player, and he had set his sights high when he finished high school: he wanted to attend Notre Dame. But Notre Dame didn't want him. Next was the University of Southern California but to hear Woody Strode tell the story, the USC Trojans only wanted Washington to sit on the bench so that he wouldn't play with any other team. His high school coach, Jim Tunney, was a Loyola University graduate, and coaches tried to get him to persuade Washington to attend school there. Tunney wanted him to go to UCLA because he would get more national recognition. Washington followed his advice.

Tom Bradley was perhaps more ambitious than the other four athletes who ended up at UCLA. Robinson, Strode, Washington, and Bartlett were primarily interested in sports. While Bradley loved track and was quite good at football, he saw sports only as a path to a college degree. Bradley always was a studious type who attracted a great many friends, perhaps because he was taller, stronger, and more athletic than they were. Nonetheless, he was somewhat of a loner, as we have seen.

The other four athletes gave little thought to attending secondary school anywhere except their neighborhood high school, but Bradley began looking at choices for the next level after the eighth grade. "I lived in a community where many of the youngsters just had no hope, and they turned to many things," Bradley said. "Some to a life of crime. Some were simply social misfits. Some with great talent had no way to use that talent, and they became disillusioned, frustrated, wasted."

Bradley admitted that others had tried to get him to join them in criminal activity, but he declined. "I knew what was necessary for me," he said. "It was clear that I had to disassociate myself from those who didn't have ambition and those who would turn to illegal activities." He saw the answer at Polytechnic High School, one of the city's best schools. He wanted a "clear break, to try to find some new identification, new associates." He could have chosen Jefferson, Strode's former high school. Instead he decided on a predominantly white school of thirteen hundred students with only one hundred and thirteen African American students and a handful of Hispanics and Asians. It helped that he was recruited by track coach Ed Leahy. "At that time a number of the young fellows that I associated with were either demonstrating, in my mind, a lack of ambition, or in some cases they were beginning to get into some trouble with the law, and I just felt that it would be healthier and better for me to break off that kind of regular association by going to a different school," Bradley recalled.

Bradley had high expectations for himself, but a school counselor wasn't encouraging. He was told not to attend college and instead to seek a career with the post office. "This was presumed to be the most promising future to which black youth could aspire," he explained. "'Don't settle for being a janitor,' I was told—'aim high. Become a postal carrier.' However misguided, this advice was in fact quite commonly dispensed to even the bright black students then."

While at Poly, Bradley ran into no serious racial conflicts but soon learned that African Americans had no access to various service organizations. His leadership abilities became evident when school officials chose Bradley to mediate whatever racial conflicts did arise. He decided to run for the presidency of the Boys League— the equivalent of student body president—"an unheard of thing" for a black student to seek in a predominately white school. As a campaign issue his opponent pointed out that whoever was elected would have "to represent the student body downtown and should be properly dressed." Bradley conceded that point "because I really didn't have a suit to my name." He wore his brother's suit, even though it was too big for his lanky frame. He surprised himself by winning the election. Years later he remarked, "I had the audacity to run for an office on that campus when we had to have separate clubs. The service clubs on campus wouldn't accommodate the young Negro no matter how popular, no matter how great his achievements."

Later Bradley broke another barrier when he was selected to join the Ephebians, an honorary society whose membership was based on academics and leadership qualities. "We never knew what Tom was doing in those days; he certainly was not out in the streets with us. . . . I guess he was back there studying," his friend Alfred Good-lowe remembered.

After Bradley was admitted to Ephebians, "it was the beginning of the end to racial discrimination at the school," his biographers J. Gregory Payne and Scott C. Ratzan wrote. "After that, no one really dared to try to keep a student out because of color or creed."

At the same time Bradley was running track and playing football. He recalled only one racial incident, in which there was name calling by players from another school, "but that was of no consequence."

Although Bradley was an all-city football player as a tackle, his first love was track, particularly the quarter-mile, which fit his loner personality. He was the city track champion in the 440-yard race in 1935 and was the runner-up in 1936. One article in the *Los Angeles Times* leading up to the all-city championships was revealing. It started off by proclaiming, "Africa Speaks! Eight chocolate-colored kinky-haired athletes from Jefferson charge into the Coliseum . . ." to participate in the races. The writer referred to their skills as "black magic." He probably thought it was "black magic" when Bradley won his race, the 440.

4

The Little Brother

"There is no question of our making a very favorable
showing in Southern California sports if we make
conscientious efforts in that direction."

—Dr. Fred W. Cozens, UCLA's first football coach

UCLA football got its start in 1919, the year the school (then known
as the Southern Branch of the University of California) took over the
two-year teachers school, State Normal School, on Vermont Avenue in downtown Los Angeles. The campus was "out in the weeds
and wildflowers," not far from where the Santa Monica Freeway
cuts through it today. Because it was a teachers college, women outnumbered men six to one among the 1,338 students. One class had a
17-to-1 ratio of women to men. The student newspaper advised its
male readers, "Select your seventeen. Girls, start early and avoid the
rush. And do your duty, boys." The school was the poor little sister
of the University of California at Berkeley and lived in its shadow
for many years. The school's provost, Ernest Carroll Moore, told
students, "You must do twenty-five percent better than Berkeley
in order to be recognized at all."

In 1924 the school became an accredited four-year institution,
and the student population reached 4,418. It was not until the fall
of 1937 that male students outnumbered coeds, 3,579 to 3,509.

Nineteen diehards turned out for the first day of the first season
of football practice on a sawdust-covered dirt field. Their uniforms

were described "as variegated as those worn by Coxey's Army [a group of unemployed workers who marched on Washington to protest the lack of jobs in 1914]. Some hopefuls appeared in the olive drab of the military, some in paint-stained overalls, some in about-to-be discarded pants and sweaters."

The Los Angeles Times reported, "And now, the southern branch of the University of California lets out a yip to let the world know that it is up and doing in the world of football." The first coach was the affable Dr. Fred Cozens, who had transferred from the UC Berkeley campus. The Cubs, as they were known, played an eight-game schedule—and not very well. In their first game, on October 3, 1919, they were trounced 74-0 by Los Angeles Manual Arts High School. The team had practiced for two weeks and hadn't scrimmaged. As the school had just opened its doors as a two-year institution, most of the players were freshmen. A few were servicemen starting school after World War I.

The team finished 2-6 that first year. Over the next five years, coached by two different men, the Cubs remained woeful. They won 4 games, lost 23, and tied 4 over that period. In 1920 they were outscored 224-21, and in 1921 opposing teams ran up the scores to 214 to the Cubs' 14. They had never beaten Pomona, Occidental, or Whittier. They lost to Whittier on November 20, 1920, 103-0. It didn't help that the Cubs also were being raided by their "big brothers" up north for their best players. With such a record and such obstacles the school was never going to reach the pinnacle of big-time college football. By 1924 Southern Branch was working on its third coach with little improvement. The school even changed the mascot's name to the Grizzlies in the hope that it would live up to its name. That didn't help either. Its record was 0-5 with 3 ties. It was time for more change.

Southern Branch recognized that college football was the most popular sport in the country, and it wanted to take part in it. College football outranked Major League Baseball because baseball teams were limited to the East Coast and Midwest. Professional basketball was still a dream, and college basketball was in its fledgling state. With a built-in fan base of students and alumni, universities and colleges drew large crowds in their communities. The Pacific Coast Conference (PCC) was no different.

The football game on a college campus was the highlight of almost a weeklong spectacle of bonfires, pep rallies, homecoming parades, bands, and card stunts leading up to the hard-hitting action. Postgame parties brought the week to a close. Southern Branch wanted a piece of the action.

Its desire to shoot for the big time in football came with the hiring of forty-five-year-old Bill Spaulding as its coach and athletic director in 1925. He had been coach of the Minnesota Golden Gophers the previous three seasons, and his record had been 11-7-4. Previously Spaulding—nicknamed "Bunker Bill" because of his love of golf—had coached fifteen years at Western State Teachers College in Kalamazoo, Michigan, where he had only two losing seasons. Spaulding had also been the head basketball and baseball coach.

At Western State Spaulding had black running back Sam Dunlap, who had been turned away by the University of Michigan because of his race. Notre Dame coach Knute Rockne called Dunlap one of the most talented players he had ever seen. In 1915 Culver Military Academy refused to play Western State if Dunlap played. He sat out the game, even though the school president said he would support him if he wanted to play. In another instance, Spaulding kicked a player off the team when he refused to play alongside Dunlap.

Two years before Spaulding's arrival, Southern Branch had fielded a black player, Jefferson Brown, who lettered at least two years in football and boxing. Little is known about Brown except that he "played an excellent game at end, and considering his light weight he was an offensive player of great ability." Next to him in a photo from that time is another African American, but it is unknown whether he was an athlete.

As Southern Branch coach, Spaulding received a five-year contract at $10,000 a year. He was soft-spoken and rarely raised his voice, but he could be persuasive. Never did he scold or ridicule his players; he maintained a good sense of humor even when they lost.

He became a beloved figure on the UCLA campus. (The Bruins' football practice field south of Pauley Pavilion is named for him.)

In the same year that Southern Branch hired Spaulding, the school also decided it needed a campus. The California Board of Regents agreed to build a new campus in Westwood, and it opened in September 1929. Writers for the Works Program Administration's Federal Writers Project described the new campus as follows: "[UCLA] stands in extensive lawns crowning a broad terraced elevation overlooking rolling valleys, plains, and low hills. Behind the blue-misted Santa Monica Mountains form an irregular skyline with ice plant, but lack the ivy and venerable shade trees of older institutions of learning; the grouping of these building has the efficiency and orderliness possible only when a full grown institution is transplanted to a new site."

On the first day of practice for the 1925 season Spaulding had the woefully out-of-shape Bruins running ten-yard wind sprints, up and back. If they didn't like that, they had to run a quarter mile around the track as a penalty.

Immediately Spaulding put together three straight winning seasons, including victories over Pomona, Occidental, and Whittier. In his first season the Cubs' record was 5-3-1, despite an 82–0 shellacking by the Stanford University Indians. "Phew," said Spaulding. "What a track meet. But we will be back." The game was scheduled too early because we weren't ready," Spaulding said after the game. While the team was gaining some notice, USC was referring to the Southern Branch school as "the Twig."

The university's goal was to join the PCC, but the Cubs had a long way to go. In 1926 Spaulding didn't do much better, finishing 5-3. After accumulating a 6-2-1 record in 1927, the Cubs felt they were ready to join the PCC. The conference thought so too, and UCLA started the 1928 season in the PCC. During that period Southern Branch changed its name to the University of California at Los Angeles and the team name to the Bruins. But the Bruins were still overmatched. They lost their only four conference games but won four out-of-conference games and tied one. Stanford manhandled the Bruins 45–7, and the two teams didn't play again for four years. The

Bruins were outscored by their PCC opponents 129–19 but trampled their other opponents 152–7. One oft-told story had it that the team was so bad against its PCC competition that Spaulding had the players spend ten minutes on workouts and two hours of practicing goal-line stands. Once during a game at the University of Oregon, the Bruins reportedly punted from behind their own goal line twenty-three times. "What they lacked in size they made up in slowness," one wag wrote.

Perhaps the lack of decent facilities hurt the Bruins. When they moved to Westwood, their practice field was no better than their previous field, and it left a lot to be desired. It was described as a "large-size honest-to-God dust bowl, in which a short player might get lost after dark and have to be searched for with dogs and flares."

In 1929, before the Bruins were to play USC for the first time, Spaulding said they "were not likely to be slaughtered as some folks suspect. I would not be surprised if there was no score in the first half." He couldn't have been more wrong. USC, which would later become UCLA's cross-town rival, ran up 712 yards of rushing. By halftime the score was 32–0. The Bruins lost 76–0 before thirty-five thousand fans. One of the UCLA players remarked, "I think we had eight or ten people on our whole team who could have made [the USC] squad."

The results the next year against USC were not much better, the Bruins losing 52–0. The two schools agreed not to play again until 1936. (Spaulding never did beat the Trojans; he did have one tie before "retiring" to handle the athletic director's job after the 1938 season.) PCC schools pummeled the Bruins, and it wasn't until 1929 that they won their first conference game, beating Montana 14–0 before forty thousand spectators at the Los Angeles Memorial Coliseum. "It helped us in getting kids to come to UCLA," one player said.

Beginning in 1928 USC and UCLA shared the Los Angeles Memorial Coliseum, drawing big crowds to see the games as the sport's popularity exploded. (The Coliseum was built in 1923 in Exposition Park, across the street from the USC campus, at a cost of more than $950,000. It held 75,000 spectators. In 1930 it was expanded to seat 101,000. It also became the home of two Olympic Games.)

In 1931 UCLA played Northern California powerhouse, the St. Mary's Gaels, and pulled off a 12–0 upset. The victory proved big because UC Berkeley hadn't been able to beat the Gaels and USC had lost to St. Mary's earlier in the season 13-7. "That was the making of UCLA," said fullback Norman Duncan. The Bruins' record that year was 3-4-1. It was not much improvement, but they were more competitive. In 1932 the Bruins won their first five games, including one over Stanford, but then lost four of their last five to finish 6-4.

In 1933 the Bruins' record was 6-4-1 but was notable because an African American played for UCLA for the first time: "Sad Sam" Storey, a transfer from Los Angeles Junior College, played guard. The *Los Angeles Times* wrote that "the big colored boy has so impressed Spaulding to date that Bill thinks the fellow may be just what is needed to put a lot of dynamite in the Bruin offense." The *Times* also ran a photo of Storey with arms up, trying to break up a pass. The caption read, "It looks as though the theme song should be 'All God's Chillun Got Wings.'"

In announcing his plans for Storey, Spaulding pointed out that he had coached Sam Dunlap at Western State. "The best player I ever coached was a Negro and oddly enough his first name was Sam," Spaulding told the *Los Angeles Times*. Storey's grandson recalled in 2014 that his grandfather had told him that "all the racism he experienced from UCLA and other teams seems unreal in today's terms, but he said it was normal back then." He said his grandfather made third-team All-PCC. He said Spaulding implied that if Storey had been white, he would have been an All-American.

By 1935 Spaulding's Bruins had improved enough, at 4-1, to finish in a three-way tie for the PCC championship with Stanford and UC Berkeley. UCLA was slowly getting better against tough PCC competition and was willing to take a chance on recruiting five black football players over the next three years. Five black players on the same team? It was unheard of in those days, especially with the racial divide that existed across the country.

While UCLA may have been more progressive toward minority students than most other universities, not all was perfect on the Westwood campus. It is a delusion to think otherwise.

Bill Ackerman noted that in the mid-1930s the political activities of a minority of students "tended to create an impression of disloyalty to California and to the country. University officials then restricted the use of campus facilities for political purposes."

As Jackie Robinson's biographer Arnold Rampersad pointed out, there were three UCLAs: the original old campus downtown, the one at Westwood, and the one for black students. Because Jackie Robinson lived in town, he attended the commuter school, the old campus, where he joined no more than fifty other African American students. If blacks experienced the most racism on campus, they were not alone. They were joined by Asian American and Jewish students, who complained they were left out of social life.

Although Tom Bradley grew up not far from Woody Strode, it is doubtful they would have known each other until they attended UCLA because Strode was three and a half years older than Bradley. Bradley may not have known Kenny Washington until they met on the football field in high school. Bradley may have known Jack Robinson in those years. Curtis Howard, a mutual friend, told an interviewer simply that "Bradley also knew Robinson."

Bradley has said he knew Robinson, Strode, and Washington, who were teammates on the track team, but it is clear that he didn't spend much time with them. When he wasn't studying or involved in extracurricular activities, he was on the track training year round. "We really didn't socialize much," he said. "There wasn't a heck of lot of social activities for us."

Bradley was one of two blacks on the relay team. The other, Tom Berkley, became a respected attorney. As noted, Robinson, Strode, and Washington were Bradley's teammates at one time or another. Robinson primarily participated in the broad jump, Strode the shot and discus and was a perfect fit for the decathlon, and Washington also put the shot.

Robinson tended not to take part in campus activities as some of the other players did. Social gatherings were pretty much off limits to the blacks, but nor did Robinson join organizations representing African Americans. Robinson also was bothered by the fact that the school newspaper, the *Daily Bruin*, referred to the black players by their race; he thought such references meant they weren't completely accepted by the student community. He remarked once that he was treated like a hero when playing in front of a huge crowd on the football field, but as soon as the game was over, he was simply Jackie Robinson, the Negro.

Blacks could not live in Westwood, were not welcomed at student parties, and were denied campus jobs. The Reserve Officer Training Corps (ROTC) never had a black member, nor were there any black professors on campus. Black athletes were somewhat of an exception to the rule. They were treated more favorably, particularly because the campus knew that they would help lift the school's sports program onto a par with other PCC schools. "UCLA was the first school to really give the Negro athlete a break," Bartlett said.

During the 1940s barbers in Westwood refused to cut African Americans' hair. Those in the Naval Reserve Officers Training Corps were severely disciplined for showing up late for muster one time. They explained that they had had to go to Santa Monica to get their required weekly haircut and couldn't return in time. That brought down the wrath of the American Youth for Democracy (a youth wing of the Communist Party) and the *Daily Bruin*, which put pressure on the barbers. Marches through the streets of Westwood got the barbers to acquiesce to student demands.

Bill Ackerman noted that when UCLA elected its first black student body president, Sherrill Luke, in 1949–50, it signaled "the explicit progress of racial acceptance" on the campus. (Luke also was the school's head yell leader. He went on to become a Los Angeles County Superior Court judge.) While Luke's election was a milestone, others preceded him in student politics. Kenny Washington was one of them. He sat on the Student Council in 1941 and became embroiled in the controversy over the school's theater production of *Uncle Tom's Cabin*. As Ackerman put it, "Outside distress was agitated by concern over the use of racial stereotypes in the play based on the famous novel." Washington was appointed head of a committee to investigate. "Kenny was a really terrific youngster," Ackerman said. "He was liberal-minded and full of common sense." Washington's committee issued a report saying that the play was not degrading to blacks and that it was "simply a play full of grand entertainment."

Obstacles to Overcome

"Somewhere behind the Sambo masks superimposed by
a racist culture were the actual young black athletes."

—Michael Oriard, *King Football*

Of the thirty-eight African Americans playing football at major universities in the late 1930s, most never started a game. The prevailing factor in whether a black would start a game was that he had to be greatly superior to the white player he would replace. That was a rare occurrence. That three blacks started for UCLA in 1939 was extraordinary and helped move college football a step closer to integration. Jackie Robinson didn't start the opening game in 1939. He had to prove his worth, and once he showed his talent in that first game, he started every game thereafter except when he was injured.

In 1936 Edwin Bancroft Henderson, the African American civil rights activist, physical educator, and sports historian, noted, "To make a success in team athletics, the colored boy must be superior. Sometimes color aids him by marking him conspicuously in the course of the activity, but frequently it identifies him as the bull's eye for the shafts of the opposition." That certainly was true of the UCLA blacks, who often faced teams whose players tried to hurt African American players by kneeing them or rubbing their faces in the lime chalk lines on the field. Certainly they heard racial taunting from the sidelines as well. Although it didn't appear to be the case at UCLA, blockers purposely failed to do their jobs so that blacks running with the ball were stopped cold for no gain

Virtually all of the black players who suited up for major universities were based in the North and Midwest. They often were subjected to the indignity of being left at home when their teams traveled to Southern schools, in a "gentleman's agreement" between the two schools. They also would be held out of games when Southern teams traveled north to play. In 1930, when the Ohio State Buckeyes were to play Navy in Maryland, Ohio State officials proffered that they planned to protect a black player from the "unpleasant experience of probable race discrimination manifested in a Southern city." College administrators used that lame excuse over the next thirty years.

The gentleman's agreements began to fade in the mid-1930s. Roy Wilkins, who was then editor of the NAACP's magazine, *The Crisis*, noted that in a 1936 game between the University of North Carolina (UNC) and New York University (NYU) in Yankee Stadium an NYU black played almost the entire game. "The University of North Carolina is still standing and none of the young men representing it on the gridiron appears to be any worse off for having spent an afternoon competing against a Negro player. It is a fairly safe prediction that no white North Carolinian's daughter will marry a Negro as a result of Saturday's play, much to the chagrin of the peddlers of the bugaboo of social equality."

Wilkins, who later became the NAACP's executive director, saw the UNC-NYU game as a momentous development. If those two schools could play without incident, so could others, especially if Northern schools demanded it, and racial equality could be attained. Such play was about to take place in the West when UCLA and its black players took on four Southern schools—the University of Missouri, Texas A&M, Southern Methodist University (SMU), and Texas Christian University—all in Los Angeles.

As Michael Oriard pointed out in his book *King Football*, the national press usually ignored the benching of black players, as did local newspapers. Only some of the biggest black newspapers, such as the *California Eagle,* the *Chicago Defender,* and the *Pitts-*

burgh Courier, brought the benching to their readers. The Communist Party's *Daily Worker* also denounced the situation, Oriard wrote. The black newspapers turned their wrath on the Northern schools but not the Southern colleges.

Henderson almost presciently saw the steps UCLA was taking when he wrote, "If Negro athletes do contribute to racial respect, and despite its nature, it is conceded by many that they do, then it behooves educators and racial agencies for uplift to make great social use of athletics." It was unlikely that the Bruins had integration in mind when they recruited five African Americans; in a more practical sense they were seeking players who would lift their success on the gridiron to higher levels.

African American players also suffered the indignities of being compared with animals or being endowed a peculiar anatomical structure that gave them an advantage over white players. Henderson noted that an Ohio State University study "had shown with painstaking research, tests, and X-rays of the body of [the 1936 Olympic track star] Jesse Owens that the measurements of Owens [fell] within the accepted measurements of white men." That controversy still exists today. A Google search of "blacks' vs. whites' athletic ability" will turn up dozens of links to sites discussing whether black athletes have special physical attributes that whites lack.

It was commonplace in the 1930s to compare blacks with animals or beasts. Arthur Brisbane of Hearst newspapers called blacks "grizzlies" and "gorillas." The "missing link," that stage between monkeys and man, was often the label cast at African Americans. Some went so far as to claim that the qualities of the genes the blacks who survived the rigors of transport to the United States as slaves carried over to African American athletes.

USC's hostility toward African Americans rose to new heights with the opening of UCLA. Several athletic officials uttered racial statements, including track coach Dean Cromwell, who said the black track star was so good "because he is closer to the primitive than the white athlete. It was not long ago that his ability to run and jump was a matter of life and death to him in the jungle. His muscles are pliable and his easy-going disposition is a valuable aid to the mental and physical relation that a runner and jumper must have."

The Hollywood Anti-Nazi League led a call for Cromwell's dismissal "for asserted anti-Semetic [*sic*] and anti-Negro utterances" in the fall of 1936. In a speech to the German-American Alliance, Cromwell said he wished he "could only be that handsome boy Hitler in New York for one hour" so that he could deal with the overwhelming "foreign population" in the city.

Unfortunately that was the pervasive thinking of the time. A syndicated newspaper columnist, Hugh S. Johnson, wrote in 1938, "The average of white intelligence is above the average of Black intelligence, probably because the white race is several thousand years farther away from jungle savagery. But, for the same reason, the average of white physical equipment is lower." Commenting on Jessie Owens's exploits at the Berlin Olympics in 1936, when he won four gold medals and set three world records and tied another, the *Atlanta Journal*'s O. B. Keeler wrote, "Our fastest runners are colored boys, and our longest jumpers and highest leapers. And now, our champion fighting man with the fists is Joseph Louis Barrow." Northern and Southern U.S. newspapers and commentators attributed the prowess of the black athletes to their "jungle ancestry" as opposed to their intelligence and strong work ethic, which led to their athletic prowess.

Such were the obstacles African Americans had to overcome to establish their right to step onto the playing field with racial equality. Progress was slow, coming in small increments. However, a significant move forward came with the recruitment of the five UCLA teammates. It was as important a step as had been taken at that time. Yet even so it was a far cry from bringing an end to the prejudice. But the awareness it spurred cannot be discounted and certainly would have helped to give Henderson more hope that the country was moving in the right direction toward racial parity, slowly but nonetheless steadily.

6

A Sorry Season

"Simply one of the most ridiculously perfect human
specimens to ever walk the Earth."

—Author Todd von Hoffman on Woody Strode

Woody Strode had followed USC as a youngster. "Back then it was
always USC; they were the machine," Strode recalled. USC and Notre
Dame, both private institutions, were the predominant football
schools in America. Neither seemed interested in recruiting black
players. USC had two African American players under coach Howard Jones—Bryce Taylor and Bert Richie. One story had it that Jones
vowed he would never have another black player on his team after
Richie allegedly became involved in a scandal with a white woman.
Strode followed USC football "because they had the only football
team that amounted to anything." But he also knew he wasn't going
to be playing there. He noted that the powerful members of the USC
Alumni Association, which recruited players, "didn't seek us out."

UCLA officials invited Strode to look over the campus when he
graduated in 1934. "I didn't realize that going to UCLA was a rare
step for a black kid," Strode said. But he "took one look at the place
and said, 'This is where I want to be. Tell me what I have to do.'"
It wasn't easy going for Strode. But he was hooked on Westwood.

The UCLA officials told him he would have to take his high
school courses over again at UCLA's extension school. Jefferson
High School had ill prepared him for the rigors of university aca-

demics. He spent two and a half years in the extension school trying to meet the academic requirements that UCLA demanded. Apparently UCLA thought enough of Strode's athletic abilities that it was willing to wait for him to qualify. That's how he wound up playing with the other African Americans who were three or four years younger than he.

"There was no bullshit from upstairs," Strode said. "We had to work to get our grades before we could play football." Strode noted that most non-qualifying athletes were sent to military prep academies to prepare for UCLA, but because he was an African American, the academies wouldn't take him. "So UCLA put me under an umbrella and hid me out in [nearby] Bel Air," where the school owned a house donated by a wealthy alumnus. There he lived with three players on the team.

Strode almost flunked out. "I needed to get a C average to get into the university, and I was far from it," he explained. He received special tutoring, which helped him get through that first semester. Then he decided to buckle down. "I concentrated hard and somehow I maintained a C average," he said.

But Strode told his parents he wanted to quit because he was exhausted, and he had accomplished at least something. His parents would have none of it. So he enrolled in UCLA in 1936, the same year as Kenny Washington, who had no trouble on the academic side. Strode was twenty-one and three years older than Washington, but they hit it off right away. "I needed a running mate, and we became very close, like brothers." They became lifelong friends. Looking back on his years at UCLA, Strode recalled that going to UCLA was the best thing that happened to him. And he found the school to his liking. "We had the whole melting pot . . . and I worked hard because there was always the overriding feeling that UCLA really wanted me."

Coach Spaulding and a graduate manager, Bill Ackerman, took in one of Washington's high school games and were sold on him. Washington was of average speed but ran with great power and shifty moves. He could run over tacklers despite being pigeon-toed and knock-kneed. He also had a strong straight-arm. And apparently he had no problems meeting admission standards.

In those years freshmen weren't allowed to play on the varsity, and the Bruin freshmen had their own games against similar teams. It didn't take long for Strode and Washington to encounter racism. "We started to hear some whispering among our teammates, 'There are some players on the varsity saying they don't want to play with any niggers.'" They learned that most of the talk came from a big tackle, Celestine Moses "Slats" Wyrick, a blond, blue-eyed farm boy from Oklahoma. (Wyrick later became an actor in *Dr. Jekyll and Mr. Hyde* and *Andy Hardy's Private Secretary*, both in 1941. He died at age thirty, a day after World War II ended, when he was accidently electrocuted while in the U.S. Army Air Corps.) His teammates told Strode that Slats wasn't going to play with him. "He called you a nigger, Woody."

The next year, when Strode moved up to the varsity, Wyrick told Coach Spaulding he wouldn't play with Strode. "I can't play next to a nigger because my folks would disown me," Wyrick said. Spaulding thought he knew how to handle the situation. He put Strode on the defensive side of the ball to square off against Wyrick, who was one of the biggest lineman in college football in the 1930s at 6 feet 4 inches and 215 pounds. On the next play during a scrimmage, Strode knocked Wyrick off his feet. "You black son of a bitch," Wyrick yelled at Strode. Strode jumped on top of Wyrick and began throwing punches. The coaches stood idly by and watched until they finally pulled Strode off Wyrick. "Slats and I became good friends after that," Strode said. "He had no respect for Negroes, but I stood up for myself and he respected that." That was the only problem he had with his Bruins teammates.

Strode said that when he and Washington were on campus, they "didn't feel racial prejudice at all. Whether we had blinders on or what, I don't know." He said when he was growing up he didn't know that football wasn't integrated. "We never thought about that. . . . When I got to UCLA I had the same right as any other student." He credited Bill Ackerman for creating a positive atmosphere. "We were not ostracized from anything."

Strode was nobody to fool with. He had chiseled his body with thousands of pushups. (Few athletes lifted weights in those days. Coaches thought the extra weight would slow them down.) He had virtually no body fat. Jim Murray, the Pulitzer Prize–winning sports columnist for the *Los Angeles Times*, wrote in 1991 that Strode "was one of the most magnificent physical specimens ever to walk on an athletic field—or anywhere else."

Not long before the 1936 Olympics, where black athletes including Jack Robinson's brother Mack excelled, the Nazis sought out Strode to model for paintings for their Olympic art show. He had previously modeled for painters at a fee of twenty-five dollars a week. Once Strode was contacted by Leni Riefenstahl, the German filmmaker who became famous for her documentary on the 1936 Olympics. She had seen a photograph of Strode and brought an artist with her to Los Angeles to paint Strode's physique. They measured him from to head to toe using calipers. "We saw your picture, but we couldn't believe it," Riefenstahl said. "You have the greatest physique of any athlete we have ever seen." Strode maintained that physique throughout his long and successful movie career. The artist painted two pictures of him, commissioned by Hitler. One showed him putting the shot, the other the discus.

Los Angeles Times columnist Murray wondered whether Strode might have been the best athlete among the five black Bruins. "Robinson's drive made it unlikely anyone short of Ty Cobb could have combined motivation with sheer talent any more successfully than Robinson," Murray wrote. Strode's "speed, loping change of direction and long arms made him a natural for basketball," Murray added. "But it wasn't an economically attractive sport in those pre-NBA days. College recruiters didn't want to win any Final Fours, they wanted to win Rose Bowls."

Strode was in training to compete in the decathlon in the 1936 Olympics but couldn't go because UCLA required that he take a summer course so that he could meet the requirements to enter UCLA as a freshman. "I don't know if I could have won a gold medal," he said. "but I had become a pretty good all-around track man." Strode would have acquitted himself well if he had made the U.S. Olympic team in the decathlon. He put the shot fifty-plus feet at a time when the world record was fifty-seven feet. He also high jumped 6 feet 4 inches, and the world record was 6 feet 10 inches. He threw the discus more than 161 feet when the world record was 172 feet 2 inches. "The only event I had trouble with was the pole vault, and I learned to pole vault eleven feet," Strode remarked.

Despite the presence of Washington and Strode, the Bruins had a poor season in 1937, with a record of 2-6-1, and they still hadn't beaten USC. If anyone stood out on that team, it was Kenny Washington—for his skill and his color. The future would be looking up.

Washington made his presence felt in the first game of the 1937 season. The second time Washington touched the ball, against the University of Oregon, he sprinted for a 57-yard touchdown. The Bruins won 26–13. United Press reported that UCLA was sparked by Washington, "who defied the superstitions of his race and wore a huge golden '13' on his blue jersey."

The Bruins weren't so fortunate in their October 9 game against the Stanford Indians, although they were favored. In preparation for the game, Stanford coaches put burnt cork on the face of their scout team halfback so he would look like Washington. UCLA threw seven interceptions—only one by Washington—in a disheartening 12–7 loss. The Indians stopped the Bruins' running game as they focused on Washington, who gained few yards. It was a tragic day for Washington off the field, but he didn't know it until after the game. His uncle Lawrence was killed in an auto wreck on his way to watch his nephew play.

In a game against the Oregon State University (OSU) Beavers on a rainy October 16, Strode showed that he was a man playing among boys. Not only was he two or three years older than a vast majority of the players, but he was also a tough, aggressive player. The *Los Angeles Times* referred to Strode in flattering terms after the game. "The towering Negro sophomore not only scored UCLA's touchdown but turned in a defensive game that defies description. He made at least 80 percent of the tackles and caught runners from behind time after time after they had pierced the secondary zone." In the OSU game Washington proved he was more than just an offensive player. His interception, which he returned 48 yards, set up the touchdown pass to Strode in the 7–7 tie. Murray described Strode's toughness on the football field this way: "He was strong enough to strangle a horse and fast enough to catch one. . . . Woody played clean, but so hard that some halfbacks got a nosebleed just looking at him over a line of scrimmage."

Strode remembered that during a game against the Washington State University (wsu) Cougars on October 23 a racial incident occurred against Kenny Washington. The big back was running along the Cougars' sideline when emotional wsu coach Babe Hollingbery called Washington "a nigger," according to Strode. "You didn't call Kenny Washington a nigger without a reaction," he commented. "Kenny stopped the whole proceedings and went after the coach." A fight broke out. "But," Strode said, "that's how we were taught, to defend ourselves."

Strode recalled that "we ran into a few problems on the road. . . . They used to mark the field and sometimes when they had Kenny down they'd try to rub [lime] in his eyes. Kenny would come back to the huddle and say, 'That son of a bitch tried to hurt me.' . . . Some players would insult me. They'd call me nigger and I'd fight over that. We had white kids on our team that would react to nigger just like I did. We got so beat up, but it was like a badge of honor." But, Strode said, "if Washington knocked a guy down he'd pick him up after a play was over. He'd hit you; he had no compunction about hitting you; he'd knock you on your ass and then he'd pick you up."

One of the biggest challenges ucla faced in 1937 with the black players was an opportunity to play the smu Mustangs on November 20. smu coach Madison Bell had no problem playing a team with black players. He had competed professionally against black stars like Fritz Pollard and Paul Robeson. Bell saw this as an opportunity to show that his team was worthy of playing in the Rose Bowl. ucla saw a chance to reap a financial reward for attracting smu to the Coliseum. The Bruins went so far as to offer to bench the black players if smu insisted. As noted, Southern schools often refused to play against black players.

Bell would have none of that. He wanted Washington and Strode to play, and the Mustangs players agreed. They figured a victory over the Bruins without the two black stars "would be a hollow triumph. We figured we wouldn't get much credit for beating UCLA without Washington and Strode," Bell said. "They are the best men they have, so we voted unanimously that they be permitted to play in the game."

The game between a team with two "dark boys," as the SMU student newspaper described them, and a team of white Southerners also would have great fan appeal. Norman Borisoff, editor of the *Daily Bruin*, recalled that during the game it seemed like eleven Mustangs would jump on Washington at the same time. "I don't know how Washington survived," he said. "And maybe the worst thing was that it was just accepted in those days."

Let's concede that it often took more than one tackler to bring Washington down. But eleven? And if the opponents had racial tendencies, the pounding got worse. "It made you sick to your stomach to watch," Borisoff said. SMU players said that "it didn't make a difference whether UCLA used white players or Negroes." Washington said years later SMU was the cleanest-playing team he had ever faced. "They sure played it hard, but they never were dirty," he said. The Bruins lost 26–13 to the powerful Mustangs, although Washington threw a 45-yard TD pass to Strode.

Washington and Strode received their due. Coach Bell called Washington "one of the best players I have ever seen." *Dallas Times Herald* reporter Horace McCoy wrote about Washington and Strode: the "two black boys were everywhere; they were the entire team; they were playing with inspiration and courage, and they cracked and banged the Mustangs all over the field." Describing a brilliant run Washington made, McCoy wrote, "In that moment you forgot he was black. He wore no color at all. He was simply a great athlete." At game's end Mustang fans gave the players a standing ovation.

Several newspapers, particularly black ones, noted that SMU had played "fair and hard" and indicated that the game showed "the sun is breaking through" on the racial issue on the football field. The following year Wendell Smith, the most influential black sportswriter of that era, interviewed the Mustang coach, who told him, "I don't believe in drawing the color line in sports." Bell went further and even predicted that sometime in the future Southern white schools would recruit black players.

On November 27 in a game at the Los Angeles Coliseum, UCLA led the University of Missouri Tigers 7–0, with the Tigers slowly marching down the field, but then Washington went to work. He intercepted a pass at the 10-yard line and ran 87 yards down the field. Just as he was being tackled, he heard Johnny Ryland, a teammate, holler, "Give me the ball, give me the ball." Washington looked to make sure it was a Bruin calling for the ball and, just as he was about to hit the ground, lateraled it to Ryland, who ran in for the score. That touchdown gave the Bruins a 13–0 lead and put the game away with just ten seconds left to play. Coach Bill Spaulding remarked, "Wasn't that last touchdown play a thriller? The boys showed some pretty good downfield blocking, and Ryland and Washington put on an exhibition of headwork."

During the game Washington returned from a minor injury and got the Missouri players looking "awful mad." After Washington ran a play, "the entire Tiger line piled up on the Negro." Quarterback Ned Mathews recalled that the game was hard played by "some redneck Missouri players riding Washington pretty good and they would take chalk from the sidelines and rub it in his face," a familiar cheap shot. The *Los Angeles Examiner* noted that after the season the Missouri players put Washington and Strode on their all-opponent team. The *Examiner* sportswriter concluded that such a move was "the top gesture of the year in fellowship and neighborliness."

Going into the USC game, Spaulding was feeling the heat from former players and school officials for the 2-5-1 record for the season. It was his thirteenth season as head coach, and although he had brought the team a long way toward respectability, it wasn't enough. Sure, there had been some injuries, and one of his best players had left the team to devote more time to his studies. In midseason his players asked Spaulding to let Washington call the signals. His players were loyal to him, but the drumbeat calling for his ouster never let up.

In a preview of the USC game, the *Los Angeles Examiner* reported that "if one man can lick a football team, Kenny Washington looks like the man to do it. But if you are going to stick to the theory that a TEAM should beat a MAN, then you have to take Howard Jones' Trojans." Perhaps Washington's greatest game in his sophomore season came against the Trojans. If it had been any other team than USC, Washington would not have played. He was beat up. He was playing sixty minutes of every game. "My ribs are really hurt," he told Strode. Washington still found time to pose for a picture of himself passing the ball in the *Los Angeles Times*. The headline read, "Westwood's Chocolate Soldier."

The best the Bruins had been able to do in their nascent rivalry was to tie USC 7-7 the year before. They took the field before eighty thousand fans in the Los Angeles Memorial Coliseum on December 4. It was turning into another no contest. USC was taking it to the Bruins offensively and defensively, holding a 19-0 lead with nine minutes to go.

The Trojans had limited UCLA to 25 yards rushing and 46 passing. *Los Angeles Examiner* sportswriter Maxwell Stiles wrote after the game that Spaulding had told Washington, "You've simply got to go back in there and do whatever you can." "'I'm ready boss,' replied the gallant son of African forefathers." Considering the state of sportswriting in those days, it seems likely that both of those quotes came from Stiles's vivid imagination. And it's difficult to believe that Washington would have referred to Spaulding as "boss," a term usually associated with what slaves called their masters.

Down three touchdowns, the Bruins made their move after recovering a fumble on USC's 44-yard line. After an incomplete pass, Washington threw a pass to Hal Hirshon, who grabbed at the 10-yard line and ran in for the score. Now it was 19-7. The Trojans didn't panic; in fact, they chose to kick off after the TD, a move that the rules allowed in those days.

With the ball on the Bruins' 28-yard line after the kickoff, Hirshon told Washington, "Kenny, I can beat their safety." Washington gave him the okay and told him, "Run as fast as you can, as far as you can, and I'll hit you." Washington dropped back to his own 15-yard line and lofted a spiral 62 yards into Hirshon's hands at the 12-yard line. "I saw the pass coming," Hirshon said, "and for a moment I was afraid it was going over my head, but Kenny had the range all right 'cause it just dropped in my arms just like that." The distance was verified by a Fox-Movietone newsreel. Hirshon ran in for the score. Few players, if any, had thrown a pass that far in those days. (Washington had a bazooka for an arm. Strode remembered when teammates and Washington would have contests to see whether anyone could throw a football out of the Coliseum. "Kenny got seventy-eight rows; there are about eighty rows altogether. Try that with a baseball sometime; I'll bet you only get halfway.")

"In the winking of an eye, black lightning struck the desolate scene," the *Los Angeles Times* reported. "Black lightning in the mighty right arm of Kenny Washington, spectacular Bruin pass thrower." USC wasn't going to make the mistake of kicking off again; it decided to receive the kickoff. The Bruins' defense held, and after a punt UCLA took over at its own 43. Washington then ran for 17 yards, then 10, and then 7 more. The Bruins were on the Trojans' 14. But after three downs when they barely moved the ball, Washington dropped back to pass with just over a minute to go, spotted Strode at the 4-yard line, and rifled a pass that Strode couldn't handle.

"I saw the ball coming at me like a bullet," Strode stated. "And like a bullet it went right through me. . . . When Kenny threw the ball, he threw it hard. . . . If I couldn't get it, nobody could. I guess it just wasn't meant to be."

Coach Spaulding went to the USC locker room to see USC coach Jones. He knocked on the closed door, but no one answered. Finally Spaulding yelled out, "You can tell Howard it's all right to come out now. Kenny's stopped passing."

A *Los Angeles Times* reporter visited the Bruins' locker room, where Washington and Strode were consoling themselves. He couldn't help himself when he started writing his story about what transpired in the locker room. "Naked as a couple of chocolate cherubs as they sat dejectedly. . . ." began the story.

At season's end Washington was named the team's most valuable player for leading the Bruins in rushing (530), passing (495), and total yards (1,025). He would continue that pattern his next two years. Strode led the team in receiving.

In the spring of 1938 Washington turned out for the baseball team, the first African American to don a Bruins' baseball uniform. The genes of his father, Blue Washington, showed up too. He hit .454 that year and followed that up with a .350 average his junior year, along with stellar defense at shortstop. Apparently, for unknown reasons, he didn't play baseball in 1940. So he never played on the same field as Robinson. Rod Dedeaux, who coached USC baseball for forty-five years and scouted for the Dodgers, said he thought Washington had a better arm, more power, and more agility than Robinson.

Strode said Robinson was faster than Washington, "but Kenny could throw and he could hit." He pointed out that Washington and future New York Yankees star Joe DiMaggio were the only ones to ever hit a home run at Saint Mary's College in Moraga, California. Washington hit a home run at Stanford that some said was the longest ever hit in that Sunken Diamond during the 1939 season. The homer cleared a tree near the center-field fence at the 425-foot mark.

"If a kid had [Washington's] ability today, they'd be waving million dollar contracts in his face. But back then, in the thirties and early forties, the hurdles were just too great for a black kid to make the major leagues," Strode said. "Next to me, Jackie [Robinson] was the best competitor I ever saw," Washington said, "but when he became a baseball star it kind of shook me up. I outhit him by at least two hundred points at UCLA." "Kenny's future in baseball . . . seemed much brighter after his brief exposure to the college game than did mine," Robinson commented years later.

7

An Easy Choice

"It just burns me up that a Negro can't play football at
places like Notre Dame. But we'll show 'em; you
just wait till next fall and we'll show 'em."

—Frank Robinson, Jackie's brother

While Washington was tearing the cover off the ball at UCLA, across town in Pasadena, Jackie Robinson graduated in midyear from Muir Tech and enrolled in Pasadena Junior College (PJC) for the spring semester. It was common for students of his time to enroll in junior colleges (now called community colleges or simply colleges). In fact the goal of Pasadena high schools was to lead students to the junior college. Robinson had several reasons for wanting to go to PJC: he would be immediately eligible to play sports, whereas at a four-year university he couldn't play for the varsity until he was a sophomore; it would better prepare him for the rigors of a four-year school; tuition was free and he could live at home; PJC had a reputation for excellence; the school was one of the most liberal junior colleges in the area—most activities were opened to African Americans; his older brother Mack was attending the school; and he received no offers from four-year schools.

Robinson looked up to Mack, whom he had also followed to Muir Tech. When Jackie arrived at PJC, he played in the shadow of his brother, who was the best amateur sprinter in the United States. He had assumed that title after Jesse Owens, who had won the gold medal in the 200 meters in the 1936 Berlin Olympics, turned professional. Mack had won the silver behind Owens.

Mack almost didn't make the Olympics. He didn't have the money to attend the trials for the U.S. team. Finally a group of businessmen raised $150 for him and a teammate. Two factors kept Mack from winning the gold: he didn't have the coaching that Owens had, and he couldn't afford to buy new track shoes. "Jesse got the coaching," he said. "I didn't. . . . And I could not even get the new pair of spikes I needed." He donned the worn-down spikes he had worn all season at PJC. Mack Robinson also said Owens had the "distinct advantage" of running in the inside lane. He said he was closing the gap on Owens before Owens crossed the finish line. Owens broke the world record in a time of 20.7 seconds, a record that stood for two decades. Robinson finished second, 0.4 seconds behind Owens. "It's not too bad to be second best in the world at what you're doing," Robinson said, "no matter what it is. It means that only one other person in the world was better than you. That makes you better than an awful lot of people."

When he returned to Pasadena, Mack felt unappreciated. "If anybody in Pasadena was proud for me, other than family and close friends, they never showed it. I was totally ignored. The only time I was noticed was when somebody asked me during an assembly at school if I'd race against a horse."

At PJC Mack participated in the 100- and 220-yard sprints, the sprint relays, the low hurdles and the broad jump. Jackie was going to focus on baseball, with some track thrown in on the side. Mack set a national junior college record of 25 feet 5 1/2 inches that spring and then transferred in 1938 to the University of Oregon, where he won a number of national collegiate and Amateur Athletic Union titles. He quit Oregon in his senior year to return home to help support his family.

Mack couldn't find a decent job. He was seen sweeping downtown streets while wearing his Olympic sweatshirt with a big "USA" on the front. "I never did understand those people," he recalled years later. "I had to take whatever I could get." Mack was fired when a judge ordered all swimming pools opened to African Americans and the city retaliated by firing all black workers, including Mack. Jackie said that incident broke Mack's spirit.

Four years after the Olympics, Cullen Fentress, sports editor of the *California Eagle*, checked in on Mack. He was out of work, and Fentress lamented that something was "radically wrong with a system wherein an athlete is the toast of a race, a nation and the world one year and a few years later a 'forgotten man.'" He noted that despite all the acclaim for the African Americans' athletic success, it did little to put food on the table.

After Jackie broke the color barrier in Major League Baseball in 1947, it was Mack who fell in his shadow. "I am getting awfully tired of being referred to just as Jack Robinson's brother," he said as late as 1968. "Why even last year, when one of my sons was killed, the story only mentioned that Jackie Robinson's nephew was dead." Over the years, though, Mack became beloved in Pasadena because of his dedication to the city and its children. The city finally came around and honored Jackie and Mack with nine-foot-high busts that cost $325,000 in a grassy area across the street from City Hall. The post office was named after Mack in 2000. The stadium at Pasadena City College (as Pasadena Junior College was renamed) also was dedicated to him in 2000. He was honored as one of the most distinguished alumni of the University of Oregon and is in the University of Oregon Hall of Fame and the Oregon Sports Hall of Fame.

While Mack was setting records at PJC, Jackie began to focus on baseball with the Pasadena Bulldogs. He showed some flashy fielding at shortstop and was the team's leadoff batter. He had a good eye for the strike zone, rarely striking out, and he would cause havoc when he got on the base paths. In the second game of the season against Modesto Junior College, Robinson stole second, third, and home. The Bulldogs went on a fourteen-game winning streak, but they lost a championship game to Compton Junior College. Robinson was considered the best shortstop in the league.

During track Jackie was the second best broad jumper behind Mack. Jackie couldn't beat his brother, but he improved steadily, and by the end of the track season he had jumped 23 feet 9½ inches.

Mack had set a national junior college record of 25 feet 5½ inches. Jackie and Mack enjoyed their competitive brotherhood.

That fall Robinson turned out for football at PJC, which had a new coach, Tom Mallory, a former star at Pasadena and USC who had been coaching high school in Oklahoma City. About ten Oklahoma players followed him to Pasadena, none of whom had ever played with or against an African American. Three blacks were to start at Pasadena: Robinson; Ray Bartlett, a pass catcher; and Larry Pickens, another end. A fourth African American, Jim Wright, also was on the team.

At one point the players from Oklahoma refused to play with the African Americans, so the black players walked off the field. "We had played with Caucasian guys here in Pasadena, so it wasn't a problem for us [black players]," Bartlett recalled. "It was a problem with them. But it seemed to kind of level itself out."

A boyhood friend of Jackie's, Jack Gordon, who was playing basketball nearby, asked the African Americans why they were leaving practice. "They don't want to play with us," came the reply. About the Oklahoma players, Gordon said, "I don't think they had ever been out of Oklahoma, their talk was just thick, thick, thick southern drawl. Man, you knew where they were coming from."

When Robinson and Bartlett threatened to quit the team and transfer to rival Compton Junior College, Mallory put down the rebellion. "Coach Mallory laid down the law," Robinson said, "and the Oklahoma fellows became more than decent. We saw that here was a case where a bit of firmness prevented what could have grown into an ugly situation." Robinson "was touchy about the racial issue," Mallory said. "We didn't have too many black players on the team in those days. Some people would say that they didn't want to play against 'the nigger.' I saw what an athlete he was and I wanted him."

Bartlett, who also would earn All-American junior college honors, recalled a different scenario. He said the players from Oklahoma refused to block for Robinson during practices. At one practice Oklahoman Dick Sieber saw Robinson race downfield behind his block. "You can sure carry that ball," Sieber said. Said Bartlett, "I think that broke the ice, and we really started to come together as a team at that point." From that Robinson learned the value of protesting injustice and realized that being an athlete gave him a platform to fight against it. He put it to good use his entire life.

Robinson was clearly going to be the best player on the field for Pasadena, but on the second day of practice he chipped a bone in his right leg and wrenched his knee. He was out for a month. The team lost its first four games. When Robinson returned, he sparked the Bulldogs with spectacular runs, passes, and punt returns as they won the remainder of their games. On a trip to play Phoenix Junior College, the black players were banned from staying at the same hotel with their teammates. "We had to stay in a place that was like a house converted to a hotel," Bartlett said. "I remember the name of it well: the Rice Hotel. The black players refused to take the rooms. I don't remember any of us going to bed," Bartlett said. "I think we just sat up and talked in the lobby areas and maybe we slept sitting up in the chairs."

At season's end a white player received the team's most valuable player (MVP) award over Robinson, but Jack just shrugged it off.

While Robinson mixed freely with whites and blacks at the school, he did not entirely escape racial overtures. Shig Kawai, a Japanese American athlete at Pasadena, played football and basketball with Robinson. He remembered that "a lot of time you would hear 'Get that Jap' and 'Get that nigger.' We had to hear these other teams making racial remarks all the time." Bartlett was not exempt from racism. "I felt that because I was a Negro I was being passed over, not considered, for many things. All the clubs were white." Once on a trip with the track team to Sacramento he and another team member were denied service at a restaurant because they were "colored."

Racism was no stranger to basketball, for which Robinson turned out as soon as football season was over. He and Bartlett were starters for the Bulldogs, and it didn't take them long to realize they were being mistreated by other teams that were virtually all white and all-white officials. As the best player, Robinson was pounded by opposing players without calls from the referees. Robinson fought back. Once he smacked a player in the face with the ball, bloodying his nose. No foul was called, and he had no further problems in the game.

In a game against the Vikings of Long Beach Junior College, a substitute Viking guard, Sam Babich, continually harangued Robinson with racial remarks. He dug an elbow into Robinson's stomach, and Robinson jabbed him back. "See you after the game," Babich said. "That's up to you," Jack replied. When the final whistle blew, he punched Robinson in the face. Robinson jumped on top of him, flailing away. Fights broke out in the stands before order was restored. The *Pasadena Chronicle* reported, "Robinson, besides coming off with high point honors for the evening, also came off top man in his personal war with Sam Babich, substitute Viking [guard]." The Long Beach student body president later apologized to Robinson and the other Bulldogs. He asked Robinson whether he would shake Babich's hand and Jackie agreed, but the other player "refused to soil his white hands on me." The student body president apologized and hoped that Robinson wouldn't hold it against the entire student body. Ray Bartlett said he became fighting mad at the bad sportsmanship in games but that Robinson sloughed it off. "Jack really didn't fight back like I thought he should have," Bartlett said. "I didn't see him as being a real fighter. I've always said that what made him such a good runner [on the football field] was that he didn't want to get hit. You couldn't get away with anything against him, but he was not dirty and he was not one to start a fight."

The Bulldogs finished third in the Western Division of the Southern California Junior College Athletic Association that year, with Robinson finishing second in scoring with 131 points in ten games, 1 point behind the leader. In a game against the USC freshman team, Robinson scored 14 points while helping Pasadena end the Trojans' 81-game winning streak.

Robinson and Bartlett almost hated to see the football and basketball seasons end. For one thing, there was a training table for participants in both sports, and it meant a hearty meal at least once a day. "Listen, we were poor, we didn't have any money," Bartlett said. "I want to tell you that right now. We didn't have any money in our pockets, and we looked forward to training table because they fed us very well, steaks and all the good heavy meat and potatoes stuff."

Then it was back to baseball, a sport in which Robinson had already established himself as one of the top players in the Los Angeles junior college system. By season's end he had been named to the All-Southland junior college team and the most valuable player in the region. For the season he batted .417 in twenty-three games, scored 43 runs, stole 23 bases, and struck out only 3 times.

Robinson's participation in track caused a conflict. In 1938 he showed up late for a baseball game because he had been forty miles away at a track meet, where he jumped 25 feet 6½ inches to set a national junior college record previously held by his brother Mack. He had been given three jumps in a row before the other competitors so that he could get to the baseball game. He changed into his baseball uniform in the car on the way to the game. He arrived in the third inning and belted two hits to help PJC win the conference championship 5–3.

Jack Gordon, a teammate as well as friend, remembered one particular play when Robinson stole a base against Glendale. "Jackie was on first, had got a hit," he said. "I remember this because the day was really windy, kicking up dust all over the place. Jack took his lead, then bent down and kept picking up handfuls of dust, which he'd toss in the air. The wind blew the dust from first to third, right in the pitcher's eyes, so he had to keep brushing it away. That's when Jack stole the base. He was so smart. Even then."

In those early years Duke Snider, who, like Robinson, went on to a Hall of Fame career with the Dodgers, idolized Robinson, who was seven years older. He remembered a game when Jackie competed in baseball and track at the same time. "Five or six of us kids from Compton watched him play a baseball game, leave [between innings] with his uniform still on, trot over to compete in the broad jump in a track meet and then run back and finish the baseball game as if nothing unusual had happened. . . . That's how great and versatile he was, and how bright the fire of competition burned in him."

In an exhibition game between a Pasadena youth team and the Chicago White Sox in spring training in Southern California, Robinson had such a good game that the White Sox manager, Jimmy Dykes, said, "Geez, if that kid was white I'd sign him right now." He said Robinson could play Major League Baseball "at a moment's notice" and that if he were white, he could get a $50,000 bonus. Such a bonus was the equivalent of $826,198 in 2015 dollars. Think of what the Robinsons could have done with that.

Later Herman Hill, a reporter for the *Pittsburgh Courier*, brought Robinson to a White Sox spring training camp for a tryout. Reportedly "several white players hovered around Robinson menacingly, with bats in their hands." Robinson was rebuffed. Dykes told him that an actual tryout would have to be up to the club owners and baseball commissioner Kenesaw Mountain Landis, who once vowed that blacks would never play in the Major Leagues. Landis was known derisively in the black press as the Great White Father.

Like Robinson, Bartlett was a member of both the track and baseball teams. He was one of the few African Americans who pole vaulted. Using a bamboo pole, he reached 13 feet 6 inches. In baseball he was a first baseman and catcher. Robinson and Bartlett were selected for the Community College Sports Hall of Fame in 1984 and 1986 respectively.

In his junior college years Robinson was growing up and filling out from the skinny kid of 135 pounds to almost 175 and stretching nearly 6 feet tall. He was in superb physical condition for his second year of football at PJC.

For one game Pasadena traveled to Taft, an oil-producing town near Bakersfield. Robinson was concerned after seeing signs on businesses that read, "We do not solicit Negro trade" and "Negroes, don't let the sun set on you here." At the game fans hollered racial epithets at him, but he ignored them. Pasadena won 27–0.

Jackie had a superb season, scoring 17 touchdowns, with the team winning all eleven of its games and scoring 369 points. In the final game against Compton, forty thousand fans turned out at the Rose Bowl—then a junior college record—to watch the game. The *Los Angeles Times* reported that with Robinson in the backfield PJC drew between twenty-five thousand and forty thousand spectators per game. "Ninety-nine percent of those present were there because they wanted to see Robinson scoot," sportswriter Frank Finch wrote.

Robinson had a sensational game in the victory over Compton. He ran for two touchdowns and passed for another. Duke Snider remembered that on a punt return Robinson "reversed his field three times. Everybody on the field took a shot at him, but nobody could touch him. He was something else."

Hank Ives, who was called the nation's leading expert on junior college football, watched that game too. "My gosh, he was something to see," Ives said. "He would catch a punt, there'd be two guys on top of him and he'd flick his hip. They'd go one way, he'd go the other. He'd fake them out of their pants. He had these hipper-dipper moves. He was poetry." Ives picked Robinson for his all-time backfield for junior colleges along with Hugh McElhenny, O. J. Simpson, and Roger Staubach, all of whom went on to the National Football League Hall of Fame.

Bartlett noted that "Jack was really pigeon-toed; he kind of wobbled and dug in his toes when he ran. He was an extremely shifty runner, very, very shifty. You didn't need to knock a guy down for Jack to get by. On a lot of runs all I would do was get out in front of a tackler because I didn't need to hit anybody. With Jack, you could block two or three guys on one run because all he needed was a little space. I've seen him literally make fools out of some defensive people trying to tackle him."

For the season Robinson scored 131 points and rushed for more than 1,000 yards. He had run for a 104-yard touchdown on a fake punt, 85 yards from the line of scrimmage, leaving would-be tacklers sprawled all over the field, and sprinting 75 dazzling yards for a score. In the school's yearbook he was described as a "one-man riot" when he got hold of a football. Along with Bartlett, he was named to the All-Southland team in 1938 and was named the MVP for the Bulldogs. He also was one of ten students named to the school's Order of the Mast and Dagger, given to students who had performed "outstanding service to the school and whose scholarship and citizenship record is worthy of recognition."

Despite Jackie's acceptance at the junior college, all was not well off campus. He and his family had run-ins with police that were based more on race than deed. Robinson loathed Pasadena, remarking at one time that if his family hadn't lived there, he would never have gone back. "I've always felt like an intruder, even in school," he said. "People in Pasadena were less understanding, in some ways, than Southerners. And they were more openly hostile."

When Robinson graduated from Pasadena, he attracted a great deal of attention for his athletic abilities. He said Fresno State College, in California's central valley, promised him an apartment for him and his mother, accommodations for his girlfriend (he didn't have one), a monthly allowance, and a lump sum to be deposited into his bank account and available when he graduated.

A Stanford alumnus purportedly offered to pay Robinson's expenses to any school outside the PCC. (Stanford didn't want him of course. The university had never had an African American player, and the academic standards may have been too high. Nor did Stanford want him to play for any other PCC team.) His brother Mack tried to get Jackie interested in Oregon but to no avail. Nor did Oregon show much interest. "I told [Oregon] he could make any team on campus. But I guess they just thought I was trying to get a free ride for my brother. They ignored him."

USC showed some interest, but Robinson thought that coach Howard Jones just wanted to put him on the bench to keep him away from other schools. "Howard Jones was a good coach, but he was a very prejudiced man," Bartlett said. A student journalist at PJC recalled that USC had offered Robinson "a real good scholarship [with] some benefits he probably wouldn't get at UCLA."

Woody Strode said USC used its money and influence to get the best athletes, "and they could get just about anybody they wanted." He observed that USC players drove brand new Fords. "I remember USC bought a house for one kid's parents, and he became a star running back and an All-American." Apparently other schools weren't beneath similar tactics. Strode noted that alumni "threw the keys to a brand-new Dodge on [Robinson's] front porch."

Finally Jackie decided to enroll at UCLA. He also persuaded Bartlett to join him at Westwood. He wrote in Bartlett's yearbook after the 1939 school year, "To a sweet player. Luck and happiness, here's hoping you come over next year. Sincerely, Jack." Bartlett joined Robinson at UCLA because "we figured we'd get a break. We felt if we played at USC, we'd probably sit on the bench because of racism." Bartlett also would become a four-sports athlete at UCLA.

Robinson liked UCLA because tuition was free except for a token administrative fee, and he could commute to Westwood from his home. In addition, he wanted to stay close to home because he wanted to be near his family, particularly his brother Frank, who had always been one of Jackie's biggest supporters. "One of my major reasons was to be able to continue to benefit from Frank's encouragement. . . . I didn't want to see Frank disappointed," Robinson said.

Jackie liked the opportunity even more when UCLA hired Babe Horrell in 1938 as its new head football coach at $17,000 a year. Horrell had attended PJC and had gone on to earn All-American honors as a center and captain of UC Berkeley's "Wonder Team" of 1923. That clinched it for the junior-to-be Robinson. But first he had to make up classes in French, geometry, and algebra that he had skipped at PJC.

Bill Spaulding, now athletic director, half wondered whether the Bruins were doing the right thing. "He [Robinson] was so good at everything, I was afraid our four coaches would start fighting among themselves," he recalled. In those days, the graduate manager ran the athletic program, and the athletic director worked under him. And when a coach was fired, the school found a job for him. That's how Spaulding became athletic director. Woody Strode remembered that graduate manager Bill Ackerman told Spaulding "what to do and Spaulding did it." Strode was sorry to see Spaulding go, but he noted, "A large part of success is timing; Bill Spaulding's timing stunk."

Bartlett stayed at PJC in the spring of 1939 while Robinson was making up needed credits. Bartlett had no trouble with school work. When he graduated from PJC, he became the first black to receive the Key Award for scholarship, citizenship, and athletic ability from the Kiwanis club. He would join Robinson in the fall for the opening of football practice.

8

Fitting in at UCLA

"The new setting [at UCLA] was different,
but it did not faze me."

—Tom Bradley

UCLA and track were a perfect match for Tom Bradley. He recalled that while most universities in America refused scholarships to African American athletes, UCLA gave him financial assistance to study and compete in track and football, although he had never played football. He also worked summer jobs. Once he worked at a used-tire and scrap-iron yard for three days before he quit. "After wearing out six pairs of gloves and putting blisters on both my hands, I realized that hard labor like that just wasn't the kind of thing that I wanted to do all my life," he concluded. One of his best summer jobs was as a photographer for comedian Jimmy Durante.

Bradley wasn't the only athlete to hobnob with celebrities. Strode and Washington worked at the Warner Brothers movie studio. "Every morning the studio would assign us to a sound stage, and we'd stand around and wait for someone to order something," Strode recalled. They dressed up in brown coats with epaulets, gold-braided ropes hanging from the shoulder, and bellhop caps. "We took care of the stars." Among them were Bette Davis, Jimmy Cagney, Ann Sheridan, and Olivia De Havilland. Once Strode encountered Errol Flynn. "Oh, you and Kenny," Flynn said. "I just love watching you guys play!" Movie stars loved football, Strode remarked. "[Once] I was told to bring a tray of food to Jane Wyman's dressing room. . . . I saw her sitting there in that powder-blue silk robe, one leg half out; I was mesmerized by her beauty; she had a face like an angel." Wyman watched Strode come in the door, and he became so flustered that he tripped on the threshold and fell down, spilling the food and coffee all over the carpet. "But she smoothed it all over for me and helped me clean it up. She said, 'You know, I'm a big fan of yours, you and Kenny Washington. How are you boys going to do this year?'"

"I didn't take any persuasion [to attend UCLA]," Bradley said. "I was just . . . anxious to be able to go to college by way of scholarship." He was recruited by another African American, quartermiler Jimmy LuValle, the international track star who was attending UCLA. LuValle had also graduated from Polytechnic High School in Los Angeles. After talking with track coaches Harry Trotter and Elvin "Ducky" Drake, LuValle told Bradley UCLA was offering him a scholarship. Bradley said years later that if it weren't for LuValle, he would not have gone to college; instead he would have taken a job out of high school. The scholarship to UCLA "was an automatic yes," Bradley said.

Bradley's long sought-after goal became a reality. He would be on a track team that at one time or another included seven African Americans: Tom Berkley, Bill Lacefield, Ray Bartlett, Jackie Robinson, Woody Strode, Jimmy LuValle, and Kenny Washington. He formed lifetime friendships with members of the track team, both black and white, and would get together with them for reunions. Carl McBain, a white hurdler on the track team, said about Bradley, "You could see why he'd do well in politics. You liked him right away, he was so easygoing."

Bradley commuted from home by bus. He found a campus with about a hundred blacks out of seven thousand students. "I don't know of any blacks who lived directly on campus," Bradley recalled. He remembered that Berkley lived near campus, "but there was nobody that lived in the dorms or fraternity houses."

While minorities were accepted on the UCLA campus, that didn't always mean that African Americans escaped some racial overtones or discrimination. In one case Bradley took the side of Arnett Hartsfield, an African American student who was denied an opportunity to take an advanced ROTC course despite excellent grades and strong leadership qualities. Bradley and Hartsfield appealed to the public on a left-wing radio station by heavily criticizing UCLA for its bias and prejudice. The school caved in, and Hartsfield became the first black in the ROTC program. He became a firefighter in the Los Angeles fire department. ("Most of the black firefighters couldn't put their food in the station house refrigerator. It would get contaminated if they did.") He later became a lawyer.

Bradley was convinced that UCLA played a vital role in setting a standard across the country for standing up for black athletes. "Some of the schools with which UCLA had an affiliation did not permit blacks to compete on the same teams," he said. "And UCLA administration made the decision that no school that would discriminate against its athletes could any longer compete in athletics with us." "UCLA, I think of all the major universities in the country, probably set standards for equality of opportunity and a demand for equal treatment of its athletes that ultimately became a matter of practice all over the country," Bradley stated.

Bradley and Washington were close while on campus. He also knew Robinson well enough to be surprised that he could take the pressure he did when he broke baseball's color barrier. "We would have thought a guy like Kenny would be more ideal because of his temperament. He was more self-contained. Jack was so volatile that he just wouldn't accept some of the abuse that was often thrown his way."

Track was the perfect sport for Bradley. For someone who was a joiner and a leader, he was an unusually private person. Track is a loner's sport, except for the relays, where runners work as a team. He could get lost in his thoughts while training or racing with no teammates to worry about, as would be the case in football. "The whole business of competition—in track, particularly because you're kind of one-on-one in track—involves a kind of discipline you have to develop for yourself. I think it really [is] part of my lifestyle."

Bradley joined Kappa Alpha Psi, one of the two African American fraternities on campus (Strode belonged to the other one), and it proved to be a strong network that he would call upon during his political career. Bradley also became a member of the University Religious Conference; the University Negro Club; and Carver Club, named after George Washington Carver, the famous black scientist. The Carver Club was a political group that worked toward integration. Bradley also was a member of the Junior NAACP and president of the Bruin Club. Most, if not all, of these organizations were concerned with discrimination issues on the campus.

Bradley and other black members of the track team were very close, and the white athletes stood up for them as well. If the black athletes were prohibited from staying at a hotel or eating at a restaurant, none of the others would use the services of these establishments. On one trip to Arizona, he and other black athletes were prohibited from riding in the passenger train, so the coaches and the entire team agreed to ride with them in the cattle cars. All track members stayed in private homes when the blacks were turned away at hotels. Bradley recalled that his teammates declared that if the blacks couldn't stay there, neither would they. "It just became that much of a common spirit among the members of that team," Bradley said.

Bradley ended his college career as a three-year letterman. He competed in the 440-yard run, the 880, and the 1,600-yard relay. The 440-yard run was his best race. His best time was 48.2 seconds in 1939, considered excellent for that time. The world record, set in 1971, is 44.58 seconds. (The 400-meter, a shorter race, has been used to determine world records since then.)

When Bradley later became the mayor of Los Angeles, he attributed his personal drive toward success to those years of running the 440. "My old track coach Ducky Drake . . . always used to push us to strive harder in the last 100 yards," Bradley recalled. "He'd tell us, 'Keep your knees up and run your guts out.' It was the toughest race. You had to sprint all the way. After running 200 yards you were really in no shape to think about putting out any more. Well, we'd gone through the [1963] election and faded in the stretch," but Bradley remembered Drake's coaching and ran the final spurt to victory.

Bradley ran track at the same time as USC track star Louis Zamperini, who would go on to world acclaim more than seventy years later as the subject of the best-selling book *Unbroken* (and movie by the same name) about his time as a Japanese prisoner during World War II. Zamperini won the mile and two-mile races while Bradley finished third in the 880-yard run in a triangular meet among UCLA, USC, and the Olympic Club on April 22, 1939. Once in a track meet against USC, Bradley, Berkley, Lacefield, and Strode accounted for 23 1/2 points of the 35 earned by the entire UCLA squad.

9

Under-the-Table Help

"When they took me out to Westwood for the first time it
was like taking a young boy to Disneyland."
—Woody Strode

UCLA knew that if it wanted to be competitive on the football field,
it would have to sweeten the pot for recruits. Several schools sought
Washington, Robinson, Strode, Bartlett, and (to a lesser extent)
Bradley.

Strode revealed in his autobiography that UCLA offered to pay for
him to attend remedial classes before enrolling at Westwood. But
the university also gave him a scholarship and financial support. By
today's standards the financial aid would be illegal, and even then
it was questionable, so much so that a widespread investigation of
all PCC football programs was launched in 1940.

If Strode's package was any indication, more than likely Washington's was even more lucrative, for he was the best player on the
West Coast, perhaps in the country. Washington never publicly
revealed what his benefits were, but Robinson's became known.

Strode wrote that UCLA "ended up taking care of me and my
whole family while I was in school." UCLA officials gave him one
hundred dollars a month and an eleven-dollar meal ticket. "Every
week they gave me twenty bucks under the table so I could pay the
bills at home." He also got a car, free books from Campbell's Book
Store, and all his clothes free from Desmond's. He also sold his tick-

ets to home games. "Well, you can imagine what a candy store that was for me," he said.

Strode noted that actor Joe E. Brown and wealthy real estate developer Ed Janss donated money to UCLA, and it was doled out for scholarships. Brown's son played second string behind Strode and was student body president in the 1938–39 school year. Janss owned a great deal of property in Westwood. Brown and Janss gave Strode a tour of the campus while recruiting him. "This is where I want to be," Strode told them. "Tell me what I have to do."

What Bartlett received to play for UCLA is unknown, but based on his career at PJC it is more than likely to have been similar to what Robinson got.

Bradley received an athletic scholarship, but he never revealed the amount. Within eighteen months after attending UCLA, he said, he had saved enough money to buy a car, which he used to commute to the campus. He also gave rides to fellow African American students for ten cents.

Alumni and boosters did most of the recruiting in those days, and that's where the problems came in with the PCC investigators. For example, Bob and Blanch Campbell, who owned Campbell's Book Store near the Westwood campus, were UCLA boosters. When Robinson was at PJC, the new coach, Babe Horrell, asked the Campbells whether they would join him in watching Robinson play . After the game, Horrell asked Bob Campbell, "Would you like to have Jack come over and play for us [at UCLA]?" Campbell replied, "Gee, that would be great. Do you think he would?"

Horrell said he was working to bring Robinson to play for UCLA in 1939. He took him to the Campbells' bookstore, and the Campbells eventually hired him to work there. Bob Campbell remembered Robinson as a dependable, charming young man. "[He] was always eager to cooperate," Campbell said. "We seemed to hit it off very well and became lifelong friends."

Washington and Strode also worked for the Campbells. Bob Campbell was a member of the Young Men's Club of Westwood Village, a booster club started in 1933. He was its first president. Before then, Campbell said, "We had been helping the football players in various ways. I'd been giving them books and supplies to help them." He and other boosters decided to form the club. "We decided to really organize, like the other schools," he said. "We aided the players substantially and gave the boys what the other schools were giving."

The help still was forthcoming when Robinson stepped onto campus. The 1931 Plymouth that Robinson drove to UCLA was replaced by a newer Ford "that somehow he had managed to acquire." UCLA was only trying to play catch-up with what other schools had been doing for years. Bartlett believed that the Campbells had arranged for Robinson to acquire the Ford. He noted that the Campbells had loaned him twenty-five dollars, interest-free and without security, to help him buy a car, "and when I paid them back, they were shocked." Providing jobs for athletes was common. Several schools in the conference allowed players to "work" for their tuition and fees in various make-work tasks on and off campus. One USC athlete's "job" was to empty the campus pay phones once a week. Athletes turned in time cards for hours not worked.

Because of such inducements the presidents of the ten PCC schools agreed to hire former FBI agent Edwin H. Atherton to investigate the California schools. (Atherton would later become the conference's commissioner.) "Atherton was one tough dude," the *Los Angeles Times'* sportswriter Melvin Durslag recalled in a 1991 column, "impressively incorruptible."

The PCC's Northwest members—the University of Washington, Washington State, the University of Oregon, Oregon State, the University of Idaho, and the University of Montana—apparently were behind the demands for the investigation because they felt at a disadvantage in recruitment and finances with the big-city schools of California. For example, PCC schools took home big paychecks— $85,000—for playing in the Rose Bowl. (Today the money is split among all the schools in the Pac-12 Conference.) Of the twenty-three Rose Bowls in which the PCC participated between 1916 and 1940, the four California schools were in sixteen of them. In addition, the California schools had a bigger population base on which to draw to fill their stadiums. Los Angeles, for example, had a population of 1.5 million in 1939, while Eugene, Oregon, home of the Oregon Ducks, had 21,000. In 1939 UCLA had gross receipts of $550,000, while Washington State in tiny Pullman (even today the population still is only about 31,500) took in about $81,500. Said one Southern California official, "The Northwest colleges are jealous of our success. They can't whip us on the athletic field, so they are trying to do it behind closed doors at conference meetings. It's just a gang-up deal."

On January 5, 1940, right after the Rose Bowl, Atherton issued a two-million-word report that cost $40,000 and had taken two years to prepare. It documented the abuses and violations of PCC rules, including high-pressure methods to attract recruits, trips and entertainment for recruits paid for by alumni, financial inducements in the form of jobs, and payment for jobs not actually worked. Atherton singled out UC Berkeley, UCLA, and USC for offering subsidies, free equipment, and entertainment to high school students. Among the violations Atherton pointed out were the same inducements that Strode had received to attend UCLA. In all, ten high school players were declared ineligible to play at UCLA, USC, and UC Berkeley. Atherton felt it was unfortunate that his actions to ban the players hurt the players more than the schools. "The sad part of it is that the schools are in no position to punish overzealous alumni or friends who make these boys ineligible by their activities," he said.

Campbell recalled that "we had a little mix-up" when Atherton began looking into alumni and booster interactions with the athletes. Campbell told Atherton that the Young Men's Club had nothing to hide. Most of the aid to athletes came not from campus sources but from booster clubs. "We decided to let him see what we were doing. Atherton told me afterward that we were the only club that let him see their books," Campbell said. "The other schools showed him a little bit, but he had to dig out all of the rest."

As a result of the investigation, Earl J. Miller, UCLA's athletics faculty representative, "cut some of the boys off when he learned [the club] was paying them for work they didn't do." Campbell called Miller to ask, "What good is that going to do if we aren't going to have any boys left?" Miller replied, "Oh, we're going to have boys left. We're just eliminating these things as we come to them. I'm sorry, but we've got to do this."

73

Campbell said all UCLA players stayed in school, "and they scraped up money from somewhere. In a few months we gave them money again without worrying about going through channels. We found out that every school was giving the boys money one way or another, so everybody went on doing just what they'd been doing before." Despite the lengthy and costly investigation it was business as usual at the California schools.

10

Filling the Coffers

"They came to see Kenny and me play."

—Woody Strode

During the years before Washington, Strode, Robinson, and Bartlett joined the Bruins, the UCLA athletic program had accumulated a net loss of $249,187 for all sports. But football was the biggest revenue producer, and those revenues soared from 1936 to 1940. That's not to say that revenues rose dramatically because of the black players alone but because of the better teams on which they played a major role. Certainly their exciting athletic ability proved a huge drawing card. Woody Strode remembered minorities flocked to the UCLA football games because of the African American players: "If we drew one hundred thousand people to the Coliseum, 40,000 of them would be black; that was about every black person in the city of Los Angeles. We received a lot of attention from the press and that added to our exposure."

In the mid-1930s the university recognized that if it were to have a financially stable athletic program, it would have to have a winning program. That meant recruiting the best players available, and those just happened to be players like Kenny Washington and Jackie Robinson.

In 1933, partly because of the expenses of joining the PCC, UCLA's athletic program had accumulated a net loss of $178,159. By the 1936–37 school year it had increased, as noted above, to $249,187.

The football team had a 6-3-1 record. By the end of the 1938–39 athletic year, when Washington and Strode played, the Bruins' record was 7-4-1, and the net loss had been reduced to $244,733. The next year, when the four African Americans played, the Bruins' record improved to 6-0-4, and the net loss dropped to $150,810. The next season, when just Robinson and Bartlett took the field, the team won one game and lost nine, and the net loss was down to $111,813. The loss wasn't entirely erased until 1944–45. While the four were playing, the athletic department's revenues offset expenses by about $133,000.

Coach Spaulding was back for his fourteenth year but announced that 1938 would be his last season. He was going to devote his time fully to being athletic director. He ended his career at UCLA with a 72–51–8 record. His PCC record was 33-34-6.

UCLA fans received a scare in mid-January 1938 when rumors circulated that Washington and Strode were considering transferring to the University of California at Berkeley. A *Los Angeles Times* reporter wrote that a "secret conference" had been held between the two players and a Berkeley assistant in Los Angeles on New Year's Day, when the Golden Bears played Alabama in the Rose Bowl. The writer claimed he was told that one player would not transfer without the other. The article remarked without explanation that "it is felt [UC Berkeley], larger of the two schools, offers greater opportunity for the future of both youths." It also noted that a "feeling of loyalty" toward UCLA was a big obstacle in making the transfer. Ultimately both players remained at Westwood.

In the first game of the 1938 season, the Bruins were favored to defeat the University of Iowa Hawkeyes, from the Western Conference (which later became the Big Ten). One reason was Washington, whom *Los Angeles Times* sports columnist Braven Dyer described as "the mighty colored boy who runs with the elusiveness of a moonbeam and throws with the power and accuracy of a howitzer." But it was Woody Strode who stood out in the dominating 27-3 win over the Hawkeyes in front of a Coliseum crowd of forty thousand. Strode, described as "the giant Negro right end," blocked a punt that led to a UCLA touchdown, recovered a fumble in the Iowa end zone for another touchdown, and partially blocked a second punt.

The Bruins traveled to Eugene, Oregon, for their next game to take on the University of Oregon Ducks. One sportswriter picked UCLA to win by three touchdowns. It wasn't to be. Trailing 14–12 with a minute to go, the Bruins' Charlie Fenenbock broke out for what appeared to be a 55-yard game-winning touchdown. A referee didn't think so. He said Fenenbock's knee hit the ground when he cut back during his run, although Fenenbock said he just put his hand on the ground to right himself from falling. The Bruins were infuriated, but the call stood. Game over; 14–12 Oregon.

Washington had a poor game. He was trapped behind the line of scrimmage several times and fumbled twice. He gained just 33 yards in 12 carries. He was becoming a target because of the hype over his talent. For the next game, against the University of Washington Huskies, Washington was moved to fullback to make room in the backfield for Fenenbock. Spaulding hoped with both of them on the field, attention might free up Washington's running game.

The Huskies had won all of the first four games against UCLA without allowing a single point to the Bruins: 19–0, 10–0, 14–0, and 26–0. This time it was UCLA's turn to shut out the Huskies. Kenny Washington scored both touchdowns in a 13–0 victory, one on a lateral after a Huskies fumble and the second on a 1-yard run. Other than that, he had a mediocre day with 22 yards on 10 carries.

Los Angeles Times reporter Dyer wrote the lateral play showed that "true sportsmanship and team play draws no color line." Jack Montgomery had recovered the fumble, and when he was about to be tackled, he lateraled the ball to Washington. Montgomery ran downfield to throw a block that made Washington's sailing clear to the goal line. The play, Dyer said, "revealed alertness of mind and body, fighting ability and co-operation to the nth degree."

Next the Bruins traveled north to play UC Berkeley, but they were overmatched. The Golden Bears ran over them 20–7 and held Washington in check. He ran for 54 yards on 13 carries and fumbled three times. The game wasn't as close as the score might indicate. The Berkeley rooting section yelled "small fry" at UCLA throughout the game in reference to the football prowess (or lack thereof) of "Cal's cousins."

In their next game, the Bruins overpowered the University of Idaho Vandals 33–0, the "marauding moleskins from Moscow." Washington ran for 123 yards on 9 carries. The Bruins beat Stanford 6–0 on October 30 in the Coliseum behind "the colored boy," Washington, who ran for 104 yards on 23 carries.

UCLA traveled to Pullman, Washington, on November 5, and Washington had runs of 24 and 51 yards in a 21–0 rout of the Washington State University Cougars. Strode, who was described as "Kenny's sun-burned playmate," blocked a punt that led to Washington's first touchdown. *Los Angeles Times* sportswriter Frank Finch also credited the "the Jewish jitterburg," Izzy Cantor, for "looking pretty good." Washington finished the game with 137 yards on 18 carries.

UCLA went out of its conference to play the University of Wisconsin Badgers of the Western Conference in a November 12 game. The Bruins fell to the Badgers 14–7 and fumbled ten times, six of which Wisconsin recovered. Wisconsin also dropped the ball eight times but retained possession on seven. After the game Badgers coach Harry Stuhldreher, one of the famed Four Horsemen of Notre Dame, praised Washington: "That Washington is a sweet football player."

In their second to last game of the regular season, the Bruins were demolished by USC 42–7 in front of sixty-five thousand fans at the Coliseum. UCLA struck first after a USC fumble on the opening kickoff. After that it was all USC. Washington had a poor game. He had three passes intercepted, one of which was returned 52 yards for a touchdown. Washington also fumbled a punt that gave the ball to the Trojans on the Bruins' 16-yard line. Total yardage favored the Trojans, 287 to 64, not a particularly fruitful afternoon for the Bruins.

The Bruins finished their regular season with a 6–6 tie against Oregon State before seventy-five hundred fans at the Coliseum. Even though they rolled up 388 yards and 23 first downs to the Beavers' 114 and 3 respectively, the Bruins had to rally to earn the tie. They twice failed to score within the 5-yard line. A missed drop-kick field goal attempt from the 17-yard line with five seconds to go kept UCLA from the victory.

UCLA still had two postseason games in Hawaii. UCLA posted lopsided wins over the Hawaii All-Stars (46–0) and the University of Hawaii (32–7) in the fourth annual Pineapple Bowl (for its first three years it was the Poi Bowl) in Honolulu. The Bruins ended the season with a 7-4-1 record.

The two games in Hawaii were a homecoming for two UCLA players, Francis and Conkling Wai, of Hawaiian, Chinese, and Caucasian descent. The Wai brothers became close with the black players because of discrimination they all faced. Francis Wai, who was the "Asian Jackie Robinson," was later killed in World War II. He was awarded the Medal of Honor posthumously in 2000, the first Chinese American to receive the award. He also was named to the UCLA Athletic Hall of Fame for basketball, football, track and field, and rugby.

Apparently it was frowned upon for Hawaiian athletes to go to the mainland to play, and the University of Hawaii players were going to let the Wai brothers know about it. During the game the brothers were injured. Conkling Wai's nose was smashed on the first play of the game, and Francis suffered a shoulder injury. Neither played the rest of the game. Strode didn't take this lightly, according to the *Honolulu Advertiser*. "Midway in the second period, Woodrow Wilson Strode, stellar visiting end, was chased from the field and the Uclans [were] penalized half the distance to the goal for [his] using his dukes too freely."

Spaulding took twenty-five of his favorite players on the Hawaii trip, which lasted from December 15, 1938, until January 11, 1939. They traveled on the luxury liner *SS Masonia* for four and a half days. When they arrived, they stayed at the Royal Hawaiian Hotel on Waikiki Beach. Strode remembered walking around Honolulu and seeing "people darker than us. Polynesians and Orientals, all manner of mixed breeds. They walked around with no restrictions." When he returned home, Strode told his mother, "I saw the people free."

While attending a luau on the beach, Strode noticed a girl looking at him, dressed as he was in a tweed suit, his hair "gassed and shining.... I could see in her eyes she loved me." The girl was Princess Luukialuana Kalaeloa, who was one of the hula dancers hired to perform at the luau. Her name meant "May the rays of sunrise forever shine on you." She was a "beautiful native girl, with dark skin and eyes that shone." At the end of the luau, Kalaeloa put a lei around Strode's neck and invited him to a party, but Strode didn't go. "I was too afraid of the interracial scene." Later she showed up at the ship as it was leaving to take the team back to Los Angeles. She made Strode promise they would meet again. And they did. Two years later they were married, an event that touched off more interracial trouble. Meeting Kalaeloa would prove to be life-changing for Strode later on.

The Wai brothers had a chance meeting with Academy Award–winning director John Ford on Waikiki Beach that indirectly led to Strode's movie career. The brothers saw a lonely looking Ford walking on the beach, and they invited him to join them for a drink. He accepted. When he was in Los Angeles, he looked up the brothers. It turned out that Ford's daughter was a friend of Princess Kalaeloa. Ford met Strode and was taken with his movie actor's physique and handsome face. Later on Strode appeared in several of Ford's movies.

11

High Expectations

"Take away the Negro stars from the UCLA
team and you would not have a team."

—*Pasadena Star-News*

While he was being hailed as an "outstanding all-around athlete,"
Jackie Robinson told newspaper reporters that he was going to focus
on football and the broad jump in track. Playing four sports would
be too difficult, Robinson said. "And besides, I think I should study.
That is why I chose UCLA. I don't intend to coast so that I can play
ball." Such comments led to speculation that Robinson may have
been limiting his sports so he could more clearly focus on the broad
jump for the 1940 Olympics.

When Robinson enrolled at UCLA in 1939, he began taking advantage of the team's training table. For a youngster who often had little to eat, the bounty on the training table was a feast. He and Ray
Bartlett chowed down.

Robinson concentrated on his studies that spring, limiting his
sports activity to playing basketball in a statewide league of Negro
fraternities. "The Black Panther," as the *California Eagle* called him,
scored twenty-five points in one game at a time when team scores
ran no higher than thirty or forty points. During the summer he
found time to win the men's singles and doubles championship in the
Western Federation of Tennis Clubs, which was restricted to blacks.
He and his doubles partner never lost a set during the tournament.

Again the *Eagle* chimed in, noting his "devilish placements, speed, and a merciless little cut, used in net play." One observer said, "The amazing thing about Robinson's performance was that although he played little tennis he nevertheless ran roughshod over players who are devoted to the sport year-round and for years on end."

Brother Frank Robinson never got the chance to watch Jackie play at UCLA. That summer tragedy struck the Robinson family. A car plowed into the motorcycle Frank was driving, critically injuring him. He died the next day. "It was hard to believe he was gone, hard to believe I would no longer have his support," Robinson said. Frank's death put him in the doldrums, during which he was often aloof. The impact of Frank's death on Jackie was misread by those who at times questioned his attitude and dour disposition.

Robinson kept busy that summer also playing golf and baseball, awaiting the start of the school year. Robinson made golf look simple. He shot a 90 at Pasadena's Brookside Park the first time he played the game. He also played badminton competitively against Pasadena's Dave Freeman, who became a world champion. Ray Bartlett recalled that Robinson also excelled at soccer and handball. "At lunchtime, we'd have a little time and get into these games. Was he good? He was good at any game he took up. I think maybe soccer and handball required these moves everybody later saw in baseball, but I don't know. He was just an outstanding athlete from the start."

Robinson found himself in trouble with the law on September 5 before he took his first class. He, Ray Bartlett, and other friends in Jackie's car got into a shouting match with a white driver who had called them niggers. When they pulled over, the white man soon was surrounded by a group of forty to fifty young black men. "Well, I'm the only white guy here, and I'm not foolish enough to try to fight all of you," he said. About that time, a motorcycle policeman arrived and drew his gun on a young black man who had just rushed up to see what was going on. Robinson jumped between the two men and urged the black man to calm down. But the policeman pushed Jackie up against the side of his car with a pistol pressed against his stomach. "You can't explain anything to a man who thinks that no Negro is up to any good and that the best place for him to be is in jail," Robinson commented years later. He was taken to jail, where he was held overnight on charges of hindering traffic and resisting arrest. The next day he posted a twenty-five dollar bail and was released after pleading not guilty.

The significance of the arrest was that Jackie had been given a suspended ten-day jail sentence for an earlier infraction on the condition that he behave himself for two years. The more recent incident happened within a year, so he was looking at jail time. That could have jeopardized his playing football at UCLA.

UCLA wasn't about to let that happen. Coach Babe Horrell and UCLA boosters hired a prominent attorney to fight the charges. When the case was heard, Jack pleaded guilty to a lesser charge of obstructing a sidewalk, and the resisting arrest charge was dropped. He forfeited his twenty-five dollar bail, and he was released without further punishment. The *Pasadena Star-News* wrote that Robinson's light punishment could have been attributed to the attorney, who requested "that the Negro football player be not disturbed during the football season." Robinson admitted, "I got out of that trouble because I was an athlete."

Nevertheless, Robinson was unhappy with the publicity the case attracted, and he was uneasy on the UCLA campus for a few weeks after. Newspapers used sports jargon to sensationalize the case. One headline read, "Gridiron Phantom Lives Up to Name." The story then continued: "City officials and UCLA's gridiron opponents were warming the same mourner's bench yesterday—and pondering the futility of trying to out-maneuver Jackie Robinson, the Bruins' pigskin-packing phantom." Robinson found it difficult to live down such stories, and they led to his somewhat standoffish behavior at UCLA. The event hung heavily over Robinson during the season and years beyond. "This thing followed me all over and it was pretty hard to shake off."

Robinson made up for his classroom deficiencies and was looking forward to the fall semester and the start of the football season. Expectations for another successful year were high after the best season in UCLA's history.

The high expectations for the football season drew a lot of press attention, particularly from black publications, because of the presence of five African American players as practice began. The *Chicago Defender* printed a photograph of Woody Strode with the headline "A Bronze Hercules," as he threw a discus in track. Robinson also was featured when he arrived on the first day of football practice. The *California Eagle* noted that five black players was "the largest number ever to play on a single university team" that did not belong to a black school. The *Eagle* wrote just before the Bruins' first game, against Texas Christian University (TCU), "We will devote a lot of space to the UCLA entry because it is the only major institution on the coast on whose football squad there are [five] Negro athletes. We hope that in the future other institutions follow the Westwood lead."

A great deal of the excitement was pinned on Robinson's talents. "All Jackie did at Pasadena," the *Los Angeles Times* wrote in a stereotypical manner toward blacks, "was throw with ease and accuracy, punt efficiently and run with that ball like it was a watermelon and the guy who owned it was after him with a shotgun." Ray Bartlett pointed out that Robinson "had the abilities to duck and dodge and stop quick and stop cold. It's just amazing what he could do with his body if he had a little room to do it in."

Robinson "was the first of the Gale Sayers/O. J. Simpson/Eric Dickerson–type running back, Woody Strode wrote in his memoirs. "He had incredible breakaway speed coupled with an elusiveness you had to see to believe. He could change direction quicker than any back I had ever seen. Stop on a dime: boom; full speed in the other direction. They didn't have to do a lot of blocking for him because he was so instinctive. He was shifty and quick and would just outmaneuver everybody."

Coaches were singing Bartlett's praises as well. They called him an underrated player for whom they had high hopes, The *Los Angeles Times* described him as "a sticky pass snatcher and a capable interference smasher-upper."

When Robinson joined Washington and Strode, white publications dubbed them the "Gold Dust Trio." The threesome took the field for the first time on September 29 against the Horned Frogs of all-white TCU, an archconservative Disciples of Christ-affiliated institution.

The Horned Frogs had been the nation's top-ranked team in 1938 and were expected to be a powerhouse again in 1939. They agreed to play UCLA—black players included—because they knew a TCU victory would appear weak without UCLA's best. Declining to play against them would hurt TCU's hoped-for Rose Bowl appearance.

Just before the TCU game the *Los Angeles Times* reported that Johnny Wynne had left school without an explanation. Wynne had been a star at Manual Arts High School and then had been a starting halfback on UCLA's 1938 freshman team. Perhaps he was disappointed in the lack of playing time and he saw himself falling behind Robinson and Bartlett.

The Bruins trotted onto the Los Angeles Coliseum field in front of a crowd of sixty thousand spectators. Curiously Washington, Strode, and Robinson were left out of the starting lineup. The reason remains a mystery, but perhaps the trio was left on the bench at the start of the game as a token response to TCU's dislike of playing against blacks. They weren't out long. The TCU game was the first showing of the new UCLA coach's offense. Horrell had implemented reverses, double reverses, and split bucks (plays designed to go against the grain).

Although the Horned Frogs were expected to win, the Bruins handed them a 6–2 loss, ending TCU's fourteen-game winning streak. TCU players lauded Washington and Robinson, one exclaiming, "We've never run into anything like them, and I hope never [to] again." Robinson handed out some praise for his teammate as well: "That boy Kenny is a really great player and if the rest of us in the backfield give him one hundred percent support he's going to get the honors he deserves." TCU's coach Dutch Meyer was almost in awe of Robinson and Washington. Robinson "is a threat every time he takes that ball. So is Washington. Oh how he can pass."

For all the hoopla over blacks and whites competing on the football field UCLA left its only black player, Clarence Mackey, home in 1941, when the Bruins, still under coach Horrell, traveled across the country to play the University of Florida. Mackey was one of four UCLA players to lead the team in scoring. Apparently UCLA and Florida had agreed several years earlier to a stipulation that no blacks would play in the game. UCLA signed the agreement because at that time no plans existed for a black to be on the team. But Mackey transferred from a junior college, a move that UCLA hadn't expected. Coach Horrell took Mackey aside and essentially told him, "You won't be able to go." The *Daily Bruin* wrote that Mackey and several other players wanted to work to make money for Christmas. As Charles H. Martin wrote in *Benching Jim Crow*, "The callous decision . . . reveal[s] that West Coast colleges were not above selling out their black players in order to schedule games against southern teams in major intersectional games."

12

A Disappointing End to the Season

"I guess you've got to have a mechanized
cavalry unit to stop this guy Robinson."

—Oregon coach Tex Oliver

UCLA's victory over TCU gave credence to expectations that the
Bruins were on the right track for a successful season. Their next
opponent, the University of Washington, sent Ralph Welch, a top
assistant, to the TCU game to scout UCLA. He reported that "Jack
Robinson is as good as he has been touted, being dazzlingly shifty.
The addition of Robinson to the UCLA backfield also adds effectiveness to Kenny Washington's play, giving the Bruins two of the
fleetest backs in the conference."

UCLA came through with a 14-7 victory over the Huskies after
trailing 7-0. Robinson got the Bruins on track by returning a punt
65 yards to the Washington 6. The Bruins scored from there to tie
the game. The *California Eagle* wrote the return was "the prettiest
piece of open field running ever witnessed on a football field." The
UCLA *Daily Bruin* cited Washington players as saying that Robinson
was "the greatest thing they have ever seen. He twisted, squirmed,
refused to be stopped."

A *Seattle Times* sportswriter described Robinson's punt return
this way: "Into midfield went the speedster. He slid past a dozen
reaching Husky arms to hug the south sideline and was clear of
the pack with a couple of protectors about him when he passed the

Washington forty-yard stripe. Twenty yards along [Dean] McAdams [the punter] angled over and cracked Robinson hard enough to make him stumble. Another ten yards and Bill Marx caught up, spilling Jack on the six-yard line. From there, it wasn't difficult for UCLA to rush for the tying touchdown." Said Husky coach Jimmy Phelan, "That run of Robinson's beat us. Until that occurred we had the game well in hand."

Robinson also caught a 43-yard pass from Washington and was part of a 52-yard pass play that featured three laterals. When Robinson left the field in the fourth quarter, Huskies fans gave him a standing ovation. One sportswriter could not resist writing, "There will be fried chicken and watermelon on the dining car table [on the way back to Los Angeles.]"

Local newspapers were finally acknowledging after the Washington game that the Bruins had black players on their team. Or maybe as Woody Strode put it, "Nobody wrote, 'A unique thing is happening in Los Angeles: the blacks are playing the whites.'" *Los Angeles Times* sportswriter Paul Zimmerman wrote, "Football is the great equalizer. You have to throw racial prejudice out the window when a couple of gentlemen like Jackie Robinson and Kenny Washington do the things they do."

The *California Eagle* took to the editorial pages on November 2, 1939, to describe the effects the black players were having on the game—in a sociological vein as much as a discussion of points on the scoreboard. The editor lauded Robinson and Washington as "glorious symbols of rising Negro Youth, harbingers of a new era of economic, political and social recognition." They would be "stalwart torch bearers in the forward march of Racial Progress (!)," the editorial concluded. If the mainstream press saw it that way, it didn't write about it.

Across the country sportswriters started to sing the praises of the three African American players, particularly writers on black newspapers. If the white papers mentioned race in their articles, it was only rarely, certainly a newsworthy event. The black newspapers were celebrating the feats of players who were the same color as a vast majority of their readers.

In the *California Eagle*, the *Chicago Defender*, and the *Washington Afro-American*, black newspapers told their readers that given a chance, black athletes could compete fairly and evenly—or better—with their white teammates. For example, the *Defender* proudly wrote that three blacks were in the game "at one time" during the TCU game, while Robinson and Washington "almost single-handedly" led the Bruins to the victory, the *Los Angeles Examiner* wrote. The *Daily Bruin* remarked, "Our Bruins have just finished astounding the football world for the second week in a row. Saturday's ball game was just a little too much Washington (Kenny), Robinson and UCLA and not enough Washington (University)." The UCLA *Magazine* wrote that the black athletes "oozed class from the moment they trotted on the greensward."

Next up for the Bruins were the Stanford Indians and their tricky quarterback Frankie Albert. Soon after the Bruins arrived in Palo Alto, Robinson and Bartlett went to a nearby restaurant with their teammates. The restaurant manager asked the black players to leave. "I'm sorry," the manager said, "but you can't eat in here." Bartlett and Robinson walked out hurt and angered. The white players sat dumbfounded for a moment, and then one by one they stood up and poured their glasses of water over their food and marched out of the restaurant en masse. The incident brought the team closer together. "Either we would eat with the team," Bartlett said, "or they wouldn't eat there." Said teammate Ned Mathews: "If they didn't fit, we didn't fit and that's the way it went. . . . We didn't worry about what color a player was. They were just players to us, important players."

Before the game, Stanford's assistant coach called Robinson "just about the best sprinter on the coast, and he's a great ball carrier. He's rugged and can play just as hard and long as anyone. We are scared to death of him." Late in the game, UCLA was trailing 14-7, with the Bruins' touchdown coming on Robinson's 52-yard run. Next Robinson intercepted an Albert pass on the UCLA 30-yard line and returned it to the Stanford 20, where Albert brought him down with a shirt-tail tackle. The Bruins went on to score, and

Robinson kicked the extra point to tie the game 14–14. That's the way it ended.

Stanford coach Tiny Thornhill called Robinson "the greatest backfield runner I have seen in all my connection with football—and that's some twenty-five years." He said that before Robinson was through, he would rank with the great runner Red Grange.

The following week against the University of Montana at home, the Bruins prevailed 20–6. Robinson didn't carry the ball once; instead he was used as a decoy that allowed Kenny Washington to score all three of UCLA's touchdowns. Robinson was limited to a 33-yard punt return. The Bruins record now stood at 3-0-1.

Robinson bristled over being used as a decoy on several occasions. In the first five games of the season he carried the ball just ten times. He thought he needed a bigger role in the Bruins' offense. Coach Horrell defended using Robinson as a decoy. He said when Robinson went into motion toward the sidelines, he took two defenders with him. "Who've we got that can take out two defending players with one block?" he asked.

One teammate, Buck Gilmore, recalled that Robinson "got a poor shake at UCLA. In my estimation, it should have been him playing tailback instead of Washington." Gilmore said that before one game, Robinson "was down in the dumps. He never complained about anything, but he told me he was going to quit the team." Robinson asked Gilmore, "What the hell am I doing here?" Gilmore, who was a co-captain, felt it was his job to "smooth things out." He told a trainer about Robinson's laments, and the trainer passed them on to Horrell. After that Robinson began getting the ball more often.

Along the way the black players were picking up nicknames—most of them racially motivated—as they attracted sportswriters to their feats on the gridiron. To describe Washington newspapers used such nicknames as "Kingfish," a character in the Amos and Andy radio show that was popular at the time. (One juxtaposition of a picture and an article in the *Los Angeles Times* nine years later stands out, although inadvertently. Washington was referred to as the Kingfish in a headline. Next to the article was an unrelated photograph of a fisherman displaying a 191-pound, 5-foot long black bass caught off Port Orange, Florida.)

Woody Strode was a "Negro Adonis." A black runner was referred to as a "sepia runner." Others were "Senegambian speed merchants," "dusky speedsters," and "the midnight express twins."

Bob Hunter of the *Los Angeles Examiner* called Washington and Strode the "Goal Dust Twins," an idea he gleaned from a box of soap powder, Fairbank's Gold Dust Twins. The box used a stereotypical picture of two black kids doing household chores together. "Kenny and I didn't really pay any attention to it," Strode said. Tom Bradley did. He wrote a letter to the editor of the *California Eagle* that said such nicknames "denigrate only Negroes. . . . We can only have a true democracy when all races are forgotten and each man is accepted as a man offering real contributions . . . to the progress of our country." Later, when Robinson joined the Bruins, he, Washington, and Strode became the "Goal Dust Trio."

Black players also were called the "dark angels of destruction." On one occasion Washington was referred to as "Shufflin Kenny Washington," an allusion to the black characters of minstrel shows. On at least two occasions Strode's name was printed in the *Los Angeles Times* as Woody "Boo" Strode. "Boo" was a racial epithet shortened from the slang word "jigaboo." A black newspaper, the *Pittsburgh Courier*, called Robinson the "cyclone-gaited hellion."

Braven Dyer, the *Los Angeles Times* columnist, wrote about Washington in black vernacular when he first moved up to the varsity:

> The lad's a wow in boldface caps, but it's mostly what he doesn't do on the football field that impresses me. He doesn't overwork, he doesn't get excited, he doesn't get those black steel muscles busy until it counts. In short, Kenny has the complete relaxation of his race. You never saw a member of his race eat a po'k chop and then go into a heavy campaign of worrying about where his next one is coming from. No, sah, he may bear down on the po'k chop, but when it's gone he just unlaxes until the next po'k chop

comes along. Well K. Washington plays football like that, if you see what I mean.

That's not to say that all nicknames were bad. "Jackrabbit" Jackie Robinson defined how he could scamper. "General" Kenny Washington linked him to the country's first president and denoted leadership. Certainly, though, the nicknames used by white newspapers were far more demeaning than any used in black newspapers.

In their next game, against the University of Oregon, UCLA surprised the Ducks at home. The highlight of the game came when Washington threw a pass to Robinson, who faked two defenders and, in the words on one reporter, "sent [them] flying on their faces with a series of hip-jiggling feints" before he crossed the goal line for a 66-yard play. He also scored on an 83-yard run down the sidelines. Oregon coach Tex Oliver remarked, "I guess you've got to have a mechanized cavalry unit to stop him. He runs as fast at three-quarter speed as the average player does at top speed, and he still has that extra quarter to draw up."

Then Robinson was injured during a practice on November 1 and missed games against UC Berkeley and the University of Santa Clara and was used sparingly in his return against Oregon State. When he was injured, one sportswriter wrote, "Bruin stock went all the way up and down the fluctuation scale." A team doctor said about Robinson, "The boy who has brought the Bruins out of hot water in every major game this year had turned his right knee."

Questions arose whether the Robinson's injury had been accidental or on purpose. Hank Shatford, a *Daily Bruin* sportswriter, wrote that Robinson was injured "when this guy came over and hit Jack on the side. He hit him on the leg, just dove in with his shoulder pads. He did it on purpose, no question in my mind. I know the guy well. The coaches were furious. There were some players on that team who weren't fans of Jack Robinson." The *Los Angeles Examiner* reported that "Robinson was tackled viciously near the sidelines [by reserves] and arose limping. Ray Richards, line coach, was actually white about the mouth and Babe Horrell and Jim Blewett were shaky for the rest of the day."

While there were racial overtones to that incident, it may well be that Robinson's personality also played a part. As noted, he tended to be aloof. "To be honest, Jackie Robinson was not that well-liked. . . . Jackie was not friendly. . . . He was very withdrawn. Even on the football field he would stand off by himself," Strode remarked. He wondered whether Robinson's trouble with the police and his brother's death were also responsible.

Because of Robinson's arrests and sullen demeanor, some whites saw him as "the stereotype of the lawless, shiftless black buck." Bill Ackerman, UCLA's athletic director, told Strode years later that "Jackie always seemed to have a chip on his shoulder. . . . Maybe he was rather ahead of his time in his thinking with regard to the black's situation. I think it hurt him emotionally to see how some of his friends were treated. The result was he kept pretty much within himself."

One rumor making the rounds was that Robinson and Washington were locked in a bitter feud and that they got into a knockout, drag-down battle one day. Robinson laughed at the mere idea that he would take on Washington. "At least you can give me credit for having common sense," he said. "And nobody with common sense is going to fight a big guy like Kenny Washington."

Robinson may have been upset that he had to take a backseat to Washington. Certainly they were two different personalities. "As far as the general public was concerned, I mean the local yokels," Strode explained, "Kenny was it. He was the main drawing card. He became quite a celebrity; people would stop him on the street to say hello. He was a handsome, clean-cut kid. He had a broad nose, warm, kind eyes, and a smile that lit up his whole face. He had a really good sense of humor. People loved to hang out with the guy. Kenny was a real class guy."

With Robinson hobbling from a sore knee, Horrell moved Bartlett from end to right halfback, but he too missed a game later against the Santa Clara Broncos because of a blood clot in a leg. The Bruins didn't seem to miss Robinson when they beat their upstate cousins, the UC Berkeley Golden Bears 20–7. The Bruins could have used a healthy Robinson against their next two opponents. They battled to a scoreless tie with Santa Clara (each team had four chances to score) with Robinson on the bench and a 13–13 standoff with Oregon State, a game in which he was not at full speed.

The *Chicago Defender* estimated nine thousand "members of the Race" attended the game against UC Berkeley, including the girlfriends of Washington, Robinson, and Strode. A description of what each of the women wore accompanied the article. For example, Washington's girlfriend wore a "smart blue skirt with matching hat and contrasting accessories and a sport coat of varied color shadings, predominately blue." The article referred to Washington's girl as his "lady love," Robinson's as a "heart beat," and Strode's as a "young chiropodist." They also listed several prominent blacks "who came to see the sepias take the day," including bandleader Count Basie and his "songbird" Helen Hume.

Without Robinson Santa Clara ganged up on Washington, often with two or three Broncos pounding on him. He still managed to gain 81 yards on 21 carries. Santa Clara coach Buck Shaw had nothing but praise for the speedy back. "Every time you get the Bruins in the hole Washington gets them out." Washington played the entire game and was so tired at the end that UCLA trainer Mike Chambers decided the Bruins' star player should spend the weekend in a local hospital. Robinson was angry after the game because he didn't get to play, but the Bruins were avoiding further injury to their elusive halfback.

Robinson was back in the lineup for the Oregon State game, but he was still feeling the effects of the injury and was a bit rusty. The *Los Angeles Times* reported that he "looked woefully weak defensively." The paper said he let the Beavers get behind him on pass plays and that when he recovered, he missed tackles. He admitted after the game that his legs weren't strong after the layoff.

Robinson was back to full strength for the Washington State game. With the Bruins trailing 7–6 in the fourth quarter, he caught a short Washington pass and "snaked his way down the sidelines and then into the center of the field, evading four Cougars on the way and going over for the touchdown standing up." The 20-yard gallop put the Bruins up 13–7. Soon afterward he dashed 36 yards to put the game out of reach. On a final TD drive, Robinson twisted and turned his way to runs of 29 yards and 32 yards as UCLA won 24–7. "Jackie was well past the scrimmage line before the harassed Cougars woke up to the fact that he had the ball," the *California Eagle* reported.

The Bruins were undefeated except for the three ties but had yet to face their cross-town rival, USC. The winner would go to the Rose Bowl. An event preceding the big game created a minor furor. To celebrate homecoming and the game, the Phi Kappa Psi fraternity on the USC campus erected a display of racial and ethnic bigotry to mock the Bruins' team. The fraternity created three grass huts and "gaudily painted figures of black savages wearing football helmets peering out of the huts. Another hut was labeled the Cantor and Cohen Food Shoppe, Inc., that referred to two Jewish players on the team. A ship replicate was placed in front of the huts with the name "S.C. Slave Ship." The fraternity members also "nailed grotesque figures to a giant palm tree in the center of the lawn" that bore the jersey numbers of Washington, Robinson, and Strode. In addition, effigies of the Jewish players were hung from the tree. The *California Eagle*, which was the only newspaper to publish a story about the display, called it Nazism, saying it was "one of the most flagrant displays of Hitlerism ever offered under the aegis of an American university group." Among those protesting the display were the NAACP and the Hollywood Anti-Nazi League. The university administration forced the fraternity to remove the display. In its place the fraternity put a "censored sign."

USC students burned the effigies of the three black football players, Woody Strode recalled. When Strode was told about the burning, he replied, "That's because we're going to kick their asses tomorrow." He recounted in his memoirs that he didn't think the burning was racial. "That was fear," he said.

Alongside that controversy another one arose: Would an African American play in the Rose Bowl for the first time since 1916?

Blacks were looking forward to showing the nation that an integrated team playing in the Rose Bowl would be a step toward advancing the race. The *California Eagle* reported that "UCLA's democratic football team should be a hint to local promoters of professional football and baseball teams. Fans turn out to watch talent, not red talent, or blue talent, but TALENT."

If the Bruins beat USC, the players would pick the opposing team for the Rose Bowl. That, wrote the *Pasadena Star-News*, would put them in "a very embarrassing position for to date the outstanding eleven in the nation is Tennessee." The University of Tennessee Volunteers were unlikely to step on the field with black players as foes. There certainly had been incidents that would back up such a likelihood. For example, Northern teams would not play black players against a Southern team if the Southern team asked. Or the Southern team could refuse to play if the Northern school would not agree to bench its African Americans. The *New York Times*'s esteemed sportswriter Allison Danzig wrote from Knoxville that he had heard from "parties in a position to know that Tennessee will not play in the Rose Bowl if UCLA, with its three colored stars, is the host team." There was no chance that the UCLA black players would sit out the game. Danzig asked Tennessee coach Bob "Major" Neyland what he would do if UCLA beat USC. He "side-stepped the issue by turning aside to speak to friends," Danzig wrote.

Later Danzig, Neyland, and Tennessee supporters gathered at a Knoxville hotel to get updates on the UCLA-USC game. Volunteers coaches were rooting for USC to win or get a tie while listening to the game on the radio. When USC moved the ball, cheers broke out, leaving no doubt they were rooting for USC to win the game, a reporter for the *Knoxville News-Sentinel* wrote.

The *California Eagle* saw such a game as having an impact beyond that of who would win the game. Its sports editor, Cullen Fentress, believed an integrated game would be good for the nation because it "is the most logical medium through which to effect world peace and all it implies." If nothing else, he wrote that if UCLA got into the Rose Bowl, it would "prove to this nation that its peoples can play together in the most approved manner as sportsmen, uphold-

ing as they do so the democratic principles as outlined by the sign-
ers of the Declaration of Independence."

The *Pasadena Star-News* wrote that the black UCLA players "could
not qualify under the strict eligibility rules made necessary by Tennessee's geographic location." A *Los Angeles Times* columnist speculated that Tennessee probably would not play UCLA.

The 1939 USC-UCLA game started a tradition that lasts today. The
UCLA Alumni Association gave the student body a 295-pound bell
that cheerleaders were to ring after each Bruin point. Two years later
it was awarded to the winner of the rivalry. But on the first matchup
with the bell in use, it didn't ring once.

A record crowd of 103,303 turned out at the Coliseum, still the
largest crowd to watch a game between these two undefeated teams.
USC was a 14-point underdog. It was estimated that fourteen thousand African Americans attended the game. Sam Lacy, the sports
editor of the *Washington* (DC) *Afro-American*, noted that the game
would be "overrun with sepia flesh." People across the nation were
taking notice of this UCLA squad.

The game ended 0–0, and the Trojans went to the Rose Bowl
because they had fewer ties during the season. USC won the national
championship by beating Tennessee, and UCLA finished ranked
no. 7 in the country.

If it hadn't been for Robinson, the Bruins would have fallen. USC's
All-American Grenny Lansdell slipped into the Bruin secondary and
looked to be on his way to a touchdown when Robinson came out of
nowhere to tackle Lansdell, who fumbled at the 2-yard line. Woody
Strode picked up the ball and ran out to the 13-yard line before he
was tackled. It was the first fumble the Trojans had committed all
season. The *Los Angeles Times* wrote "The ball shot off the Trojan's
chest like it had been blown from a gun barrel. No man's arm could
have withstood that blow from Robinson's body."

The Bruins had a chance to win the game with five minutes left.
They had the ball at their own 20-yard line. Washington threw an
18-yard completion to Strode and then hit Robinson with a pass to
the USC 26. Then Strode pulled down a pass at the 15. A pass and

two rushes put the ball on the 3-yard line. Three plays later and the Bruins had lost a yard. Field goals were rare in those days. In the huddle the Bruins took a vote: five wanted to go for the touchdown and five for the field goal. Quarterback Ned Mathews cast the deciding vote: go for 6.

It's difficult to blame the players for their lack of confidence in trying for a field goal, despite the fact that the ball was directly in front of the goal posts at the 4-yard line. The Bruins had made only one field goal all season, and they had made only 10 of 19 extra-point attempts during the season, second to last among major teams on the West Coast. Perhaps a more puzzling question is why Robinson failed to carry the ball once the Bruins drove to the 3-yard line. Another is why Washington didn't throw a high pass to his favorite receiver, the 6-foot-4 Woody Strode, who was covered by a 5-foot-11 defensive back.

Coach Horrell said after the game that he considered sending in a man to try a field goal before the Bruins made their last first down, "but when the boys made first down on the Trojans' three, I changed my mind. After all, these kids were doing pretty good without my help. Anything Mathews did from then on was good enough for me."

UCLA sent Strode and two others as decoys to the left, and Washington headed that way as well and then turned and threw a pass across the field to a seemingly wide-open Don McPherson. A Trojan defensive back was able to recover and knocked the ball away. Game over.

Horrell pulled Washington with fifteen seconds left so that the crowd could recognize him in his last game. He received a standing ovation from the spectators, and several Trojans shook his hand and hugged him. "It was the most soul-stirring event I have ever seen in sports," Strode said. "I have never been so moved emotionally," Washington said, "rarely so proud of my country."

After the game Horrell was asked why he had declined to go for a field goal. "The game is over now; it makes little difference, don't you think?" Robinson was devastated to miss out on the Rose Bowl game. He broke down in tears in the locker room.

The *Amsterdam News* of New York editorialized in an article reprinted in the *California Eagle* two weeks after the game that "every red-blooded American must have felt proud" of Washington, whom it called "a great back, a good student, and a manly youth who had brought credit to his school, his race, and his country." The editor noted that despite the love shown, Washington was "denied many privileges and rights . . . which make U.S. citizens the most blessed in the world." Because he was black, jobs, including in the NFL, would be "closed to him." The next day, when Tennessee was selected to play the Trojans, the *Amsterdam News* wrote a headline over the article that read, "And Rose Bowl Remains White as a New Lily."

More than four hundred thousand fans watched the Bruins that year—by far the most of any university in the country—and millions more tracked them by listening to the radio or reading newspapers. A week after the game a group of local businessmen invited the four African American Bruin football players and Tom Bradley to attend a banquet celebrating their accomplishments.

Toastmaster Paul R. Williams, a noted architect and a USC graduate, told the players that the businessmen had arranged the banquet so that they could show appreciation to the UCLA coaches and the black athletes for their achievements on the field and in the classroom. He said the businessmen promised "to offer encouragement and assistance, financial and moral, in seeing that they get off on the right foot in pursuing their life's work."

Coach Horrell attended the banquet and urged the black stars to complete their requirements for graduation, noting that "only about six percent of the athletes, otherwise eligible, are able to come up to UCLA's scholastic requirements." Washington spoke for his teammates when he responded, "There is so much to be said I hardly know where to begin, but I am certain I express the sentiments of the rest of the fellows when I say that we certainly appreciate this manifestation of interest in us. We want action and the opportunity to put our foot in the door. We will do the rest." They spent the night playing ping pong and badminton during the banquet, which was held at Williams's house. They put away steaks "suited to their he-man appetites."

Washington and Robinson were slighted in postseason honors, despite the backing of the mainstream and black press. Washington was particularly proud that he had played all but twenty minutes of the season on offense and defense during the 1939 season. "Records are made to be broken," he said, "but when somebody breaks my endurance record, let me hear about it."

Washington led the nation in scoring and total offense. He ran up 811 yards rushing and 559 passing. He scored 5 touchdowns and threw passes for 7 more. His total offensive numbers were 1,370 yards. Robinson finished the season third in the PCC with 514 yards rushing in 42 carries, for an average of 12.23 yards a carry. He was second in punt return yards with 281 yards in 14 returns, for a 20.07-yard average per return. He also caught 6 passes for 145, a 24.17 average per pass.

The *California Eagle* wrote that the black athletes "had done more to make the road of the Negro athlete easier to travel than a thousand sermons, proclamations or treatises." It's unknown if any of the help that was mentioned at the Williams banquet came about, but one thing is certain: those athletes had trouble moving on to their early careers because of racial discrimination. Looking back over the season, astute fans might also have noticed that despite their contributions to the team, neither Robinson nor Washington nor Strode was ever named team captain, a position that was determined by their teammates.

13

Decision Time

"I guess we realized one of the most exciting times
of our lives had just come and gone."

—Woody Strode

Jackie Robinson had vowed when he arrived at Westwood that he would concentrate on football and track, but when the 1940 Olympic Games were canceled because of the war in Europe, he had no reason to focus exclusively on track in the spring. So when basketball season began in the winter, he was right there, ready to go.

The team, loser of twenty-eight consecutive games, could use his help. Coach Wilbur Johns had seen Robinson play at Pasadena when he had helped defeat USC's heralded freshman team and "was sold on the boy." Johns said Robinson was "a great player. He has a world of natural ability." His Pasadena coach, Carl Metten, predicted in September 1939 that Robinson would be one of the best players in the PCC. "He has wonderful speed and coordination," Metten said, "and can dribble and shoot equally well with either hand. If he wants to make a basket he'll do it." Johns couldn't wait for basketball season to start.

The UCLA losing streak went to thirty-one games when the season started after two losses at Stanford and one at UC Berkeley. Robinson stood out in both Stanford games, scoring 23 of the team's 28 points in the first game and 12 of the 36 in the second. The Bruins lost to the Golden Bears 39–33 despite Robinson's 15 points.

Robinson was unhappy with the pace of the game the Bruins were playing. Johns liked a slow-down, half-court offense while Robinson preferred a fast-break offense. The coach and player clashed. Robinson's frustration and a couple of skipped practices brought the two together to work out a solution. Robinson agreed to be more cooperative—and the Bruins began playing a faster game.

The change put an end to the losing streak when the Bruins beat UC Berkeley 35–33 with Robinson making a game-winning layup. Berkeley coach Nibs Price raved that Robinson had "more natural talent, speed, and spring than any man in the conference." He called Robinson the best basketball player in the United States. But Price left Robinson off his all-conference team at the end of the season despite praising "the speed and shooting ability of the Bruin Negro," and he picked another player on "basketball ability alone."

Shav Glick, a reporter for the *Daily Bruin* who had attended PJC when Robinson was there, said in 1997 that he marveled at "those hands, he was so quick. He'd steal balls so easily and just take off. He was very intelligent as an athlete. He could jump for a guy who was only six-foot and had that incredible quickness. He also had a good shot. Without any doubt, he could have played in the NBA." Glick remembered that Wilbur Johns credited Robinson's athletic talents to "beautiful timing and rhythm and ability to relax completely whenever he wished. Robinson was always in perfect condition and was a great team player despite being an outstanding player."

Robinson wound up leading the PCC with 148 points, 10 points ahead of USC's Ralph Vaughn. Because of his prowess on the basketball court, sportswriters sometimes called him the "Ebony Luisetti." (Stanford's Hank Luisetti was the first college basketball player to use the running one-handed shot that led to today's jump shot.) About Luisetti, Robinson remarked, "Wear Luisetti's shoes? Why, I couldn't even carry them." Ray Bartlett was a seldom-used player on that Bruins team.

Coach Johns became Robinson's biggest booster. Although Robinson liked to play a fast-paced game, if the situation called for it, he could slow down to help the Bruins hold a lead. "He might have been the greatest of all basketball players," Johns said, if he had focused only on basketball. "His timing was perfect. His rhythm was unmatched . . . [and] he always placed the welfare of the team above his chance for greater stardom."

No sooner was basketball season over than Robinson left his gym shoes for his baseball cleats. On March 10, 1940 Robinson and Bartlett joined the baseball squad, and with little practice Jackie played his first game.

Booster Bob Campbell remembered Robinson pitching part of one game against UC Berkeley:

> It had started to rain in the top half of the fourth inning. Cal was way ahead, and UCLA was trying to keep the game going so that they wouldn't complete five innings and make it a game. . . . Cal came to bat in the first half of the fifth. UCLA had a little consultation and Jack went in to pitch. He pitched high and outside to them so they couldn't possibly hit them; the catcher couldn't catch them, and he took his time about going to the backstop to get the ball. And they couldn't be called strikes, so they got walks. Cal protested against it, and the umpire said there was nothing they could do about it, that Cal had swung at everything in the top half of the fourth inning to hasten the game. They couldn't do anything to make him pitch better to them. Finally, it got to raining so hard that they called the game off and started over again the next day with a doubleheader.

Robinson batted .097 with 6 hits in 62 at-bats, 1 home run, and 1 RBI that season. (He got 4 of those hits and stole 4 bases, including home, in his first game.) He also made 10 errors, with a .907 percentage for the season. Robinson told sportswriter Roger Kahn thirty years later that he "was dog tired. Playing and practicing all the sports I did without a break just wore me out."

Despite his errors Jackie was a "hell of a defensive player," Bartlett said. "He could field so well that he stayed in the lineup, and they hoped that he could get on base. At the time it was his worst sport, but he developed his talent after he left." Nonetheless, the sports editor of the *Los Angeles Daily News* said that if there were no boycott of black players in Major League Baseball, Robinson "would have been sought by a half dozen major league scouts."

Carl McBain, a hurdler on the track team, knew what made Robinson a great athlete: "As a track man, he was outstanding. And why he was so good in all sports, I'll tell you. His first two or three steps were so much faster [than those of other athletes]; he would go off and he was ahead of everybody. Like, every time. At fifty yards he could beat anybody. At one hundred yards, I could catch him. In basketball, is that important? Football? Baseball?"

On May 25 Robinson won the PCC broad jump championship with a leap of 25 feet even, a jump that broke the conference record by two inches. He later won the broad jump championship of the National Collegiate Athletic Association (NCAA) by jumping 24 feet, 10 1/4 inches.

Daily Bruin sportswriter Milt Cohen, who was graduating that summer, submitted one final column that turned out quite prophetic. He wrote that he hoped the black athletes would be given a chance to show their skills in professional sports. He pointed out that fans might welcome an opportunity "to see men like Jackie Robinson and Kenny Washington play big league baseball." It seemed unlikely they would be given that chance. "Someday a man will come along who will sign a Negro to play for his team—and then this so-called tradition [of barring African Americans] will be shattered."

The summer of 1940 also was a turning point for Tom Bradley: he decided to leave the university a year shy of graduation. He had been contemplating becoming a teacher, but in his junior year he decided, along with three of his friends, to take an exam for entrance into the Los Angeles Police Academy. "I had no dream," Bradley said, "no thought of becoming a police officer but I went along just to keep them company."

Bradley and his friends joked that if they were admitted, they would find themselves on the right side of the law. Bradley thought he would spend a couple of years on the police force and return to school. He told no one—not even his mother or his wife-to-be, Ethel

Arnold—that he had taken the test. He told them only after he had accepted a job. "My mother had such total faith and confidence in me that she might discuss a decision, but she would never really argue with a decision that I made," he said. His trusted adviser at UCLA, Adaline Guenther, told Bradley she thought his being a police officer was "a tragic waste of my talents."

Bradley decided he needed a police job for when he and Ethel were married. That summer he received notice that with a score of 97 percent on the written examination he had finished near the top of the five thousand candidates taking the test. Then he had to take an oral examination. "I remember very well telling the oral board . . . [that] I wanted to do something to help change the image of law enforcement," Bradley said. "And they looked at me as though I were crazy—one man who's going to change the whole image of the police department." He passed that exam too and was told he could start the academy without finishing college.

Bradley was aware that there was an "unofficial quota" on the number of black officers hired and promoted in the department, but he wasn't deterred. He noted that it was difficult to weed out black candidates when they had finished high on written and oral examinations but that it could be done with a medical examination. A police department physician told him he had a heart murmur that might keep him off the force. He was incredulous because of his many years of sports. So he appealed to an outside physician and was termed fit. He was asked by a *Los Angeles Times* reporter in 1982 why he bothered. He replied, "Because I decided I was not going to let anybody tell me no."

The job at the Los Angeles Police Department (LAPD) paid $170 a month and came with a good pension plan. Bradley never regretted his decision. "I always had the most interesting and challenging assignments, and it became a great joy for me to work as a police officer," he said.

Strode's last year at UCLA proved difficult for him and his family. In late December, Strode told Davis J. Walsh, a columnist for the *Los Angeles Examiner*, that before football season he and his family "had nothing to eat but beans. For breakfast. And dinner. And supper." Once the season began, Strode ate with the team, but his family still went without. He gave some of the money he earned at on-campus jobs to his family. At one point he sold his tickets to the UCLA-USC game "for what they'd bring. . . . I'd like to see anybody with a well-filled belly and a righteous sense of ethics try to make anything out of that."

After the season Strode realized he would have to earn money to help his family. He left UCLA without his degree. He had been a student at UCLA for six and a half years, including his extension years. He had been planning on competing in track in the spring of 1940 and graduating. But when the Olympics were canceled, Strode said tongue-in-cheek that "I wasn't ever going to be a brain surgeon. I was an athlete so . . . I decided not to hang around."

14

Passed Over by the NFL

"You know . . . [Washington] would be the greatest
sensation in pro league history with any one of your
ball clubs . . . [yet] none of you chose him."

—NBC Radio commentator Sam Balter to NFL owners

The local media began stumping for Washington to be named a first-team All-American soon after the 1939 season ended. The *Los Angeles Examiner* opined that Washington was an obvious pick and "one gent who just won't miss" the honor. The *Los Angeles Times* wrote that Washington deserved the honor because his "passes are poison, his tackling fierce, his blocking 'heavy' and his squirming, shifty fast-away running a despair to defenders."

Although statistically Washington was ahead of Tom Harmon, the Michigan standout, Harmon was named a first-team All-American while Washington was selected for the second team. The press called the slight laughable and lamentable. But none referred to it as racism, blaming instead East Coast bias. The *Los Angeles Examiner* thought that Washington had been passed over because he had often been overshadowed by Robinson, "which is bad for ballyhoo." Teammate Woody Strode said, "Kenny didn't make the first team because of prejudiced voting. . . . The whole thing was a big joke."

The *Daily Bruin* came to Washington's defense as well. "It's with a distinct sour taste in our mouth that we read the lists of All-American selections that are now pouring out of all sections of the country," columnist Milt Cohen wrote. "We don't care what they do with any other ball player in the nation—but we don't like the way they're treating our Kenny Washington."

Washington had "put to shame those All-America pickers who inexplicably failed to include the great Negro halfback on their 'must' list," the *Los Angeles Times* wrote. The *Pasadena Star-News* joined in: "Anyone who picks an All-America team and leaves [Washington] off needs to have his head examined."

Crisis, the NAACP magazine, also weighed in on the controversy. In the January 1940 edition Roy Wilkins wrote in an editorial that Washington had been more than slighted. He stated that Washington was well worthy of the honors except for the "one thing wrong with him: he was several shades too dark."

Washington also was passed over for the nationally prestigious annual East-West Shrine Game on January 1 in San Francisco. The United Press noted that Washington was a "conspicuous absentee" from the team. No black player had ever been invited to the game. The committee making the player selections acknowledged that the decision to exclude Washington was made because his appearance "might cause friction with the Southern players on the Eastern team." His exclusion came despite the fact that in a *Liberty* magazine poll that asked college players to select an All-America team, out of 664 nominees, Washington was the only one to receive the votes of every player who had played against him.

The mainstream and the black press were outraged that Washington had been left off the squad. The *California Eagle* noted that several organizations protested his absence, including "sports scribes, labor unions, college societies, leading citizens and others." One labor union noted that it was obvious he had been left off the team "solely because he was a Negro." The UCLA Student Committee wrote that leaving him out was "unsportsmanlike, un-American and a threat to democratic procedure." The *California Eagle* remarked that if players selected for the team had "not learned . . . the spirit of tolerance and fair play then education . . . is a failure."

Even the lieutenant governor of California, Ellis E. Patterson, who called himself an "old football player," joined the cry. In a letter to the *Los Angeles Sentinel,* Patterson wrote that the snub "was not the sentiment of the majority of the people. Such prejudice is un-American. If we believe in Democracy there must be equal justice to all people irrespective of color and creed."

Governor Culbert L. Olson, however, refused to get into the fray, claiming he didn't have enough information to determine why Washington had been overlooked and said he doubted Washington would have accepted because he wanted to play baseball at UCLA. But Washington had made it clear before the selections were made that he was foregoing baseball that spring. A month after the East-West Shrine Game, Washington was the guest of honor at the Islam Temple Shrine luncheon in San Francisco, an afterthought and a minor salve on a major wound.

Washington received some consolation for being snubbed by the East-West game when he was selected to play for the College All-Stars against the Green Bay Packers, the National Football League (NFL) champions, in a charity game in 1940 sponsored by the *Chicago Tribune.* In a scrimmage nine days before the game, "the fleet, shifty Negro half back," Washington, "stole the show," the *Tribune* wrote. "Washington's running measured to the tall tales of his prowess which have been told by the Southern California boys, Los Angeles neighbors of Kenny." Charles "Buckets" Goldenberg, the stocky guard who met Kenny Washington head-on on the 1-yard line but was bowled over as Washington scored, termed the former UCLA star "the finest man on the college squad," the *Tribune* reported. Another Green Bay player, end Carl Mulleneaux, said he did not believe a "better back ever would play on the college side in the All-Star game," the *Tribune* wrote.

The Packers beat the All-Stars 45–28 in front of 85,567 fans at Chicago's Soldier Field, with Washington accounting for one touchdown. Jimmy Powers, a *New York Daily News* columnist, noted that Washington had played in the *Tribune*'s charity game with no problems. "He played on the same field with boys who are going to be scattered throughout the league. And he played against the champion Packers. There wasn't a bit of trouble anywhere. Kenny was tackled hard once or twice especially after he ran a kick-off forty-three yards right through the entire Packer lineup. But that's routine treatment for jack-rabbits. You slam your opposing speed merchants about, hoping to wear them down. Kenny took it all with a grin."

What Chicago Bears coach George Halas saw of Washington impressed him. Halas kept Washington in Chicago for a week while he tried to get the NFL to reintegrate the league, but he didn't succeed. (African Americans had played in the NFL in its early years but were kept out from 1933 to 1946.) Washington Redskins owner George Preston Marshall, a noted bigot, was the lone holdout. After all it had been Marshall's idea to ban African Americans from playing in the NFL, and he was not about to back down now.

The prevailing thought has always been that Washington was kept out of the NFL because he was black. But in the opinion of another sportswriter, Fay Young of the *Chicago Defender*—a black sportswriter at that—Washington may not have been good enough to play in the league. Young agreed that Washington's offensive prowess was excellent but believed he was lacking on the defense side: "[Washington] just wasn't in there to nail the Green Bay ball toters when the chance was his." He said one missed tackle "was the kind of play one would expect to see in a high school contest." Young added that players for traditionally black colleges were just as good as Washington and were much better on defense. "Washington's play didn't stamp him of the caliber of an all-round player whom we expected to see—and far from the caliber which is demanded by the professional football clubs." Young wrote that if anyone were to break the color barrier, he would have to "stand head and shoulders above the rest." About the color barrier, Young concluded, "As it is we will have to wait another year to put Jackie Robinson in there in the starting lineup and then watch things hum."

NBC broadcaster Sam Balter blasted the NFL's black ban. In an "open letter" over the airwaves he asked NFL owners why "nobody chose the leading collegiate ground gainer of the 1939 season." He remarked that those who had seen Washington play agreed that he was "not only the best football player on the Pacific Coast this season, but the best of the last ten years and perhaps the best in all that slope's glorious football history—a player who has reduced to absurdity all the All-American teams selected this year because they did not include him—and all know why. . . . You have scouts—you know this better than I—you know their unanimous reports: he would be the greatest sensation in pro league history with any one of your ball clubs—you got that report. He was No. 1 on all your lists." Balter expressed bitter disappointment "on behalf of the millions of American sports fans who believe in fair play and equal opportunity." He concluded by offering air time to owners to explain why neither Washington nor another black player, Brud Holland, was "good enough to play ball on your teams." The offer was rejected.

"There are ten teams in the league that can use this one hundred and ninety-two pounder without a doubt were there some way to remove the Ifs, Ands and Buts that the managers and owners and coaches of these teams hide behind when confronted by the facts," the American Negro Press wrote. In December 1940 African American journalist William A. Brower in the magazine *Opportunity* put the blame squarely on the owners. "There is no record of any authenticated commitment by them on the issue [of a color barrier]," Brower wrote. He added the "action towards the Negro somewhere along the line is transparent."

What Washington was facing was often equated with the color ban in Major League Baseball, and while they had a commonality, there also were differences. African Americans had been blocked from playing baseball from the late 1800s until Jackie Robinson broke the color barrier in 1947. Professional football was a newer sport, with the NFL established in 1920. For the first thirteen years several talented black players such as Duke Slater, Joe Lillard, Charles Follis, Henry McDonald, Fritz Pollard, and Paul Robeson suited up for the pros. One school of thought had it that players from the South wouldn't want to play with African Americans, a reason that was never proven. That color barrier remained in effect until 1946.

After football Washington found himself searching for a way to make a living. Over the next two or three years he tried acting in movies, playing semi-pro football, and becoming a policeman all while trying to finish his studies at UCLA.

Washington took a short venture into the boxing ring, but little is known about his success other than that he didn't last long. The crooner and movie star Bing Crosby thought Washington might make it as a prizefighter. As his promoter, Crosby no doubt believed that because of Washington's gridiron fame, he would be a big draw in the ring. "He needs experience, of course," Crosby said, "but in my opinion he might be heard from as a fighter in less than a year. And there is no doubt but what he will be a big drawing card."

Crosby sent Washington to a veteran manager and trainer, George V. Blake, who gave him a workout and a good review. "I think well of Washington's chances," Blake said. "He looks like he has very good prospects. He showed speed and punch. . . . He is a very intelligent fellow and picks it up quick, and with it he has the speed and the build. In fact he looks way above the average for one of his limited experience. He likes to fight, which is a good thing. What he showed me in a couple of rounds of boxing was plenty." Blake said Washington "might be heard of" within the next year. Apparently not.

It appears that Washington had other thoughts for a career. He signed a contract with Million Dollar Productions to star in a movie playing the hero in a football scandal movie. His uncle Rocky was his agent. A promotion poster from the film *While Thousands Cheer* gives a good indication just how far blacks could go in sports and entertainment in the 1940s. The film had a low budget and a nearly all-black cast, and it was designed for an exclusively African American audience. Kenny Washington's co-star was actress-dancer Jeni Le Gon, one of the few African American actors under contract in Hollywood.

The sixty-four minute black-and-white film had Washington playing a star football player at a fictitious college who hopes to lead his team to the "Peach Bowl," the championship playoff game of the Western Conference. But a mobster tries to bribe him with $25,000 to not play in a key game leading to the playoff game. He turns the mobster down and goes on to be the hero of the movie. Washington invited the entire freshman team at UCLA to attend the final showing of the film, as well as former classmates and alumni. The *Los Angeles Times* apparently didn't review the movie.

In mid-September 1940 Washington played for the semi-pro Chicago Black Panthers, which had a black coach and a black squad. They beat an all-white team 42–0 in the inaugural year. After the game Washington jumped on a plane and returned to Southern California, where he and June Bradley of Long Beach, California, were married in a private home. Nine months later he finished his studies in history and physical education and graduated from UCLA. Immediately afterward he left for a film role in Acoma, New Mexico, where the British war opera *Sundown*, which also featured old friend Woody Strode, was being filmed. They played officers of the British-controlled Kenya, Africa district. The film starred George Sanders and Bruce Cabot.

While Washington was earning his degree, he was named an assistant coach of the UCLA freshman team. It was another move that broke a racial barrier. No black man had ever been a coach of any kind at a major college. The black newspaper *Plaindealer* of Kansas City, Kansas, in an editorial praised UCLA for hiring him, calling it a demonstration "to the world that the color-line should be wiped out and a democracy can be practiced. . . . It took a lot of gumption and real sportsmanship on the part of UCLA authorities to make the 'General' their frosh coach." The *Plaindealer* noted that Washington was appointed more than "just to kick the Kluxers in sports in the pants." He was picked because he was "a tireless worker, patient, and one of the brainiest players on the West Coast."

Washington was "an inspiration to all youth. . . . He knows the game at which he is so adept. We take this opportunity to suggest that it would be entirely fitting that he become a member of the coaching staff at the Westwood institution," the *California Eagle* wrote. For Washington, the coaching job was a chance to bring his enthusiasm for the sport to the fledgling class of 1944–45. It also was a chance for Washington to be on campus so he could finish his degree.

After leaving UCLA Strode landed a job with the Los Angeles County District Attorney's Office as an investigator. He had hoped to get into coaching and never thought of becoming a professional athlete. But Strode was soon out of a job after less than a year when the district attorney lost his reelection. He didn't mind. "The D.A.'s office was using me, but I was too naïve to notice," Strode said. Then he was lured into playing in two exhibition football games for the Hollywood Bears in the Pacific Coast Professional Football League at $750 a game. (Washington was paid $1,000 a game to play as well.) They were to play the game as college all-stars against semi-pro players. "The guys who played football after college played because they loved the game," Strode said. Everybody had regular jobs, and after work they would practice at Griffith Park.

Washington and Strode were making more money than some NFL players, primarily because they took home a cut of ticket sales. Crowds reached twenty thousand or more at their games, drawn in part by Washington and Strode. Strode would get paid after each game. "That's all the money I needed," he said. "The money gave "my family some decent food and at least some measure of comfort in the home," Strode said.

Strode and Washington led the Bears to an 8-0 record. Washington was exempt from the military because of damaged knees. He was playing for the Bears when he went to make a cut, planted his foot to push off, and his leg collapsed. "I could hear that thing go clear across the field; it sounded like a guitar string popping," Strode said. "I used to laugh about that; Kenny wasn't physically fit for the armed services, and he ended up making a fortune playing football during the war," Strode said.

After graduation Washington looked without success for a head coaching job at one of Los Angeles's high schools. With the help of his uncle Rocky he landed a job as an officer on the Los Angeles Police Department. He was one of 147 new officers on the force. Said the American Negro Press, an international news agency, "Persons who break the law when Kenny is pounding a beat had best not run as the former football great is a vicious tackler."

Washington and Strode continued to play football for the Hollywood Bears in the fall of 1941. In one game they beat the league rival Los Angeles Bulldogs 24–7, a team that featured former Stanford quarterback Frankie Albert, who later played the position and coached the San Francisco 49ers.

Washington's knees were so banged up he missed the entire 1942 season. Strode played that year while Washington went on tour with the United Services Organizations in 1942 and 1943, entertaining troops. He became used to talking with the segregated black athletes stationed throughout the world. Strode said the idea behind the tour was "to keep the black soldiers quiet by promising them things would get better after the war."

Mulling over the war, Strode recalled that World War II was a racial war "and what it did was pull the blanket off America's race problems. . . . The Negro American [Press] said, 'I fought for liberty; now I want to enjoy some,'" Strode wrote in his autobiography. That certainly was true for him, Washington, Robinson, Bartlett, and Bradley. Their time was coming.

The Indispensable Robinson

"Jack was dedicated to being the best athlete he could
possibly be because he saw that as an escape."

—Ray Bartlett

The 1940 football season held great promise for UCLA—and Jackie
Robinson. This season he would be the star, the player who would
draw attention now that Kenny Washington had used up his eligibility. The *Daily Bruin* wrote that Robinson's "colossalness is almost
universal knowledge among football fans all over the country." It
said he was "beyond a doubt the Coast's No. 1 candidate for All-
America honors" and that he would be "the greatest drawing card
in the nation."

Robinson became a one-man show in the 1940 season for the Bruins, who lacked the versatility of the previous year's team. He was
so valuable to the team that coaches would run behind Robinson in
practice yelling to his teammates, "Don't hit him, don't hit him," to
avoid injuries. Robinson was almost indispensable to the Bruins; no
one on the team was capable of stepping into his spot. His value to
the team made him a marked man. The Bruins' opponents recognized they had a better chance of winning if they knocked Robinson out of the game. In a game against the University of Oregon, the
Ducks knew about the dangerous Robinson. *The Oregonian* reported
that Robinson "was inevitably double teamed, face-guarded, blan-
keted, hornswoggled, clotheslined, and otherwise neutralized."

"There were a number of games where [opponents] just crucified him," said former teammate Don McPherson. "They just knocked the hell out of him." They ganged up on him to the point that he was held to 3.64 yards per rush for the season. Some of the toughest linemen had graduated as well, making it difficult for Robinson to get past the line of scrimmage. But once in the open field he was extremely dangerous. For the season he had 19 punt returns for 399 yards, an average of 21 yards a return. That was a college record for many years. Despite the difficulties Robinson finished second in the conference in total offense. His standing earned him only honorable mention as an All-American.

Ray Bartlett also figured prominently in the Bruins' chances. Coaches "figure he'll prove as able a decoy as Jackie and probably as potent on pass catching, blocking and occasional ball packing," a *Los Angeles Times* reporter wrote. "But will he come through on defense? Horrell thinks so, that his experience at end will have polished his tackling and that his basketball playing will have sharpened his eye and glued his hands for pass defense. He didn't do a bad job during limited service last fall."

In the season's opening game against SMU at the Los Angeles Coliseum, Robinson returned a punt 87 yards for the Bruins' only score in a 9–6 loss. They led 6–0 going into the fourth quarter but could not stop the Mustangs from scoring a TD and a field goal. Bartlett started at right halfback but didn't carry the ball. He was used primarily as a blocking back. Afterward Coach Madison Bell and the entire SMU team congratulated Robinson and Bartlett for their play.

Next the Bruins fell 9–6 to the Santa Clara Broncos, who kicked a field goal to win the game. The *Los Angeles Times* wrote that the backfield of Robinson and Bartlett, plus two others, "ain't got it." Robinson had trouble passing, continually trying to escape the Broncos' pass rush. The Bruins ran for only 35 yards and passed for a dismal 63 yards. Santa Clara punted the ball away from Robinson except once, when he returned the pigskin for 24 yards.

Coach Horrell was upbeat after the loss. "We're coming along all right. It was a tough one to lose. I plan to go ahead with the same backfield combination." Broncos coach Buck Shaw had nothing but praise for Robinson. "Naturally, we had expected more trouble from Jackie Robinson, but he still gave me enough scares for one evening," he said.

Los Angeles Times columnist Dick Hyland was not sold on the talents of either Robinson or Bartlett. He was particularly hard on Bartlett, who he said, "looked very . . . mediocre" in the SMU game. "Bartlett was not up to snuff, there was no doubt about that," he wrote. But he noted that Bartlett had been an able substitute the previous year against UC Berkeley when Robinson was injured.

Despite Horrell's support for Bartlett as part of his backfield, Ray was on the bench for the Bruins' next game against the Texas A&M Aggies at the Coliseum, another loss for punchless UCLA, 7–0. The only score came from All-American John Kimbrough, who ran in from 9 yards out. Robinson, who was moved to the right halfback position, carried the ball only three times for 9 yards. Angry UCLA fans accused the Aggies of dirty play by using "back-alley tactics" in an attempt to put Robinson and several other Bruins out of the game.

The Bruins lost their first three games by a total of 13 points. They scored only 12. It wasn't going to get much better. The UC Berkeley Golden Bears were up next, and Robinson would be sidelined with a hip injury suffered when he was knocked around by the Aggies. He was starting on the bench, and Horrell wasn't sure he would play at all. Bartlett was back in the starting lineup. Once again the Bruins fell victim to a late field goal, losing 9–7 this time. The Bruins got to the 5-yard line in the final minute but couldn't push across the winning TD. Robinson never got in the game.

Next up was Oregon State at the Coliseum, and the results weren't much different as the Bruins lost 7–0. Robinson started on the bench but entered the game later, although he didn't show much of his talent as he was still suffering from the hip injury.

The undefeated Stanford "Wow Boys" were next in line for the Bruins at the Coliseum. The Indians were under the guidance of Clark Shaughnessy, who reintroduced the T-formation that season. The flashy formation baffled PCC opponents, and UCLA was no exception. The origin of the term "Wow Boys" apparently came about because of the team's colorful uniforms and a play on words of

Stanford's three-time Rose Bowl teams, the Vow Boys, who vowed never to lose to USC, a promise they kept.

The Bruins were ready for the Indians. Horrell held secret practices and indicated the Bruins would pass the ball more. "We'll open up," he said. "All of our former cripples are now in good shape. If we lose, no alibis." Robinson would be starting at right halfback.

The *Stanford Daily* "welcomed" Robinson with a cartoon that showed a Stanford Indian waving a tomahawk while traveling in a race car headed on the road to do battle with the Bruins. On a hill above the race car, a Bruin is pushing over a boulder while saying, "O.K. Jackie Boy. Let Him Have It!" On the road in front of the car stands an African American man, clearly a reference to Robinson, getting set to push a plunger down on TNT. The stereotypical caricature with the addition of a tail, replies to the Bruin, "Yas suh boss."

The cartoon was typical of the brazen attempts to characterize blacks as still unequal. Another example occurred on September 20, 1940, when an Associated Press story carried a typographical error. The *Stanford Daily* ran the story with the error, which claimed that Kenny Washington, then playing for the Hollywood Bears, had broken away for a "330-yard run." The headline over the story read, "Kenny Washington Sho' Do Travel."

The Bruins gave the Indians all they could handle but still came up short 20–14. Robinson kept UCLA in the game with his terrific all-around play. On one play a Stanford punt rolled to a stop at the 16-yard line, and Indians gathered around it. Out of nowhere Robinson streaked, in scooped up the ball, and took off running. At the UCLA 45, All-America fullback Norm Standlee grabbed Robinson by the leg, but he broke free, looped back to the UCLA 35, and then headed toward the goal again. He was finally tackled at the Stanford 43 for a 41-yard return. Robinson may have covered 100 yards during the return. He also had a 40-yard punt return keyed by a Bartlett block. But the Bruins' drive stalled.

With the Bruins trailing 20–7, Stanford was on the move again until Robinson stepped in front of an Albert pass at the UCLA 20 and returned it to the 33. Robinson ran the ball three times after dropping back to pass, moving the ball to the Indians' 19. He then threw a touchdown pass to end Milt Smith with a minute to go—not enough time as Stanford ran out the clock.

Shaughnessy said about Robinson, "Once a year is too much for me with that boy on the other side. A very dangerous back. One of the best I have ever seen. We saw two of the best backs on the Coast out there today. Robinson and Standlee." The *Los Angeles Times* described Robinson as being a "tormentor of old getting away not once but several times on those typical dipsy do dashes that send everyone into hysterics."

The 0-6 Bruins next headed to Eugene, Oregon, to take on the Ducks, who would hand UCLA its worst defeat of the season, 18-0. Coach Tex Oliver was apparently worried enough about Robinson to lock reporters out of practice. The Ducks took great advantage of typically horrible conditions on a rainy afternoon and a muddy Hayward Field. This was UCLA's only game outside California, and Coach Horrell said afterward that many of his players had never played a game in the rain. To top it off his starting quarterback, Ned Mathews, suffered a knee injury in the second quarter, forcing Robinson to move from halfback to quarterback—a position at which he wasn't very good (he completed 2 passes in 11 attempts for 13 yards and 1 interception). On UCLA's last drive he was tackled for a 12-yard loss, throwing the ball halfway into the mud in frustration.

Although the Ducks bottled up Robinson, "the Negro boy nevertheless kept them in a constant sweat lest he break away. He was frightfully dangerous even on the shoe-deep wet turf," a sportswriter for *The Oregonian* wrote. The reporter pointed out that Robinson was hard to tackle. "To stop him, they had to grab him above the waist, or still better around the Negro boy's neck and headlock him out of bounds. . . . When he finally left the game late in the fourth period, the customers not only heaved sighs of relief but gave him the tribute of a cheer."

As *Los Angeles Times* sportswriter Al Wolf put it, the only real excitement came when Ray Bartlett and Oregon's Bill Regner got into a fistfight. It was unclear whether the fight was owing to a racial issue or just hot tempers. Wolf noted that Bartlett "exhibited a fair left jab and [Regner] a pretty good roundhouse right." The Bru-

ins made only one first down in what was described as a "hog wal-
low." Wolf wrote that the Bruins "didn't seem to have their hearts in
the [game]." The Bruins blamed "that cold, wet, slimy mud which
utterly bogged them down," Wolf added. Robinson had 38 yards on
15 rushes, and Bartlett gained only a yard on one carry.

Robinson and his teammates were now 0-7. Back home UCLA
finally found its groove against Washington State with a 34-26 victory. The Bruins scored just two points shy of what they had scored
all season. And they allowed the most points to an opponent in any
of their games.

They had to come from behind 20-6 to do it, and it was all thanks
to the heroics of Jackie Robinson. "They had everything in the ball
game except the bearded lady and free lunch," Wolf wrote. Robinson scored 3 TDs, passed for another, set up a fifth, and kicked 4
conversions. He accounted for 339 yards of total offense. On defense
he intercepted 3 passes. His touchdowns included a punt he ran
back for 60 yards "by doing figure eights all over tarnation" and a
75-yard touchdown run. "I still marvel at the way Jackie Robinson
evaded three Cougar tacklers who apparently had him cornered
on his first touchdown run," remarked Bob Ray, a *Los Angeles Times*
sportswriter. "They all wound up falling flat on their faces, grabbing
nothing but night air. Jackie has more than a change of pace—it's
a chance of space."

The following week against the University of Washington the
Bruins were back to their old habits, getting trounced by the Huskies 41-0. The Huskies wound up second in the league with a 6-1
record, behind undefeated Stanford. Washington led only 7-0 at
halftime, but the Bruins fell apart in the second half. Robinson was
a marked man and had little impact on the game. Nor did Bartlett.
Robinson inexplicably left the game early, dressed hurriedly, and
headed home before his teammates ever left the field.

Coach Horrell had little to say after the game except that he was
looking forward to the USC game the following weekend. "If we
can get some of our cripples back and regain our spirits we have a
chance," he said. The Bruins' chances against the Trojans didn't
look good. Certainly the game might have been considered a rivalry,

but it was nowhere near the rivalry that exists today between the two schools. The Bruins had never beaten USC—and they weren't going to do so on this date either.

As Robinson bowed out, the press heaped plaudits on his two years as a Bruin, calling him one of the most feared backs in the PCC and one of the outstanding players in the country. But newspapers noted that he was not the same player without Washington to take some of the pressure off him.

The Trojans weren't about to let Robinson beat them. Practice revolved around how to stop the fleet running back. And they planned to punt away from him to keep the ball out of his hands. One of the ways USC prevented Robinson from handling the ball was to keep possession with long, grinding drives that ate up the clock. The Trojans won 28–12 while throwing only 4 passes. They had touchdown drives of 67, 62, 61, and 34 yards, all without throwing a pass. The Bruins had led the game 6–0 on Robinson's 6-yard touchdown run. The loss marked the end of a long season for Robinson. The Bruins finished the season with one victory and nine defeats.

Robinson thought of dropping out of school, but in the end he decided to play one more season of basketball. Coach Wilbur Johns was glad to have him back, noting that if Robinson had not devoted so much time to football, he could have been "the greatest of all basketball players."

It turned out to be another hapless year for UCLA basketball, despite Robinson's once again leading the Southern Division of the PCC in scoring with 133 points. After a game at UC Berkeley the *Daily Bruin* complained that Robinson was "viciously treated." Racial taunts from Berkeley fans marred the game. They abused Robinson because of his race, and he provoked the crowd by talking back instead of laughing off or ignoring the taunts. The fans chanted, "Take the nigger out of there," "Down with the colored race," and "Look out, eight ball," according to Tom Berkley, a black UCLA graduate and former track star currently attending Hastings Law School.

Again Robinson was left off the all-conference team; every player from Stanford's championship team was named to the first team.

1. Woody Strode, Jackie Robinson, and Kenny Washington were starting players for UCLA during the 1939 season at a time when few college teams had African Americans who suited up. Photo courtesy UCLA Library Archives.

2. (*opposite top*) Although an all-city football player in high school, Tom Bradley chose to focus his attention on track. He competed in the 440-yard run, the 880, and the 1,600 relay. Photo courtesy University Archives Record Series 100, UCLA Library Archives Special Collections.

3. (*opposite below*) Jackie Robinson was a cunning runner whose quickness and speed helped the Bruins get within one game of the Rose Bowl in 1939. Photo courtesy ASUCLA Photography.

4. (*above*) Jackie Robinson was a threat on the football field whether he was running, passing, or kicking. He was the lone bright spot in 1940 for the Bruins, who finished with a record of one win and nine losses. Photo courtesy ASUCLA Photography.

5. As they were at Pasadena Junior College, Jackie Robinson and Ray Bartlett were teammates at UCLA, this time under basketball coach Wilbur Johns. Bartlett was a rarely used substitute. Photo courtesy Pasadena Museum of History Archive.

6. (*opposite top*) Jackie Robinson's best sport may have been basketball. He led the Pacific Coast Conference in scoring in his junior and senior years. Photo courtesy University Archives Record Series 100, UCLA Library Archives.

7. (*opposite bottom*) Ray Bartlett was a valuable backup runner in his junior year and a part-time starter in his senior season at UCLA. Photo courtesy Pasadena Museum of History Archive.

8. Woody Strode, a football as well as a track and field star, worked as an attendant at a Signal gas station while at UCLA. Photo courtesy Walter L. Gordon Jr., William C. Beverly Jr. Collection, UCLA Library Archives.

9. Ray Bartlett, the second African American on the Pasadena police force, served for twenty years before retiring at the age of forty-seven. Photo courtesy Pasadena Museum of History Archive.

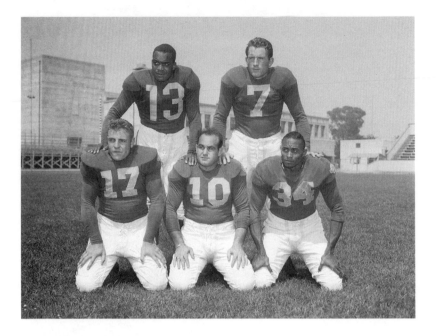

10. Kenny Washington (13) and Woody Strode (34) were among five UCLA players invited to the first Los Angeles Rams training camp in 1946. The others were Bob Waterfield (7), Jack Finlay (17), and Nate DeFrancisco (10). Photo courtesy *Los Angeles Times* Photographic Archive, Charles E. Young Research Library, UCLA Library Archives Special Collections.

11. (*opposite top*) Kenny Washington, who was active in Republican politics, meets with California governor Earl Warren. Photo courtesy *Los Angeles Times* Photographic Archive, Charles E. Young Research Library, UCLA Library Archives Special Collections.

12. (*opposite bottom*) Los Angeles mayor-elect Tom Bradley reaches into the crowd in 1973, offering well wishes after becoming the first African American to hold the job. He remained in office until 1993. Photo courtesy *Los Angeles Times* Photographic Archive, Charles E. Young Research Library, UCLA Library Archives Special Collections.

13. Woody Strode might best be remembered for his role as a powerful gladiator battling Kirk Douglas in the 1960 movie *Spartacus*. Film still from *Spartacus* (1960).

14. After leaving the Pasadena Police Department, Ray Bartlett devoted his time to civic and religious endeavors in Los Angeles County. Photo courtesy Pasadena Museum of History Archive.

15. Jackie Robinson was inducted into the National Baseball Hall of Fame in 1962. He played ten years for the Brooklyn Dodgers after breaking the baseball color barrier in 1947. With him are Branch Rickey and Robinson's wife, Rachel. Photo courtesy of the National Baseball Hall of Fame Library, Cooperstown, New York.

Robinson was chosen for the second team. The *Daily Bruin* called it a clear case of prejudice. Berkeley coach Nibs Price, who had praised Robinson the previous season, left him off his first, second, and third teams. "It's purely the case of a coach refusing to recognize a player's ability purely out of prejudice," one person was quoted as saying.

Robinson decided he had had enough and quit UCLA short of his degree. He wanted to earn money to help his mother, who was still just getting by. He also wanted to find a decent job and wasn't convinced that a college degree was all that important. "I was convinced that no amount of education would help a black man get a job," he said. "I felt I was living in an academic and athletic dream world. . . . My brothers, their friends and acquaintances, all older than me, had studied hard and wound up as porters, elevator operators, bellhops. I came to the conclusion that long hours over books were a waste of time."

Robinson also realized that baseball was his weakest sport. UCLA officials begged him to stay and graduate, even offering him financial help. His mother begged him to stay in school, but to no avail. Jackie remarked, "I wanted to do the next best thing—become an athletic director. The thought of working with youngsters in the field of sports excited me." He also was acutely aware that professional sports—the NFL, the National Basketball League, and Major League Baseball—were off limits to a black athlete.

The day Robinson departed UCLA, the *Daily Bruin* wrote, "Yes it was his speed, his lightning-like reactions that brought the oohs and aahs from the crowd and dollars through the box office. Whether the Bruins won or lost, the people would still come just to watch him. . . . Few can deny that he brought spirit and hope to a Bruin student body that had only known pessimism."

In his senior year Robinson met his future wife, Rachel Isum, at UCLA. Ray Bartlett had introduced them, and now they were a steady couple. ("He was big, he was broad-shouldered, he was very attractive physically, and he had pigeon toes you couldn't miss," she said at the time.) Rachel was shocked when she heard Jackie was leaving school. It was the first she had heard of it. "I was aghast," she said. "I tried to talk him out of it. He was so close to finishing. He put it all on mother Mallie, that he wanted to help her financially, because she was still working very hard. But I think he would have left in any case. He had had enough." Jackie and Rachel's relationship and marriage proved a bedrock of strength for Robinson during the tumultuous times ahead. Her calm demeanor helped keep in line Robinson's often heated temper. Their bond of mutual support was steadfast throughout their marriage.

One of Rachel's observations about Robinson is telling. She noted that Robinson almost always wore a white shirt. "I thought to myself, 'Now why would he do that? Why would anyone that dark wear a white shirt?' It's terrible. He wore his color with such dignity and pride and confidence that after a little while I didn't even think about it. He wouldn't let me. He was never, ever, ashamed of his color."

Newspaper sports pages effused over Robinson's career. George T. Davis, a sportswriter for the *Los Angeles Evening Herald and Express*, wrote that "Jackie Robinson will go down in history as the greatest all-around athlete in Pacific Coast history." Not to be outdone, the *Los Angeles Times*' Al Wolf wrote, "There may have been better footballers, better basketeers, better baseballers and better track men, but cudgel our memory as we will we can think of nobody more able in the four put together." Of the great all-around athletes like Bo Jackson, Jim Thorpe, Deion Sanders, and Glenn Davis, none had ability at such a high level as Robinson.

World War II Beckons

"Things I had been doing all my life I could not do now."

—Woody Strode, on his life in the military

It didn't take Robinson long to find a job. The National Youth Administration (NYA) hired him as assistant athletic director at its work camp in Atascadero, California, on the coast about midway between San Francisco and Los Angeles, for $150 a month. The NYA was founded in 1935 as part of President Franklin D. Roosevelt's New Deal to provide jobs, job training, and relief. Robinson was hoping that the job would help him prepare for a future career.

The NYA saw a need to announce his hiring as news because he was a black man in a position of authority over whites. (Only 2 of the 109 boys were African Americans.) The NYA reported that it was "fortunate, indeed to secure the services of this outstanding athlete." Robinson found the job rewarding, working with boys and men ranging in ages from sixteen to twenty-five from poor or broken homes. "I realized that I had been no different than many of these kids, who would make good if given half a chance," Robinson said.

While he was working at the NYA camp, UCLA held its annual football banquet, during which Robinson was given the coveted award for outstanding service to the university. Robinson had sent a letter ahead of the banquet saying, "Thank you," and it received loud applause.

Only once during his time on the job was Robinson subjected to racial discrimination. A white associate took him along to a camp dance, but when they sought entrance, Robinson was turned away, and the two left.

Because of the war in Europe the government closed all NYA projects in July 1941 as the United States moved closer to joining World War II. The job had lasted less than six months.

Robinson was having trouble finding another job when he was invited to play in an annual charity football game sponsored by the *Chicago Tribune* that matched an all-star college team against the NFL champion Chicago Bears. The all-stars practiced three weeks leading up to the game. "It took one scrimmage to establish the Negro boy's rightful place among the All-Stars," the United Press reported. Babe Hollingbery, the Washington State coach who was helping prepare the team, called Robinson "the best athlete I ever saw. Why, he could play shortstop on a major league team right now, and he is plenty uncanny on a basketball court."

In one scrimmage "the lithe, twisting" Robinson broke away for a 60-yard touchdown run. A *Tribune* story made no mention of his race. But he wasn't in the starting lineup come game time. Ironically two of his teammates played for Tennessee, the school that had hoped to avoid playing against black players in the Rose Bowl.

On August 28 the Bears beat the all-stars 37–13, a game in which Robinson caught a 36-yard touchdown pass in front of 98,203 fans at Soldier Field. "The play easily was the most thrilling of a thrilling game," the *Tribune* wrote. The Bears were wary of Robinson. "The only time we were worried was when that guy Robinson was on the field," Bear defensive end Dick Plasman said in 1977.

Robinson then sought a job in professional football, but not the in the NFL, where some of his all-star teammates, such as Heisman winner Tom Harmon, would ply their trade. Robinson landed a spot on the semi-pro Los Angeles Bulldogs' roster of mostly white players. He played one game before pulling up lame in the first quarter and sat out the rest of the game. A week later he and Ray Bartlett received offers to play for the Honolulu Bears, a semi-pro football team. They would work construction during the week and play football on Sundays. Robinson received $100 a game plus the construction job money. "The construction job was a very important part of the package," Bartlett remembered. "We could use the extra money, because we were both trying to help our mothers. But because the construction job involved defense, it also meant we wouldn't be drafted—at least, not yet."

Robinson and Bartlett were treated like heroes by Hawaii football fans; Robinson had his picture on page one of the *Honolulu Advertiser*, which called him the "Century Express." Nonetheless, Robinson and Bartlett were barred from staying at Waikiki hotels; instead they were housed at Palama Settlement, a social service agency in Honolulu.

The team worked by day, practiced by night, and played games before crowds of as many as twenty thousand on Sunday night. But construction work didn't suit Robinson. "Jack didn't like to work," Bartlett noted. "Jack didn't last long on the job. Either he quit or was fired."

Robinson continued to play football, however, and his star quality brought legions of fans to games. Promoters called him "the sensational All-American halfback" in publicity for the games. Robinson was his typical hip-swiveling self, but his passing faltered. Then he hurt his leg, and the Bears found themselves on the losing side of their record. By December attendance had dwindled to less than six hundred a game.

Robinson headed home on December 5, 1941, by ship. Bartlett stayed on Oahu for another month. Robinson remembered he was playing poker on the ship when he heard of the Pearl Harbor bombing. "We saw the members of the crew painting all the ship windows black," he said. That was to reduce the light and thus ward off possible attacks by air or submarine. Robinson knew that when he got home, that he was likely to be drafted, and he was willing to do his part.

On December 7 Bartlett was about twenty-five miles from Pearl Harbor when the Japanese began bombing Oahu. "I saw a plane flying low above where I was sleeping. When I looked up I saw a red dot on the plane. I didn't know it was a Japanese fighter until later. I turned on the radio and they were announcing that entire island was under attack." Many of the construction workers were taken to Pearl Harbor the next morning to help clean up. They had to retrieve bodies of dead U.S. Navy men from the water. "I still remember the terrible sight of the bodies bobbing in the water. I saw the USS *Arizona* burning in flames for days after the bombing," Bartlett said.

Bartlett returned to the mainland, secured a job in a naval shipyard, and completed his degree at UCLA, graduating with a psychology degree before being drafted into the army in 1944. Bartlett became an army first sergeant for an all–African American unit. He served in Europe and later was sent to the Philippines and the Pacific theater. After the stint with the army Bartlett joined the U.S. Army Reserve Corps and served in Korea and during the Berlin Wall crisis. He retired as a chief warrant officer in 1979.

When Robinson returned, he took the field for the last game of the season for the Los Angeles Bulldogs, who were playing the Hollywood Bears, the team of Washington and Strode. Robinson helped the Bulldogs to a 10-7 lead, but Washington rallied the Bears to a 17-10 victory. If the war had not intervened, the course of history might have changed if Robinson had continued to play football as a career.

Robinson took a job with Lockheed Aircraft in Burbank, a hiring that is noteworthy because the aircraft industry hired few blacks. To meet the military's need for equipment, Lockheed relented and put blacks to work. Robinson drove a truck, earning $100 a month. Looming over him was the possibility that he could be drafted into the service. He sought an exemption based on being his mother's sole support. He doubted whether his bad ankle would make him fit for the service, and, moreover, he questioned his patriotism after learning how African Americans were treated in the military.

Robinson's bid for an exemption was turned down, and he received his induction notice on March 23, 1942, just about the time that Jimmy Dykes of the Chicago White Sox, who had seen Robinson play several years earlier, was holding tryouts. Dykes was supportive of blacks playing in the big leagues. "I would welcome Negro players on the Sox, and I believe one of the other fifteen big league managers would do likewise. As for the players, they'd all get along too." But it was too late for Robinson to try out. He was dispatched to Fort Riley, Kansas, for basic training.

During the football offseason Strode took a crack at professional wrestling, the exhibition kind where the bad guys seemed to always win. Fans hated the villains and would turn out in droves in the hopes they would lose. A promoter at the Olympic Auditorium in Los Angeles agreed to give Strode a shot. He trained for eight months. He went on tour to San Bernardino, where, he said, "we paraded up and down the streets just like the circus had come to town. That would attract fans because television hadn't hit yet."

Strode became the good guy, "the baby face." He couldn't be the bad guy because there would be a "race riot" if he pummeled the white wrestler. Strode dressed all in white. "I was the clean colored boy," he said. Once when he was wrestling, the bad guy was "doing all this nasty stuff to me, gouging and punching." Strode's father was in the audience and couldn't take it anymore. He jumped into the ring and told the bad guy to "get the hell off him." Strode said he got up off the mat and told his father, "It's only a show Daddy."

Then football season resumed. At halftime in one game they learned about the attack on Pearl Harbor. Strode was drafted and wound up playing football for the March Field Fliers team near Riverside, California. The football team was organized to raise money for the Army Emergency Relief fund, which helped the families of killed or wounded soldiers.

Segregation was in force in the military during World War II. On the base whites and blacks lived in separate barracks. The blacks would work in the mess hall and clean latrines and officers' quarters. "What a slap in the face that was," Strode said. "For twenty-seven years I thought I was equal. Now we had the goddamnedest war going and I find out how bad things really are."

But being an athlete brought him privileges that other blacks were denied. An officer who supported the football team talked the commanding officer into letting Strode stay with the other football players in the base gym. None of the athletes had played with an African American before. "Some of them white boys from the South didn't know we could talk except for 'Yassuh!' But before the year was out, we were good friends and teammates," Strode recalled. "We started to have a good time, and they saw I didn't have any scars on my back." One player told him, "I had no idea you guys were like this."

The army football team played other service teams, semi-pro teams, and colleges up and down the Pacific Coast and as far east as Colorado, holding its own with most of them. "We were all grown men; a lot of the team was from the NFL," Strode noted. Once a general who had placed a bet on the March Field team went into the locker room at halftime when the team was losing 6–0 and told them if they didn't win the game, they would be shipped overseas. That did it. They won 32–6. "That was pressure football," Strode said. "We played for our lives."

Strode played for three more years before a stepped-up war effort called for an end to football. This time Strode was going overseas for sure. "They were going to ship me off with the rest of the black soldiers to Europe, and boy, that was the butcher shop," Strode remarked. But the officer who had landed him on the football team stepped in. He asked that Strode be kept with the athletes going overseas. "They do everything together," he told the commanding officer. "I sure would hate to get Woody killed with some other outfit."

Strode was sent to Guam, where he wound up guarding B-29s on an airfield for the duration of the war. When the war was over and he arrived in San Francisco, he discovered the Hollywood Bears playing the San Francisco Clippers. Washington had been playing for the Clippers the year before, leading them to a 7-3 record. Strode called the Bears owner, who told him Kenny Washington was once again playing for the Bears and that a uniform was waiting for Strode. The owner asked him, "Are you in shape?" Strode told him he was. "I suited up and played forty minutes." The Bears went on to win the Pacific Coast Professional Football League championship with an 8-2 record. Washington led the league in scoring, was second in rushing, fourth in passing, and second in total offense. He may have been the most dominant pro football player outside the NFL.

17

Moving Up in the Ranks

"When I followed [Bradley's] career it was obvious to me
that he was the most qualified black officer on the force
and one of the most outstanding of any color."

—Attorney and friend Charles Lloyd

Not long after Pearl Harbor Tom Bradley sought to enlist in the Coast
Guard. He was rejected "on the grounds I was too tall"; he was 6
feet 4 inches. "They said I'd just be bumping my head on things." It
was a clear signal to him that it was because he was black. Then he
inquired about joining the Army Air Corps, but "they just laughed."
Soon thereafter he received his draft notice from the army, and it
came during the week that his wife, Ethel, learned she was preg-
nant. Bradley now had second thoughts about joining the military.

At the time Los Angeles was experiencing an increase in violence
and vandalism, as well as the Zoot Suit Riots, so called because U.S.
sailors and Marines attacked Mexican youths, who were wearing
wide-cut zoot suits, for their being "unpatriotic." Coincidentally
Bradley's status came before the draft board, where he found a
friendly face. He was a Watts real estate broker who was familiar
with Bradley's work with juveniles. The man was influential in getting the draft board to waive him from military duty because of his
pending fatherhood and his need to work with youngsters.

Bradley knew it would be difficult to advance in the police department because of his race, but he was confident that he could over-

come that hurdle. Of the 72 police recruits in the academy only 4 were black. When Bradley started out, there were about 100 African Americans on the forceout of about 4,000 officers. Twenty-one years later Bradley noted that only about 150 officers were African Americans, a ratio that was far below the 14 percent of the black population of Los Angeles in 1960.

Bradley's first assignment was to work traffic, "and that was the worst of the assignments I was to have in twenty-one years," he said. But to his relief, three days later he was assigned to work patrol in the Newton Street Division, which today encompasses nine square miles and 150,000 residents in the South Central area of Los Angeles. Newton was where all the African American officers were sent. The watch commander was Lieutenant Roscoe "Rocky" Washington, Kenny Washington's uncle. "Blacks had been excluded from the normal activities of the department, and it was literally a department of double standards," Bradley commented, one standard for whites and one for blacks.

That assignment lasted three months before Bradley was enlisted to work in the juvenile delinquent program. Department officials saw his youth and college background as perfect qualifications to work with youngsters. Bradley agreed: "I think my age and background really helped provide me with the needed insight to make a difference with these kids. I often knew only too well the answers to come of the very questions I would be asking them." Moreover, Bradley's abilities as a track star came in handy. Troublemakers often took off running when they created mischief. "Well, I guess my record in track paid off," he observed, "because I would always catch them. They would be out of breath and just gaze up at me in disbelief."

Bradley organized sports programs in cooperation with local colleges to get the youngsters involved in football, basketball, baseball, and track. He remembered how important those activities had been when he was growing up. "It really marked the first time that some of these kids were not in the ever-present company of dropouts and more hardened criminal elements," Bradley said. "Having some of the college coaches and stars involved—successful people whom these kids saw pictures of in the papers or heard about over the radio—really help the kids to develop a 'can-do' attitude."

After five years with that program Bradley was promoted to sergeant and assigned as a detective for five more years. There were few black sergeants at that time. He went to work in the vice squad, where he helped clean up prostitution, bookmaking, and other illegal activities in the South Central and Wilshire areas of Los Angeles. About this time Bradley also was taking an interest in the Democratic Party. Bradley worked on future governor Edmund G. "Pat" Brown's unsuccessful attempt to become attorney general in 1946. He also helped Ed Roybal become the first Hispanic member of Congress from California in 1962.

Bradley became a mentor for many of the black officers, encouraging them to seek higher ranks. His leadership was characterized by his quiet style and reserved nature. "He just had that leadership ability without appearing to be an obvious leader," fellow officer Maria Thomas said. After four years in vice Bradley needed a new challenge. He proposed the position of community information officer, a post that he said no other department in the country had. The job led to a base of support for him later when he entered politics.

While Bradley was moving through the ranks, Jackie Robinson was having problems with the law—military law. It was Jim Crow raising his head once again. Although Robinson had been subjected to racism all his life, he had never seen what came with being in the U.S. Army.

After basic training Robinson received his first lesson on being a black man in the military. He applied to Officer Candidate School. He and other blacks in his unit had passed tests for the school, but nothing happened for three months. "We could get no answers to our questions about the delay," he said. "It seemed to be a case of buck passing all along the line." Finally in January 1943 Robinson became a second lieutenant.

Robinson was put in charge of an all-black transportation battalion at Fort Riley, Kansas. Some of the men complained about being allowed to sit in only seven seats in the post theater even when other seats went empty. Robinson telephoned a major who told him there was nothing he could do. The major thought he was talking to a white man, so he said, "Lieutenant, let me put it to you this way. How would you like to have your wife sitting next to a nigger?" When Robinson went into a rage, the major hung up on him. The seating arrangement soon was changed by a colonel to allow for more seats, even though they remained in the rear of the theater.

Robinson also was playing for the post football team. Its first scheduled game was against the University of Missouri, which refused to play if a black player—that is, Robinson—took the field for Fort Riley. The army solved the problem by giving Robinson leave to go home so that the game could be played. After that Robinson never played in a game for the post. He told the colonel in charge of the football program that he would not play. The colonel said he could order him to. Robinson said, "You wouldn't want me playing on your team, knowing that my heart wasn't in it." The colonel let it go, but Robinson concluded, "I would never win a popularity contest with the ranking hierarchy of that post."

The army barred Robinson from the base's all-white baseball team, on which a future Brooklyn Dodger, Pete Reiser, was playing . "One day we were out at the field practicing," Reiser recalled, "when a Negro lieutenant came out for the team, [and] an officer told him, 'You have to play with the colored team.' That was a joke. There was no colored team." The lieutenant walked away. "That was the first time I saw Jackie Robinson," Reiser said. "I can still see him slowly walking away."

Robinson was soon transferred to Fort Hood in Texas. He hopped on an army bus to go to a nearby hospital for a checkup on his ankle to see whether he was fit for overseas duty. While on the bus, he talked with the wife of a fellow lieutenant. "We sat down together in the bus, neither of us conscious of the fact that it made any difference where we were sitting," Robinson said. The bus driver glanced in his rearview mirror and thought he saw a black man talking with a white woman. He stopped the bus and ordered Robinson to move to the rear of the bus. "I didn't even stop talking, didn't even look at him," Robinson recalled. He knew that the army had put out a regulation prohibiting racial discrimination on post vehicles. "Knowing about these regulations, I had no intention of being intimidated into moving to the back of the bus," Robinson said. Robinson and the driver got into a verbal squabble. The driver drove on, and when Robinson was getting off at the next stop, the driver went to get a dispatcher. "There's the nigger that's been causing me trouble," the driver said, pointing at Robinson. Robinson told the driver to get off his back. Seconds later two military policemen arrived and asked whether Robinson would talk to their captain. Robinson agreed, but "I was naïve about the elaborate lengths to which racists in the armed forces would go to put a vocal black man in his place."

The upshot was that the army brought court martial charges against Robinson, charges of which he was eventually acquitted. The accusations came about because of his "insolent, impertinent and rude manner" when addressing a superior officer about the incident on the bus. Robinson was fed up with the army, and he had a plan: he would violate military procedure by going over the head of his superiors and send a letter to the Adjutant General's Office in Washington DC. The letter asked that he be retired from the army because there were no openings for black officers. "I feel I can be of more service to the government doing defense work rather than being on limited duty with an outfit that is already better than 100% over strength in officers." Robinson was hoping the top brass would see him as a potential troublemaker. "I guess someone was really anxious to get rid of me fast," he said, because not long afterward, on November 28, 1944, the army gave him an honorable discharge.

Good fortune was about to come Robinson's way. While waiting for his discharge, he met a black soldier who had played for the Kansas City Monarchs of the Negro National League, one of the top teams in professional black baseball. The soldier, Ted Alexander, told him the Monarchs were looking for top players. The pay was good and so was the baseball life, he told Robinson. Robinson wrote a letter seeking a job with the Monarchs. They agreed to pay him $400 a month if he made the team during spring training in April 1945.

During the winter Robinson's Pasadena mentor, Karl Downs,

sent Robinson a telegram asking him to teach physical education at Samuel Huston College in Austin, Texas. Downs had been hired as president of the black college a year earlier, and he was reputed at the age of thirty-two to be the youngest college president in the United States. Robinson wanted to repay Downs for all the help he had been given and eagerly accepted the job—although only until spring training began.

The college had virtually no athletic program, so Robinson put out a call for students to try out for a basketball squad. Seven students showed up, most of whom knew little about the game. Robinson set up a schedule against teams in the Southwestern Conference, including Grambling, Southern University, Bishop, Wiley, Prairie View, and Arkansas A&M. Huston didn't fare well.

Southern humiliated outmanned Huston in a tournament. On hand to watch the game was a Langston University player whose team would play Southern in the next tournament round. That player, Marques Haynes, was repulsed by Southern's treatment of Huston and vowed to pay it back. With two minutes to go in the Langston-Southern game and Langston leading, Haynes went into one of his dribbling routines to run out the clock and keep the ball away from Southern. Haynes later became famous for his dribbling prowess with the Harlem Globetrotters and was inducted into the Basketball Hall of Fame in 1998. Robinson's team won one game that season, a stunning defeat of defending league champion Bishop 61–59

In March Robinson headed off to Houston for spring training with the Kansas City Monarchs. He discovered spring training consisted of playing games rather than preparing for the season. At the same time as Robinson was with the Monarchs, the Red Sox were under pressure from a Boston city councilman who was fighting Jim Crow in baseball. After a month of "spring training" Robinson was surprised by the Boston Red Sox, who offered him a tryout. He joined two other African Americans on April 16, 1944, at Fenway Park.

The Communist Party newspaper, the *Daily Worker*; the black press; and to a much lesser degree the white press were joining in an effort to bring racial equality to the big leagues. Pressure from an angry white Boston city councilman, whose district encompassed a large black population, persuaded the Red Sox to hold the tryout. Neither the manager nor any players attended. Robinson banged pitch after pitch off and over the Green Monster, the famous left-field fence. "What a ballplayer," scout Hugh Duffy said. "Too bad he's the wrong color." The two other black players, Sam Jethroe and Marvin Williams, also fared well, but none of the three heard anything from the Red Sox ever again. Robinson headed back to the Monarchs. It wasn't until twelve years later that Pumpsie Green was hired to play for the Red Sox, the last team to include an African American on its roster.

Perhaps the most influential sportswriter to put pressure on big league baseball was Lester Rodney, a white man who relentlessly led the drive. "Nobody was making any fuss about the fact that the great black players—we called them Negroes at that time—were not allowed to play in the big leagues," Rodney said in 1996.

Rodney, a popular young reporter for the *Daily Worker*, chided his readers eleven years before Jackie Robinson broke the color barrier. "You pay the prices," he told his readers. "Demand better ball. Demand Americanism in baseball." In those days communism was not the feared enemy that it became during the 1950s and the Cold War. Thousands of people read the newspaper. (Rodney later denounced communism.) Rodney once told the famed sportswriter Roger Kahn of an encounter he had with New York Giants manager Leo Durocher. "For a fucking Communist, you know your baseball," Durocher said.

Rodney's "work, with an audience, encouraged black writers," said University of Pittsburgh historian Rob Ruck. "The two big impacts were with black writers and in mobilizing people." Rodney and the *Daily Worker* led petition drives that Ruck said generated more than a million signatures urging baseball commissioner Kenesaw Mountain Landis to integrate the game. "Rodney made it seem that this was the 'American Way,'" says Mark Naison, Fordham University professor of African American studies.

As early as 1934 Rodney (then aged only twenty-three) and the *Daily Worker* had begun pushing for the integration of baseball.

On August 13, 1936, Rodney wrote, in the promotion of an upcoming series of articles about Jim Crow in baseball, that he was going to "rip the veil from the 'Crime of the Big Leagues'—mentioning names, giving faces, sparing none of the most sacred figures in baseball officialdom." He wrote that mainstream newspapers had carefully hushed up the Majors' bigoted stand against blacks in baseball and called it "one of the most sordid stories in American sports.... Read the truth about this carefully laid conspiracy." Rodney's articles received wide attention but no action from the "officialdom" of baseball.

Outside of the black press, few white newspapers except the *Daily Worker* were covering the issue of a boycott on African American ballplayers. J. G. Taylor Spink, editor of *The Sporting News*, once wrote that there "was no good" to come from raising the racial issue. "The conscience of American journalism on baseball apartheid, sorry to say, was not in the hands of America's big daily newspapers," Rodney retorted. Rodney and the *Daily Worker* never quit trying to end baseball segregation.

Robinson always was appreciative of Rodney's efforts. He testified before Congress two years after he broke the color barrier that "The fact that it is a Communist who denounced injustice in the courts, police brutality, and a lynching when it happens doesn't change the truth of his charges. Negroes were stirred up before there was a Communist Party, and they'll stay stirred up long after the Party disappeared—unless Jim Crow has disappeared as well."

Sports historian Larry Lester told ESPN in 2010 that he believed Rodney's efforts had a significant effect on Brooklyn Dodgers president and general manager Branch Rickey's move to sign Robinson. "It made his job easier to sell the signing of Jackie Robinson to the American public, because Lester Rodney had already planted the seeds for this historic event to happen." Rodney said in 1996 that the *Daily Worker* didn't do it for credit, and "I don't know how much we specded up the inevitable." As for Rickey, Rodney said, "He was going to be the big hero and baseball legend in history—he is, and rightfully so, because he did it ... and once he did it, he fought for it."

In his biography Rodney recounted the scene in a jammed-packed

Ebbets Field press box on April 10, 1947. Brooklyn announced its historic call-up of Robinson to the Dodgers as he batted against them for their Montreal farm club in an exhibition game. Three writers, Rodney said, approached him and said something like, "Well, you guys can take a lot of credit for this."

Life was not easy in the Negro leagues. The teams were poorly financed, the schedules created chaos, and black players had trouble finding places to eat and sleep on the road. Robinson missed the structure he found in college athletics and was appalled by gambling interests in the league. "[Playing in the Negro leagues] turns out to be a pretty miserable way to make a buck," Robinson said. "When I look back at what I had to go through in black baseball, I can only marvel at the many black players who stuck it out for years in the Jim Crow leagues because they had nowhere else to go."

Robinson questioned what his future held. He saw that a white ballplayer could achieve fame and fortune, but a black player could not. "I began to wonder why I should dedicate my life to a career where the boundaries for progress were set by racial discrimination," Robinson noted. He also worried that he would lose Rachel, the love of his life, who was growing impatient that he was not returning to California to settle down.

Robinson played in sixty-three games for the Monarchs—the most any member on the team played that year was eighty—and batted .414. He was twenty-six years old. At the end of the season Robinson was so fed up with black baseball that he was ready to return to Los Angeles, look for a job coaching baseball in high school, and marry Rachel. But his fortunes were soon to dramatically change.

18

Making NFL History

"From 1933 to 1946, major league professional football
was as lily-white as a Klansman's dancing partner."

—A. S. "Doc" Young, writer for *Ebony* magazine

The year 1946 was Kenny Washington's and Woody Strode's time
to make sports history. They would be the first blacks to end the
thirteen-year unwritten boycott by the NFL that banned African
Americans from playing in professional football. Up until 1933 seventeen African Americans had played in the NFL. The last was Joe
Lillard of the Chicago Cardinals. He was a shifty runner, an excellent passer, and a skilled defensive back and kicker. He had been
involved in at least four fights during the 1932 season, none of which
he started. Yet there is little doubt those skirmishes had a major
impact on the NFL owners who started the boycott. When the Chicago Bears' founder and coach George Halas was once asked why
there were no black players, he remarked that the game "didn't have
the appeal to black players at the time." That doesn't explain why
Halas tried to sign Washington and then changed his mind after
talking with other owners; perhaps it was in a show of solidarity.
NFL owners never acknowledged publicly that there was a ban, but
it was apparent to all, particularly the black race. Sometime after
the boycott was lifted, an NFL executive, Tex Schramm, recalled,
"You just didn't do it [hire blacks]. It wasn't the thing that was done."
   Two owners of football teams—one a racist and the other not—

signed Washington, Strode, and two other blacks to contracts. The Los Angeles Rams (originally the Cleveland Rams) were the first to break the NFL boycott, not necessarily because their owner, Dan Reeves, wanted to but because he was forced to. The Cleveland Browns of the new All-American Football Conference (AAFC) signed two black players, Marion Motley and Bill Willis, to contracts because they were among the best players available. The conference was new, and it had no boycott, so Motley's and Willis's contributions to breaking the color barrier are less strong than those of Washington and Strode. Nonetheless, the new teams in the AAFC were in no hurry to hire blacks. Cleveland Browns coach Paul Brown read about the Rams' signing of Washington and Strode and months later took the first courageous step toward integrating the AAFC by signing Motley and Willis.

When the fledgling AAFC opened the franchise in Cleveland under Brown, who was to become pro football's Branch Rickey, the Rams decided to move from Cleveland to Los Angeles and its burgeoning population. The Rams, despite being NFL champions, were drawing fewer than twenty thousand fans to home games. Two major factors made the Rams pick Washington to be the first player to end the boycott: they were concerned that the new competition would sign black players, Washington among them, and that Los Angeles city officials would prohibit them from using the Coliseum if they didn't let blacks play. They also were feeling heat from three prominent African American sportswriters: Halley Harding of the *Los Angeles Tribune*, Edward Robinson of the *Los Angeles Sentinel*, and Herman Hill of the *Pittsburgh Courier*. These journalists took up the challenge of persuading the Rams to sign Washington despite his age and injury-prone body. They wanted Coliseum officials to know that if they didn't sign Washington, "there will be no pro football in the L.A. Coliseum."

African American leaders in Los Angeles put pressure on Coliseum officials by pointing out that under the Supreme Court's 1896 "separate but equal" ruling the Coliseum could not have a segregated sports team playing in a stadium supported by public funds. It left Coliseum officials no choice but to prohibit the Rams from playing in the stadium unless they had black players. The Rams "didn't take Kenny because of his ability," Strode said. "They didn't take me on my ability. It was shoved down their throats."

Reeves reluctantly agreed to sign blacks, particularly when he recognized that Kenny Washington, although age twenty-seven and often injured, could be a big draw at the box office. "The people out there loved Kenny, and they wanted him to play for the Rams," Strode said. On March 21, 1946, Washington signed a contract with the Rams. No terms were announced, but a Rams' source said, "Kenny asked for plenty and got it."

Reeves also knew that the rest of the league couldn't stand in his way if he signed black players because he was opening new territory for the NFL. "Reeves had the league over a barrel," Washington said later. "The Coliseum people warned the Rams if they practiced discrimination, they couldn't use the stadium. When those NFL people began thinking about all those seats and the money they could make filling them up, they decided my kind wasn't so bad after all."

Head coach Bob Snyder also admitted that the Rams would have been denied a Coliseum lease if they hadn't signed Washington. "I doubt we would have been interested in Washington, if we had stayed in Cleveland," Snyder said.

It took two more years for another NFL team to sign a black player. The Detroit Lions signed end Bob Mann and halfback Mel Groomes, and the New York Giants signed defensive back Emlen Tunnell, whose career led him to the Hall of Fame.

Ironically while the Rams were forced to sign the first two black players and break the boycott, the same procedures were used sixteen years later to integrate the last NFL team—the "lily-white" Washington Redskins. Their bigoted owner, George Preston Marshall, wanted to lease federal land for a new football stadium. But Secretary of the Interior Stewart L. Udall said that would happen only if Marshall would agree to a non-discrimination policy. Jackie Robinson applauded Udall's stand, calling it "inspirational and encouraging." Marshall fired back at Robinson: "Jackie Robinson is in the business of exploiting a race and making a living doing it. I'm not. He doesn't qualify as a critic." But Marshall reluctantly agreed.

Washington's uncle, Rocky, acted as his agent, assuring that Washington would get a full year's pay under a no-cut clause if he was used by the Rams only to generate ticket sales. When Jackie Robinson signed with Brooklyn, the Dodgers took steps to see him succeed. The Rams didn't give Washington the same chance.

The Rams decided it would be best if Washington's roommate on the road was a black player. When asked whom he would like, Washington without hesitation picked Woody Strode. Ram officials questioned Strode's interracial marriage in an effort to keep him off the team, but Washington would not relent. "I want my buddy," he said. That was enough. The NFL then signed its second African American.

"My signing with the Rams wasn't a package deal *per se*," Strode said, "but they realized that Kenny would be a loner on the road. They didn't want Kenny to face it by himself. . . . Sometimes the team would stay at the Hilton and Kenny and I would have to go find somewhere else to stay. If we were lucky, we'd stay with a friend or relative."

Strode said he had the ability to play in the NFL, "but the Rams weren't concerned with that. They spoke badly of my marriage to a Hawaiian, and I think if they had their choice they would have selected someone else." Strode spent most of his playing career sitting on the bench and "collecting my $350 a week." He would remark when his career was over, "Integrating the NFL was the low point of my life. There was nothing nice about it."

Strode said he didn't realize what he and Washington had accomplished. "We discovered that very few blacks received the opportunity Kenny and I received," he said. "I never became bitter over it, maybe at a few individuals, but never at the total picture."

Dick Hyland, a sports columnist for the *Los Angeles Times*, called Washington the greatest football player he had ever seen, better than Red Grange, Tom Harmon, and Ernie Nevers, but he questioned whether Washington's "break" had come five or six years too late.

"Washington has become a beaten-up ballplayer who is neither so strong nor so quick in his reactions as he was before the war." He noted that because of Washington's trick leg he had lost "just enough of his speed to enable tacklers . . . to nail him with punishing tackles—which in turn cut down his speed, strength and effectiveness." Hyland saw Washington as no more than a "spot" player. "Kenny Washington will work his head off to prove this predication wrong, and I hope he does," Hyland wrote.

Washington made the team, and his first appearance in the NFL in 1946 was in Los Angeles in an exhibition game against the Washington Redskins; it was a replay of the championship game won by the Rams the previous year. A crowd of one hundred thousand was expected to attend the game. Such a number was more than the Rams had attracted during their entire season. Surely Kenny Washington had a lot to do with the size of the crowd, and Angelinos were eager to see top-flight professional football.

The crowd fell below expectations at slightly more than 68,000, but fans saw a great game with the Rams winning 16-14. If Washington played, he had little impact on the outcome as he wasn't mentioned in press accounts in the *Los Angeles Times*. According to Strode, Washington got in for one play in the first half plus a few minutes toward the end of the game. Strode said he never got into the game. The Rams wound up the year drawing almost 215,000 spectators in five games, a huge boost over crowds in Cleveland.

Gordon Macker of the *Los Angeles Daily News* wondered why the duo didn't play. "The scam of advertising names to hustle the chumps and then letting the names be only numbers in the program (25 cents please) seems to be an accepted practice with the pro promoters. Well, this town won't go for it." It didn't bother Strode much. He was making more money than he had in semi-pro football, and he wasn't getting beat up. "I was in the NFL and that was like a prize," he said.

Although Strode played a few minutes in some games, he thought he could have helped the team more. But he quietly accepted the situation. "Well, I had to sit and suffer those lashes because I opened the door," he said. "Kenny and I opened the door. Soon, every black with the ability was running up and down the field." Looking back on those days, Strode remarked, "If I have to integrate heaven, I don't want to go."

Traveling with the Rams made a big impact on him and Washington, Strode said. "We discovered how popular we were across the country. The black kids outside of California used to tell Kenny and me how much they enjoyed listening to our games on the radio while we were still playing at UCLA. Until that time, we didn't realize what a unique thing we had done."

On one trip to Chicago Washington and Strode tried to stay at a white hotel. The hotel offered Washington and Strode $100 each to find someplace else to stay. "Well, what the hell, let's be segregated," Strode replied. "It was great," Strode said. "I discovered my own people." They got to listen to Count Basie's jazz band in the hotel to which they moved. But the black press heard about the incident and criticized Washington and Strode. "Look," he said, "do me a favor and mind your own business. We get $200, we don't have to stand curfew. I hear the white guys on the club are about to mutiny to get the kind of a deal we got. Now, you're going to louse it all up."

Strode wrote in his memoirs that he could not recall many racial incidents on the field. "You're out there trying to beat each other up; how do you know when a guy's trying to hurt you because you're black?" He acceded that occasionally some players would take a cheap shot at them. At times white players hit Washington after the whistle had blown to stop play, and no penalty was called. It did little to help his aching knees.

In a game against the Chicago Cardinals, Washington hurt his knee again. The *Pittsburgh Courier* wondered how long Washington could keep taking the punishment. His knee, it said, "will only hold together for so long. . . . One hard tackle at a certain spot . . . and the former Bruin is generally through for the day." Bob Snyder noted that when Washington first began to play, "They'd tee off on him. They'd drop knees on him."

Snyder recalled that Washington and Strode were well accepted by their teammates but not so much by other teams. He remembered when a big Green Bay tackle hit Washington in the jaw with an elbow. Apparently the player also called Washington a "black bastard." Washington started to go after him but regained his composure. Then he said, "Listen, that was a pretty good shot. I want to tell you something you white trash. If you want to wait till the game is over, meet me under the stadium and I'll knock your goddamn block off." Snyder said, "Well, our other players heard about that, and I think if we had an election, he would have been elected captain."

Strode played little that year, catching just four passes. Strode said he was put in as a 200-pound defensive end "in the butcher shop. . . . It was a joke." Teammate Tom Harmon called Strode "one of the greatest defensive ends I ever saw, but he never got a chance to prove it because of that fool coaching staff. In practice you could never get near him. You never saw a man in better shape."

The next season, after an exhibition game in which he got in for only one play, the Rams released Strode. Line coach George Trafton told him, "Woody, it's not because of your ability that you're getting fired. They're trying to say you're too old [thirty-two] and that they're trying to rebuild. I tried to tell them Negroes don't age like white people." Later, when Strode was talking with Washington, Kenny told him, "It's not your ability; it's your lifestyle. Dan Reeves does not approve of your marriage to Luana and your Hawaiian lifestyle." It wasn't the first time Strode's mixed marriage had been an issue. When they were married, Strode remarked, "You'd have thought I was marrying [actress] Lana Turner."

On the field Washington was the target of slurs and cheap shots in pileups unseen by officials, who often overlooked them. Washington found himself "turning the other cheek" more often than he would have liked. "I think he endured it but there were times like anything else where he would have to get in somebody's face to challenge somebody," his grandson Kirk Washington said. "It got to him at times. It was hard to be a Negro during that time trying to play football. He endured a lot."

In limited action in 1946 Washington ran for 114 yards, caught 6 passes, and scored a touchdown. The following year he ran for

for 144 yards for a league-leading average of 7.4 yards a carry. His final year, when he put in some time as a defensive back, Washington gained 301 yards on the ground. He then decided to call it quits. He was no longer the healthy player who had thrilled UCLA crowds ten years earlier. He was thirty years old. Time had passed him by. For his career he had carried the ball 140 times for 851 yards, or 6.1 yards a carry, and 8 touchdowns. He had caught 15 passes for 227 yards and a touchdown.

But Strode's and Washington's mark in pro football was greater than their performance on the field. They had broken the barrier, and eventually every NFL team became integrated. Washington recalled in 1971 that it "was just as important for a colored player to break into pro football as it was in baseball." The next year the Rams signed African American Tank Younger to the team and went on to win three straight champions beginning in 1949.

Washington left football with the same grace that he had maintained throughout his life. During halftime of his final game at the Los Angeles Coliseum, Washington was honored for his career. He was given a number of lavish gifts, including a new Ford sedan, a combination radio-television set, and a $500 savings account for his seven-year-old son Kenny Jr. His teammates presented him with a watch. While thanking the crowd, he remarked, "The cheers you fans have given me went to my heart, not to my head." The crowd roared.

Strode's football career was far from over. Not long after he was cut, a former Rams teammate who was a player-coach for the Calgary Stampeders in Canada asked him to join his team. He offered him $5,000 for the eighteen-game season and $100 a week in expense money. Strode likened playing in Canada to the Old West because Canadian football was so far behind U.S. football. But nowhere did he find the Jim Crow discrimination he found in the states. The Canadians loved Strode.

The former teammate and now coach installed plays that the Rams used, a system far advanced for Canadian football. The Stampeders went undefeated, with Strode scoring the winning touchdown in the championship game when he returned a fumble 45 yards. The next season the Stampeders made it to the championship game again but lost. Strode suffered a separated shoulder and sat out most of the second half. In his third and final season in Canada he suffered two cracked ribs over his heart and called it quits. "I loved football, and I probably played longer than I should have," Strode said. "When you start getting injured like I did towards the end, that's a sign to hang 'em up." It was 1949, and he was heading back home for good.

19

The Negro League Years

"The plate is the same width. The bases are the same—
ninety feet apart. I've got to make good."

—Jackie Robinson

Jackie Robinson was fed up with playing in the Negro Leagues. The travel was fatiguing, and the meals were lousy. "You were lucky if [restaurants] magnanimously permitted you to carry out some greasy hamburgers in a paper bag with a container of coffee," he recalled. "You were really living when you were able to get a plate of cold cuts. You ate on board the team bus or on the road." The players often slept on the rickety old buses on the way to the next town because hotels wouldn't take them. If there were hotels that took blacks, they had no eating facilities. Robinson was ready to return to California. He saw no future in black baseball. He wanted to marry his college sweetheart, Rachel, and still sought to land a job as a high school coach.

On August 24, 1945, Robinson was at Chicago's Comiskey Park, home of the White Sox and also where the black teams played when the White Sox were on the road. Clyde Sukeforth, a Brooklyn Dodger scout, walked onto the field to talk with Robinson. He told Robinson that Branch Rickey had heard of Robinson's talents and wanted to talk with him. Sukeforth asked to meet with him that night. Then he asked Robinson to travel to Brooklyn to meet with Rickey on the pretense that the Dodger boss wanted him to play for the Brook-

lyn Brown Dodgers in a new league being formed for black players. It took some talking, but Robinson finally said he would come.
"I was thinking that this might be a gag, a cruel gag," Robinson
said. "I didn't dare think of becoming a Dodger. Hundreds of things
entered my mind, and I was still thinking when we got off the train
in New York."

Who was this Branch Rickey he was going to meet? As the great
sportswriter Red Smith described him, he was "a player, manager,
executive, lawyer, preacher, horse-trader, spellbinder, innovator,
husband and father and grandfather, farmer, logician, obscuran-
tist, reformer, financier, sociologist, crusader, father confessor,
checker shark, friend and fighter, Judas Priest, what a character."
The sixty-four-year-old Rickey wore a hat most of the time under
which bushy eyebrows wiggled up and down. A gruff voice came
out over his bowtie, while his pudgy body strained the buttons on
his natty suit. He often held a cigar in his hand, from which he took
an occasional puff. He neither drank nor cussed. He amassed a fortune during his baseball years.

What transpired was an intense three-hour meeting in which
Rickey was going to get his way. Rickey "just stared and stared,"
Sukeforth recalled. "That's what he did with Robinson—stared at
him as if he were going to get inside the man. And Jack stared right
back at him. Oh, they were a pair, those two. I tell you, the air in
that office was electric." Rickey told Robinson that he wanted him
to play for the National League club, not a black team. Mentioning a
black team as a reason was just a ruse to get him to meet with Rickey.
"My reactions seemed like some kind of weird mixture churning
in a blender," Robinson said. "I was thrilled, scared, and excited. I
was incredulous. Most of all, I was speechless."

Rickey told Robinson he had considered several players who
could become the man to break the color barrier, but they didn't
match up to Robinson. But, he warned, "We can fight through this,
Robinson. We can win only if we can convince the world that I'd
doing this because you're a great ballplayer and a fine gentleman."
He told Robinson he would face terrible problems on and off the
field and asked him how he would handle them. "They'll taunt and

goad you," Rickey said. "They'll do anything to make you react. They'll try to provoke a race riot in the ballpark. This is the way to prove to the public that a Negro should not be allowed in the major leagues. This is the way to frighten the fans and make them afraid to attend the games."

"Mr. Rickey," Robinson asked, "are you looking for a Negro who is afraid to fight back?" Rickey flew out of his seat and replied, "Robinson, I'm looking for a ballplayer with guts enough not to fight back. . . . We've got no army. There's virtually nobody on our side. No owners, no umpires, very few newspaper men. And I'm afraid that many fans will be hostile. We'll be in a tough position."

Rickey told Robinson he would have to play hard to win people over. "You've got to do this job with base hits and stolen bases and fielding ground balls, Jackie." Rickey drew on the New Testament passage to stress that Robinson had to turn the other cheek. Robinson had never backed away before, and to do so at this point in life would be foreign to his nature. But he agreed to embark on the new path for two years until Rickey released him from his restraints.

Robinson withheld from Rickey that he wondered whether he could restrain himself, but he knew that he had to. He said he had to do it for black players who might follow him, for his mother, for his girlfriend, for himself—and "for this spellbinder I had just met." He agreed to a contract that included a $3,500 bonus and $600 a month in salary to play for the Montreal Royals, a team one step from the Brooklyn Dodgers. But he was to tell no once except Rachel and his mother.

Rickey recalled, "Surely God was with me when I picked Jackie. . . . He really did understand the responsibility he carried. . . . He had the intelligence of knowing how to handle himself under adversity. Above all he had what the boys call guts, real guts." A childhood friend, Gloria May, recalled that she was surprised when Robinson signed with the Dodgers. "And amazed, just like the rest of the public was," she said. "But I think a lot of people were behind him, and they appreciated the fact that he gave of himself, which must have been a very traumatic experience. And nobody can realize it unless you have been through it. We felt it, but, you know, he had to live it."

On October 23, 1945, Robinson was introduced as a new player for Montreal at a news conference attended by more than two dozen members of the press. The room "exploded" as flash bulbs popped and reporters headed to tell their newspapers the story. When order was restored after several minutes, the club's president, Hector Racine, expressed confidence that Montreal fans were not racially biased and that they would judge Robinson on his playing ability. "We made this step for two reasons," he told reporters. "First, we are signing this boy because we think of him primarily as a ball player. Secondly, we think it is a point of fairness."

Branch Rickey Jr., who was then in charge of the Dodgers' farm teams, said he expected some reaction from areas in the United States that had not accepted blacks into their culture. "My father and Mr. Racine are not inviting trouble," he said, "but they won't avoid it if it comes. Jack Robinson is a fine type of young man, intelligent and college bred, and I think he can make it, too." He predicted that some players from the team would "steer away from a club with Negro players on its roster. Some of them who are with us now may even quit, but they'll be back in baseball after they work a year or two in a cotton mill."

When Robinson spoke before the reporters, he told them he knew he was a "guinea pig" and that he was delighted to have been picked to break the color barrier. "Maybe I'm doing something for my race," he said. Rickey also defended his position. "I have never meant to be a crusader," he said. "I hope I won't be regarded as one. My purpose is to be fair to all people and my selfish objective is to win baseball games."

The announcement met with an avalanche of news coverage, from critics to backers. Most coverage contained negative comments ranging from sportswriters' opinions to ballplayers' distaste for the idea. "Ball players on the road live close together," Texas-bred Rogers Hornsby, a Hall of Famer, commented. "It won't work." Dixie Walker, a popular Dodger who was born in Georgia, said, "As long as he isn't with the Dodgers, I'm not worried." The editor of a black New York weekly wrote that Robinson "would be haunted by the expectations of his race. . . . White America will judge the

Negro race by everything he does. And Lord help him with his fellow Negroes if he should fail them."

Future Hall of Fame pitcher Bob Feller doubted that Robinson would succeed in the Major Leagues because he had "football shoulders." He said Robinson "couldn't hit an inside pitch to save his neck. If he were a white man, I doubt if they would even consider him as big league material." Robinson replied that he wished Feller hadn't mentioned his shoulders. "What are football shoulders?" Robinson asked. "I don't think anybody knows. If it means muscle-bound I don't have them. . . . It was a shot in the dark, because football players don't set big league baseball afire. Maybe I won't but I'll make a good living by trying. Anybody who says I can't make it doesn't know what I've gone through, and what I'm prepared to go through to stay up."

Sportswriters Dan Parker of the *New York Mirror* and Red Smith of the *New York Herald-Tribune* were supportive, but not so Jimmy Powers, sports editor of the *New York Daily News*, who wrote that Robinson wouldn't succeed "next year or the next. . . . He is a 1000-to-1 shot to make the grade." An editorial in the Bible of baseball, *The Sporting News*, deemed Robinson a player of Class C ability and predicted, "The waters of competition in the International League [Montreal's league] will flood far over his head." *Atlanta Journal* sports editor Ed Danforth wrote, "I don't see why a top flight Negro ballplayer would be anxious to play in the white leagues when he is doing so well in his own organization." George White of the *Dallas News* said that signing Robinson was unfair to him as well as to the South. Bud Seifert of the *Spartanburg Journal* in South Carolina wrote, "Segregation in the South will continue. We live happier with segregation in athletics as well as all other activities."

Some supporters saw Ricky's and Robinson's efforts as an affirmation of the World War II fight for freedom. Lee Dunbar of the *Oakland Tribune* said it was "fitting that the end of baseball's Jim Crow law should follow the conclusion of a great war to preserve liberty, equality and decency." Elmer Ferguson of the *Montreal Herald* wrote, "Those who were good enough to fight and die by the side of whites are plenty good to play by the side of whites." The black press, of course, was ecstatic, but Ludwig Werner of *The Sporting News* wrote that he felt sorry for Robinson. "He will be haunted by the expectations of his race." Another sportswriter, Will Connolly of the *San Francisco Chronicle*, wondered whether Rickey had picked the wrong man to break the color barrier. It should have been Kenny Washington, he wrote. "Kenny is a 'white man,' a nice guy. Robinson, he's a troublemaker."

It is interesting that black players were surprised, and some, like pitcher Satchel Paige, thought Rickey had picked the wrong man. "I'd been the one the white boys wanted to barnstorm against," Paige said. "I'd been the one everybody said should be in the majors. . . . It was still me that ought to have been first." Even so, Paige was uncertain whether integration was a good idea for the black ballplayer. He criticized black reporters who were advocating integration "without thinking about our end of it . . . without thinking how tough it's going to be for a colored ballplayer to come out of the clubhouse and have all the white guys calling him nigger and black so-and-so. . . . What I want to know is what the hell's gonna happen to good will when one of those colored players, goaded out of his senses by repeated insults, takes a bat and busts fellowship in his damned head?"

Major League officials were less than forthcoming with what they thought of Robinson's signing. They voted fifteen to one against Rickey's effort to integrate baseball. Commissioner Albert Benjamin "Happy" Chandler, National League president Ford Frick, and American League president Will Harridge were "unavailable for comment." The venerable owner of the Philadelphia Athletics, Connie Mack, replied, "I'm not familiar with the move and don't know Robinson. I wouldn't care to comment." Others went so far as to deny a color barrier existed.

Rickey traveled to Louisville, Kentucky, to persuade Chandler, a former U.S. senator and two-time governor of the Blue Grass State, to allow Robinson to play. Much to Rickey's surprise, Chandler disagreed with the owners' vote. "Mr. Rickey, I'm going to have to meet my maker some day," he said. "If He asked me why I didn't let this boy play, and I answered, 'Because he's a Negro,' that might not be

a sufficient answer. I will approve the transfer of Robinson's contract from Montreal to Brooklyn, and we'll make a fight with you.
So you bring him on in."

Before spring training began, Robinson and Rachel were married in
California. A few weeks later they headed to Daytona Beach, Florida, to begin his stint with Montreal. It wasn't going to be easy, and
they knew it. She worried that her husband's temper would get the
best of him. "I could not be sure what was going to happen," Rachel
said. "I worried that something might happen, some incident, and
we would be harmed, or killed." As the Robinsons tried to travel
to Daytona Beach, airlines bumped them from their seats twice in
favor of white passengers. They had trouble finding a place to eat
and to sleep. Time and time again they ran into Jim Crow. Robinson thought he might lose his temper, but he remembered that he
and Rachel had agreed "that I had no right to lose my temper and
jeopardize the chances of all the blacks who would follow me if I
could help break down the barriers."

At Daytona Beach they were given "special accommodations"
with a local black political leader while white players lived in a hotel.
After several days in Daytona the club moved to Sanford, Florida,
where there were two hundred players, most of them Southerners. Robinson was reticent when he was in their presence, but they
seemed to go about their jobs. "But there was a mutual wariness
between us, a current of tension that I hoped would lessen in time,"
Robinson recalled.

The Robinsons faced discrimination at virtually every turn. They
hated it but were not discouraged. They gritted their teeth and carried on. "What it did for us was not only enlighten us and open our
eyes to what things were going to be like, but it also mobilized a
lot of fight in us," Rachel said. "We were not willing to think about
going back. It gave us the kind of anger and the rage to move ahead
with real determination."

Robinson's manager at Montreal was Clay Hopper, a forty-four year-
old cotton broker from Greenwood, Mississippi. Hopper reportedly

told Branch Rickey that he didn't want to manage Robinson. "Please don't do this to me," he pleaded with Rickey. "I'm white and I've lived in Mississippi all my life," Hopper said. "If you're going to do this, you're going to force me to move my family and home out of Mississippi." Some questions have arisen whether that quote was accurate. Hopper, however, was open-minded. Rickey had hired Hopper as Montreal's manager after Robinson signed with the Dodgers. Rickey had hoped that hiring Hopper might show that a white Southerner was willing to manage a black on his team. Hopper's actions after he became manager show tolerance and then acceptance.

Rickey had placed Hopper in this difficult situation because he had great faith in Hopper's leadership and his ability to develop young players. Hopper had been with Rickey in the St. Louis and Brooklyn franchises for seventeen years and had produced eight championship teams. "I didn't need an introduction when [Robinson] came through that door," Hopper said. "I said to myself, 'Well, when Mr. Rickey picked one he sure picked a black one.'" Hopper greeted Robinson and shook his hand. Robinson was surprised by the handshake, "for even in those days a great number of Southerners would under no circumstances shake hands with a Negro."

After Robinson's talents began to show, Hopper seemed to agree that Rickey had made a positive decision. Robinson's teammates weren't hostile toward him, nor were they friendly. "Tolerant" might be a better description. "They seemed to have little reaction . . . one way or the other," Robinson said. One white player was an exception. Lou Rochelli and Robinson were competing for the same position, second base, and Rochelli had no animosity toward Robinson. He even helped him to learn a position that was new to Robinson.

Although Robinson's hitting was weak, he fielded and ran the bases well. The continual tension Robinson lived with no doubt sapped his strength as a hitter. "Jackie couldn't perform well that spring," Rachel recalled, "because the pressure was unbearable. . . . He was trying too hard; he was overswinging; he couldn't sleep at night; he had great difficulty concentrating." She said they were afraid Jackie wouldn't make the team, "that he would be cut in spring training. Every day without a hit made Rickey's experiment seem more risky."

During spring training Robinson heard good news about a friend: Kenny Washington had signed with the Rams. "That's great," he told the press. "He's a great football player and Los Angeles will make a lot of money with him in the lineup."

Toward the end of the training camp, the nervousness had calmed down, and Robinson's hitting began to improve. There was little doubt he would be in the starting lineup on opening day. His turnaround may have been because Robinson had found some acceptance among his fellow players. "Those who had no prejudices acted toward me the same as they acted toward other fellows they were meeting for the first time," Robinson wrote in a newspaper column several months later. "And those who, because of Southern descendancy, had certain feelings about race quickly set those feelings aside. There were some recalcitrants, of course, but they were in such a minority that they were inconsequential."

Along the way, Robinson's morale was stoked by two "glorious" events. One was during a spring training game between the Dodgers and the Royals. He had steeled himself for jeers, taunts, and insulting behavior. Instead he was greeted with only a few weak and scattered boos. He made decent plays and smacked his first base hit of the spring. The second event was in the opening game of the International League season in Jersey City, New Jersey, when he homered with two men on in the third inning on the way to a Royals' 14–1 win. "This was the day the dam burst between me and my teammates," Robinson said. He ended the game with 4 hits, the home run, and 3 singles, and he had stolen two bases. His bluff dashes from third caused pitchers to balk twice, allowing him to score. "He was amazingly fast and agile," teammate Al Campanis said. "If he were caught in a rundown, the odds were in Jackie's favor to get out of it." Robinson began to believe in Rickey's prediction. "Color didn't matter to fans if the black man was a winner," Robinson said.

"He did everything but help the ushers seat the crowd," said sportswriter Joe Bostic, writing for the black periodical the *Amsterdam News* of New York, in summing up that first game of the regular season. Bostic called Robinson's performance that day "the most significant sports story of the century." He said baseball had taken up "the cudgel for democracy and an unassuming but superlative Negro boy ascended to heights of excellence to prove the rightness of the experiment. And prove it in the only correct crucible for such an experiment—the crucible of white-hot competition."

Montreal's early schedule seemed to be designed almost to test Robinson's courage. After the series with Jersey City, the Royals played in Newark, New Jersey; Baltimore (the southernmost city in the league); and Syracuse, New York. League officials were concerned that Robinson's appearance in Baltimore would create "rioting and bloodshed," but Rickey thought they were overreacting. Besides, he told the league president, "We solve nothing by backing away. In fact, we'll encourage every agitator in Maryland if we show fear." Robinson was greeted with "the worst kind of name-calling and attacks on Jackie that I had to sit through," Rachel Robinson recalled. But he got through it.

The Royals returned to Montreal, where Robinson found a welcoming environment. He was encouraged to find an "atmosphere of complete acceptance and something approaching adulation." Said a Montreal sportswriter, "For Jackie Robinson and the city of Montreal, it was love at first sight." Another sportswriter wrote, "The absence here of an anti-Negro sentiment among sports fans . . . was what Mr. Rickey doubtless had in mind when he chose Montreal as the locale of his history-making experiment."

Although his manager tolerated Robinson on his roster, he had difficulty accepting him. Prejudice was ingrained in him from his Southern upbringing. Once Robinson made a terrific play at second base as Rickey and Hopper watched together. Rickey called the play "superhuman." Hopper turned to Rickey and said, "Do you really think a nigger's a human being?" As noted, however, Hopper eventually came around to accepting Robinson, at least on the surface.

The warm atmosphere Robinson felt in Montreal didn't extend to games in the United States. In Syracuse, New York, a player for the opposing team threw a black cat out on the field and yelled, "Hey, Jackie, there's your cousin." After Robinson doubled and then scored, he ran by the Syracuse dugout and replied, "I guess my cousin's pretty happy now." Nevertheless, similar incidents were taking a toll on Robinson, who was having trouble sleeping and eating. But by season's end he was leading the league in hitting and received a standing ovation in Baltimore after he stole home in one of the games. A Montreal sportswriter even gave him a nickname–"the Colored Comet."

The season was not without incidents on the field. When a fight or a dispute broke out, Robinson was told to stay out of it. "I've reminded him several times," Hopper told the press. "'Jackie, you stay out of the arguments no matter what they are.'" Pitchers threw at his head, runners aimed their spikes at his legs and arms, and players baited him unmercifully from the opposing dugout. At season's end one Montreal sportswriter wrote, "Because of his dark pigmentation Robbie could never protest. If there was a rhubarb on the field . . . he had to stay out of it. Otherwise there might have been a riot." Robinson was consistently the target of bean balls. "You never saw anything like it," said Dixie Howell, Montreal's catcher. "Every time he came up, he'd go down."

The Royals won the International League championship by 18 1/2 games and appeared before eight hundred thousand fans at home. Up next was the Little World Series against Louisville, champions of the American Association. Three games were played in the Kentucky city, and Robinson said the visit "turned out to be the most critical test of my ability to handle abuse." The tension was terrible, and Robinson was greeted with some of the worst vituperation he had experienced. He managed only one hit in eleven trips to the plate, a performance that only raised the loudness of the taunts and insults from the crowd.

The Royals lost two of the first three games; if they were to capture the best-of-seven-game series, they had to win three games in Montreal. Canadians were livid over the treatment Robinson had received in Louisville. During the games the Montreal fans loudly booed the Louisville players. The support they showed Robinson and his teammates boosted them to three straight victories and the championship. Robinson wound up hitting .400 despite his poor start in Louisville, and he had two hits and started two double plays that helped to give the Royals a 2–0 victory in the final game.

Robinson and his teammates were mobbed after the game. In the locker room Hopper held out his hand to Robinson and said, "You're a great ballplayer and a fine gentleman. It's been wonderful having you on the team." After he showered, Robinson had a plane to catch for a barnstorming tour and had to tear through the crowd to get to the airport. One sportswriter wrote, "It was probably the only day in history that a black man ran from a white mob with love instead of lynching on its mind."

Robinson finished the season with a league-leading .349 batting average and 111 runs scored; he stole 40 bases (second in the league) and drove in 66 runs. Sportswriter Dick Young of the *New York Daily News* wrote, "Jackie Robinson led the league in everything except hotel reservations." Next stop: Brooklyn.

20

End of the Line at LAPD

"The only thing that will stop you from
fulfilling your dreams is you."

—Tom Bradley

If Tom Bradley encountered racial discrimination in the LAPD, he faced it as a citizen trying to make his way in a hostile environment in Los Angeles. He was refused credit at a downtown clothing store even though he was a police officer, restaurants and hotels turned him away because he was black, and he and his wife had to use a white intermediary to buy their first house in virtually all-white Leimert Park. When the Bradleys and their two children moved in, neighborhood children looked on and chanted, "The niggers are coming, the niggers are coming." Bradley never forgot the names of Los Angeles restaurants that had turned him away in the 1940s and 1950s, and he boycotted them all. "I have a long, long list."

He refused to let such setbacks wear him down. "For one thing, I have never let an experience with discrimination or prejudice embitter me," he said in 1984. "I have always tried to rise above that kind of situation. . . . It was hard. My attitude was, 'That's the other guy's problem, and I'm just going to keep pushing on. . . .' Like a Sherman tank, I just kept rolling over the opposition and the obstacles." On another occasion he remarked, "I can tell you in all candor, I don't see people, individually or in crowds, in terms of their color."

When he was appointed as a lieutenant, one of the first issues he took on was to allow blacks to work together with whites in patrol cars. That got him labeled as a troublemaker. "Anyone who had the courage and the guts to speak out against the status quo and against the injustice in the department was looked upon as a troublemaker," Bradley said.

Until then blacks had been assigned to street duties. Once Bradley set out to desegregate the patrol cars, it didn't go well. In 1960 he persuaded the chief to allow an experiment that would put a white officer into a patrol car when one of the black officers was on vacation. Several officers volunteered, knowing that the plan would be soundly rejected. When white and black officers were in a car, they began getting calls that were a "very sick kind of treatment and abuse" from their fellow officers from all over the city, Bradley said. "It became such a nasty situation that the white officer who was involved in this particular unit came to me and asked if he could be relieved of that assignment." Bradley had predicted the experiment would fail and that it would become a reality only if the police chief ordered it. After Bradley retired, it became official department policy, but it still didn't happen until 1963 or 1964, Bradley said, and not before the police chief told white officers to turn in their badges if they refused to cooperate.

Off duty Bradley suffered the humiliation of discrimination on road trips across the country when he was turned away from motels with blinking vacancy signs and restaurants that were half full. One Texas motel let him stay if he promised to leave by daybreak before other customers saw him and his family. Once when they were turned away, he became angry, a rare show of emotion. "And it was more a matter of frustration. But I didn't even let on to my children or my wife."

In the 1950s Bradley wrote a letter to the Gillette Corporation protesting that it was failing to show black athletes, like his friend Jackie Robinson, in advertising. "I thought that was wrong, so I wrote and told them so." He never received a reply. He never bought a Gillette product after that.

The rank of lieutenant was the end of the line for Bradley. His superiors told him that he "had gone as far as an African American could go." In 1974 Bradley revealed his approach in a racially hostile environment in the city and within the police force: "If you treated everybody, no matter what the circumstances, as you would like to be treated, . . . one could do his job with dignity and honor and receive respect from the citizenry he serves. . . . It was that kind of philosophy which carried me twenty-one years in the department without ever having to draw my gun, without having to engage in physical abuse or parading of the persons with whom I came in contact."

Knowing that he could not move up any higher in the police department and that he had never been satisfied with police work, Bradley sought a career change. He was greatly discouraged by his lack of success in bringing changes within the department. "I knew the obstacles were so great that I did not see it was worth the investment of time with so little promise of success," Bradley concluded.

While still on the force, Bradley began attending law school at night. He first attended Loyola University and finished up his degree at non-accredited Southwestern University in 1956. He passed the California bar examination a year later. In 1961 he retired from the police force and began practicing law full time. Bradley commented that he had no resentment toward the police department. "If they hadn't had such racist policies I'd probably still be there," he said, "so it was actually a blessing in disguise."

He was hired by Charles Matthews, considered to be the dean of black lawyers in Los Angeles. Matthews saw a promising career ahead for Bradley if he stayed in law, but law was no more satisfying to him than his years on the police force. He thought public service "was going to be more exciting and more satisfying to me."

Bradley joined the liberal California Democratic Council and became active in the City Council's Tenth District. In June 1961 a group of businessman urged Bradley to seek appointment to the vacant seat from that district on the council. One of them, Bishop H. H. Brookings, thought Bradley was the "right person at the right time. He was a moderate and forthright individual, a lawyer and competent about city government. He had strong support in the black community and credentials that brought him support from the white constituency as well."

Bradley agreed to seek the appointment, but he was just one of thirteen candidates, some of whom were African Americans. He thought he might have more influence in that position than on the police force or as a lawyer. He collected seven thousand signatures supporting his appointment, but the council appointed a conservative white Republican. Bradley was convinced he had been rejected because he was black. It was a slap in the face to all blacks who had been passed over. Bishop Brookings remarked, "We are delayed, but not defeated."

Two years into practicing law Bradley again sought (this time in an election) the City Council Tenth District seat, which represented a multicultural constituency in the Crenshaw area of central Los Angeles. A campaign worker, Maury Weiner, commented on Bradley's strengths and weaknesses: "Blackness in and of itself was considered radical. His not being publicly associated with any great controversial cause . . . was a plus [because] the insiders knew of his conscientious efforts, but the general public did not. There was very little negative stuff they could throw at Tom Bradley." Among the campaign workers and supporters were athletes and fraternity members from Bradley's UCLA days.

Prejudice, however, followed him on the campaign trail. One black precinct walker, Leroy Berry, remembered when he (Berry) would walk up to houses and residents would open a small window in the front door to see who was there and then slam the window shut without opening the door. "They were really disturbed that blacks had moved into their neighborhood," Berry said. "A black person coming to the door and ringing the bell reminded them that blacks had invaded their community."

This time the voters spoke, not the City Hall politicians. Bradley won the election by a two-to-one margin over the Republican who had earlier been appointed over him. He became one of three blacks elected to the fifteen-member council. (The others were Billy Mills and Gilbert Lindsay.) African Americans now had some political clout. Weiner thought Bradley may have been the first black elected to office from any predominantly white constituency in any state west of the Mississippi River. After Bradley won the election, a blind campaign worker heard on the radio that Bradley was an African American. He called Bradley over to him and told him that was the first time he knew Bradley was black. "That said a great deal to me," Bradley said, "because it was the way in which we tried to run the campaign; not on the question of color, just on the basis of the issues, of qualifications, and what I'd like to see done in the district."

Bradley had said during the campaign that the police department had taken "great strides" in working to end discrimination, but once on the council he became a strong critic of the police force. "Some police officers are bigoted," he stated, but "it is not a majority, but a small minority. I think the public should be aware of it. I think there is obvious segregation in the Los Angeles Police Department."

Much of Bradley's term in office was spent criticizing the police department, especially during the Watts Riots in 1965, even though Watts was outside his district. Blacks were rioting because of police brutality, overcrowding, and high unemployment. Bradley became the voice of opposition to Mayor Sam Yorty and Police Chief William H. Parker. Blacks were outraged when Parker blamed the riots on "monkeys in a zoo." Yorty was not much better, blaming the riots on Communists "for agitating Negroes with propaganda over police brutality."

At the same time Bradley tended to hide behind his stoic demeanor. "One of the most difficult [things] to learn in dealing with Tom Bradley is that you go in and he listens with a sphinx-like expression and you don't know whether anything you have said has registered and you certainly don't know whether he agrees with your assessment of the situation," said Anton Calleia, a top assistant to Bradley. Bradley lacked charisma, a shortcoming that was often met with criticism. Once a student who was referring to this shortcoming asked Bradley whether he was a black Gerald Ford rather than a black John Kennedy. Bradley shot back, "I'm not a black this or a black that. I'm just Tom Bradley."

Slowly but surely Bradley was making his mark as a city councilman. He was often at odds with Yorty, who Bradley believed was showing a lack of direction and vision. In 1969 Bradley decided to take on Yorty, the Democratic mayor who had been elected in 1961 with strong black support. The odds were against Bradley. Initial polls showed he was not well known outside his district, and the field of thirteen challengers—two congressmen were running, for example—made the chances daunting. But Bradley was working eighteen-hour days lining up support for his race. Contacts made while he was a police officer helped a great deal. Meanwhile, Yorty was putting minimal effort into his reelection campaign.

In Los Angeles primary elections are open—that is, all candidates (Republican, Democrat, or whatever) run, and the top two vote getters run against each other in the general election. As election results came in on April 2, 1969, Bradley was showing surprising strength. At final tally he pulled off a stunning win with 42 percent of the vote while Yorty came in second with 26 percent.

If Bradley had won a majority of the vote, he would have been elected outright, but he had to face Yorty in a runoff. Campaign organizers were fearful that Yorty was capable of rebounding. "I knew, as did Bradley and the staff, of Yorty's history of negative campaigning and ruthless smearing of any opponent. I knew that he would run a racist campaign," Maury Weiner said.

Weiner was right. The race proved one of the most bitter in the city's history. Yorty painted his opponent as a dangerous radical, alternately of the black power or Communist revolutionary variety. The charges were not plausible, but they resonated among fearful voters. Bradley refused to lower himself to Yorty's mud-slinging level, but his not responding may have cost him the election. Bradley was ahead in the polls until the "constant, vicious campaign of . . . fear" began catching on. Yorty predicted—among other racial attacks—that if Bradley were elected, white police officers would quit and blacks would take over the police department. The voters bought it; Yorty was reelected by 55,000 votes out of 850,000 cast.

"The voters have approved corruption in government and racism in America," former mayor Norris Poulson remarked. "The city now has an awful black eye." Bradley pledged to work with Yorty to end the "bitterness and divisiveness," but Yorty rejected Bradley's attempt at reconciliation. Yorty commented, "The attempt to form a racial coalition and conduct a partisan campaign for the nonpartisan office of mayor was certain to be divisive. This attempt has been rejected by voters and it is time to forget recrimination and work for the best interest of our self-governed city." Even the John Birch Society joined the fray. Its leader, Robert Welch, called Bradley's defeat the biggest setback for the Communist Party in fifty years.

No sooner was the race over than Bradley decided he would take on Yorty once again in four years. "I pledged to myself that I would do whatever I needed to, to ensure that the next time I ran, people would know me for my record, for what I could provide the city," he said. He was relentless in pointing out for four years, whether in council meetings or on the campaign trail, that the city lacked leadership. Yorty kept up his attack on Bradley, to which the councilman replied on one occasion, "We ought to be tired of a mayor of the city who every time he opens his mouth has an oral bowel movement."

In formally announcing his intention to run for mayor in December 1972, Bradley admitted that his "low-profile campaign" in 1969 had been a mistake. . . . I think a much more vigorous and hard-hitting campaign is necessary. We plan to engage in that kind of campaign." And it worked. Bradley again finished on top of the nonpartisan ballot with 35 percent of the vote (down from 42 percent in 1969), and Yorty increased his percentage from 26 to 29 percent. Bradley's lower total was in part due to the fact that powerful state legislator Jesse Unruh also was in the race. He took votes away from Bradley by garnering 17 percent of the total. Again a rematch was on between Bradley and Yorty.

Little changed in Yorty's campaign, with attacks on Bradley's honesty and integrity still evident. This time Bradley answered the charges and switched the talk to the issues facing the city. He outspent Yorty by a two-to-one margin, and the polls began to show a shift. When the results came in, Bradley had won by 100,000 votes and 56 percent of the total cast. "I iz da may-your," Bradley jested with his press secretary. Later he summarized: "Yorty failed to realize that time had not stood still. People knew me and what I stood for. His old tactics simply didn't work. . . . [He] failed . . . to motivate the fears and hate in people. The racial campaign didn't work because people were interested in the issues and the vision of what the city could become to all people, and not scare tactics."

When Bradley moved into the mayor's office, he found all files had been shredded and all cabinets emptied. A staff member found one key with a note attached. It said, "Here is de key to da Mayor's office, Sapphire."

Now it was time to begin a program that would see Los Angeles transform "from a conservative, provincial city to one of the most diversified and inclusive cities in the world."

21

Leaving Athletics

"It would be a shame if [Washington] were to be
forgotten. I know I never will forget him."

—Jackie Robinson

In 1950, when Kenny Washington was thirty-one years old, the New
York Giants baseball team offered him a tryout after a recommen-
dation by former Los Angeles Rams teammate Tom Harmon, the
Heisman Trophy winner at Michigan. They had played together on
a softball team, and Harmon was impressed. Washington was confident he would succeed despite the fact that he had played only
semi-pro baseball after leaving UCLA and that he had not played in
two years. He had been working out five days a week for five weeks
and had lost 22 pounds to get his weight down to 210 pounds. "I feel
great. My legs never felt stronger," he said.

Washington said that if his batting eye was as good as it was when
he was laid off, "I'll make the team. I'm not too worried about my
hitting." He preferred playing the infield, "but I think my chances
will be better in the outfield. I am larger now than when I played reg-
ularly. But, I am stronger." The *Chicago Defender* wrote that Washington "may have been one of the game's biggest name players
and home-run hitters today" if he had been allowed to play in the
1940s. Giants manager Leo Durocher was eager to see Washington
play. "I hope he can make it," he said. "I've got only eight outfield-

ers on the roster and I'll probably carry seven during the season so he stands a good chance."

The chance came too late. Three weeks into spring training, a scout told the *Los Angeles Times* he doubted Washington would make the team. "Kenny can hit a fast ball as far as the greatest sluggers, but his throwing arm is just so-so and he has only fair speed. All those years of football took too much out of him." The scout did say Washington might make it in AAA baseball, a step down from the Major Leagues.

Five days later Durocher dropped the news. Despite the fact that no one had worked harder in training camp than Washington, his lack of experience would keep him off the team. "Make no mistake, Kenny can really rap the ball," Durocher said. "But his speed is only fair and I've been disappointed in his throwing. His fielding has been adequate." Durocher also thought he had "a fine chance" to play for a Pacific Coast League (PCL) team. "Some . . . club is missing a bet if it doesn't give him a trial."

Washington did play for the PCL's Los Angeles Angels, but he appeared in only nine games, failing to get a hit in nine at bats. He struck out four times and walked once. Apparently he appeared only as a pinch hitter and played but three games in the field, at third base. He had four fielding chances and made an error on one of them. He was released and never stepped on the playing field again. After Washington's failed tryout with the Giants, his participation in professional sports was over. Washington said in 1952 that he came within twenty-four hours of going into baseball at the same time as Robinson. He had agreed to play football for the Los Angeles Rams on March 21, 1946, a day before Robinson called him to say that Dodgers general manager Branch Rickey wanted to have a look at him too. "I never regretted joining the Rams," he said, "but I often wonder how I'd have done in baseball when I was young."

It was time for Washington to settle down. He took several jobs, including one as a scout for the Los Angeles Dodgers, a sales representative for a wholesale food company, and a public relations representative of a scotch whiskey company, and he became active in civic affairs in Los Angeles.

Between 1941 and 1950 Washington appeared in seven movies, including *The Jackie Robinson Story*. In 1949 he acted as a physician in the acclaimed and controversial movie *Pinky*, about a light-skinned African American woman (played by Jeanne Crain) passing for white. It was the top-grossing film of the year. Crain and two other women who had starring roles in the film, Ethel Barrymore and Ethel Waters, were nominated for Academy Awards. In other movies Washington appeared alongside such actors as Rex Harrison, Burt Lancaster, Victor Mature, Bette Davis, and Bruce Cabot.

Washington became active in the Republican Party, supporting Congressman Richard Nixon in his landslide defeat of Congresswoman Helen Gahagan Douglas in their bid for the U.S. Senate in 1950. According to Nixon's biographer Roger Morris, Nixon spent election night at Washington's home playing music and trying to relax. In 1952 Washington took a stab at politics, entering the race for the Los Angeles Board of Supervisors. He finished third with 18,261 votes, not enough to qualify for the November ballot.

In 1956 UCLA retired Washington's No. 13 jersey, and he was inducted into the College Football Hall of Fame. The hall noted that Washington "was nearly unstoppable. In 1939 the running back played five hundred and eighty of six hundred minutes and led the nation in scoring. That same season he became the first UCLA player to be named an All-American."

In December 1970 Washington was honored by about one thousand friends from sports, entertainment, business, and government at the Palladium in Los Angeles. Among the attendees were Mike Frankovich, who had played football at UCLA in the early 1930s and had gone on to become a major movie producer; comedian Bill Cosby; and NFL commissioner Pete Rozelle. Funds raised were to help defray Washington's medical expenses. He was suffering from polyarteritis, a serious blood vessel disease in which the small and medium-sized arteries become swollen and damaged. "I can take a little exercise, walking around, but I get tired pretty easily," he said. "I think I'll whip it."

When Woody Strode heard about Washington's illness, he grabbed a plane from Italy, where he was making spaghetti westerns, to be by his side. Strode couldn't believe how skinny his friend had become or how pasty and ashen he looked. His eyes were sunken in, and he had dark circles under them. "They'd lost their spark. . . . I had to hold the tears back," Strode recalled. During other visits he could see Washington fading. "I sat and cried as I watched him getting weaker and weaker because Kenny was always the Big Bad Wolf, the Kingfish." Washington died on June 24, 1971, at the age of fifty-two, of polyarteritis after thirteen days in the hospital. "I just wasn't prepared for him dying," Strode said. "That was one of the saddest moments and saddest days of my life."

Bob Waterfield, who had also played at UCLA and is in the Pro Football Hall of Fame for his years with the Rams, called Washington the best football player he ever saw, "and that includes everybody I ever knew. He also was a great gentleman. If he had come into the National Football League directly from UCLA, he would have been, in my opinion, the best the NFL had ever seen."

When Robinson heard of Washington's death, he remarked, "I'm sure he had a deep hurt over the fact that he never had become a national figure in professional sports. Many blacks who were great athletes years ago grow old with this hurt." Strode wrote years later, "I guess you've got to feel a little sorry for yourself when you're one of the greatest football players of your day and you don't get a chance to show it. . . . But Kenny was never bitter."

A. S. "Doc" Young, a columnist for the *Chicago Defender*, wrote a week after Washington's death, "He wasn't one to complain. But he knew life, too, had curved him. He was born too soon. He died early. Life beat him up. Death kicked him when he was down."

Many former teammates and sports figures attended the funeral, including Don Newcombe, Buzzy Bavasi, Tank Younger, Rafer Johnson, and Strode. "You've never seen more people at a funeral in your life," Strode recalled. Politicians and UCLA people also were in attendance. Robinson didn't attend, probably because his health was in a sharp decline at the same time. Not only that, but his son Jackie Jr. had died a week earlier in an auto accident.

Ray Bartlett was the least heralded of the five athletes but led an extraordinary life of community service in Southern California. After the war, Bartlett returned to Pasadena and began a twenty-year career as a policeman, the second African American to join the police department in Pasadena. He eventually became a detective in burglary but not before being "passed over for promotion eight times" by his superiors "because of prejudice" in the department.

At the age of forty-seven, Bartlett left the police force to become an assistant deputy for Los Angeles County Supervisor Warren Dorn in 1967, a job that lasted six years. In 1983 he was given the Golden Goblet Award by the Los Angeles County Recreation and Youth Services. In 1985 the Pasadena YMCA named Bartlett Man of the Year. There was a certain irony to the award because the Y hadn't allowed the nineteen-year-old Bartlett to become a member in 1938, even though he had volunteered to clean the facilities. Bartlett was a president of the YMCA board in Pasadena. He also found time to serve on the Pasadena City College (its name had changed in 1948) board for more than twenty years. A bronze bust of his likeness is in the college's Court of Champions, one of sixteen of the college's most famous athletic alumni, including Jackie and Mack Robinson. Bartlett, Jackie, and Mack also were inducted into the California Community Colleges Hall of Fame.

In 1999 Bartlett represented Jackie Robinson as the grand marshal at the Tournament of Roses parade. He called it one of the greatest moments in his life. "That was so special and fantastic," he said. "What an honor to be able to represent my friend, and to do so while riding down the streets of my hometown." Bartlett said he had Robinson's widow, Rachel, to thank for being named marshal. She recognized that Bartlett and Robinson had grown up together and had starred on the athletic field as well. "And I think Rachel was thanking me, since I was the one who first introduced Jackie to Rachel when we were all attending UCLA." Said his son Bob, a former mayor of Monrovia, "He absolutely loved being grand marshal. I don't think there was a bigger highlight in his life."

Bartlett also was chosen as one of Pasadena City College's seventy-five distinguished alumni during the college's seventy-fifth anniversary. In addition, he was a pioneering member of the Pasadena City College Foundation board. He was active in the Fellowship of Christian Athletes and the American Legion. He also served on the UCLA Jackie Robinson Foundation Scholarship Selection Committee.

Bartlett was a past president and member of the Los Angeles County Human Relations Commission for twenty-seven years, the longest-serving member of the commission. He was commended for being an "advocate for civil and human rights, no matter the race, gender, or religion." When he retired, he was appointed an honorary member of the commission. In 1993 his alma mater, UCLA, presented him with its prestigious Community Service Award. In 1987 Pasadena City College honored him with its Presidential Award for his support and his bringing recognition to the school. "I've received so much from [the college] and this surrounding area," he said, "that I feel privileged to be in a position to give something back." Said his son Bob, "My dad was always striving for a perfect world. He'd always say, 'You never lose, you just run out of time. You keep playing until the end.'" Bartlett was married four times, twice divorced and twice widowed. He died of complications of outpatient surgery in Lynwood, California, at the age of eighty-eight in 2008.

22

Movie Star in the Making

"I was strictly a mechanic. They told me what to do and I
did it, took the money, and got out of there."

—Woody Strode

When Woody Strode returned from Canada, he went into wrestling full time. Strode had to learn how to perform—that is, act in the ring. He didn't hit the big time until he let his opponent throw him out of the ring or he landed with his feet first when he was body slammed. When he became a headliner, he said, "I would walk into the ring like I was going on stage to perform Hamlet." He wrestled the likes of the immensely popular Gorgeous George, who Strode said was actually not "gorgeous" but a "block of granite" with long, flowing blond curls. George Raymond Wagner was his real name, but he changed it to Gorgeous George. He once said, "I do not think I'm gorgeous, but what is my opinion against millions of others?"

Professional wrestling was the number 1 show on television in the late 1940s and 1950s. George, Strode said, "became a master at antagonizing the crowd. That was the key to success in the wrestling business. And that's how the greatest villain in wrestling history was born." Strode wrestled George several times, with George winning most of the matches. "He won. Of course, I knew in advance who was going to win—the box office. Everybody made money when they wrestled Gorgeous George." Strode said the fans came to see

George, not him. "It was like dancing, and he was leading. You had to allow him to perform."

When wrestling in Dallas, Texas, Strode remembered going into the ring with a referee who had a pistol and a blackjack in his pocket. Strode asked him what was going on. The referee told him that there had been a race riot at the arena a week before. "There I was stripped naked except for my white shorts and shoes, standing out there like a neon sign," Strode recalled. He told his opponent, "Listen you son of a bitch. We're going to wrestle from the floor." No way, Strode said, was he going to give fans a clear shot at him. Fans had never seen a white man wrestle a black man before. By the time Strode was finished wrestling, he had entered the ring in Canada, the Midwest, the South, and Hawaii.

On May 20, 1950, Strode was honored at a dinner sponsored by the First Thought, Last Word program, which brought together influential community members from the media and entertainment industry to discuss pertinent business issues and provide learning and networking opportunities with industry peers. It was held at the Olympic Auditorium, where Strode had often wrestled, and it was attended by a galaxy of sports stars and sports-minded people, including Kenny Washington, Tom Harmon, Rams assistant coach Red Hickey, journalist Halley Harding, and state athletic commissioner Norman O. Houston. Strode received a trophy presented by Lieutenant Governor Goodwin Knight.

Strode's fortunes soon changed again when a Hollywood theatrical agent watched him wrestle on television. He saw Strode's statuesque body and his acting ability and thought he would be a good candidate for the movies. "You have a look I think I could sell," said the agent, Sid Gold. "Would you be interested in making some money?" He didn't have to ask twice. "And slowly, Strode said, "[I] fell into the acting business. After a certain point, I realized I could make a living at it, and I never looked back." Gold lined Strode up with a job in the TV show *Ramar of the Jungle*, in which he played an African native. "With me, all they had to do was give me a loin cloth and put a spear in my hand." He ended up doing nine *Ramar* shows. Next he appeared with Johnny Weissmuller in the TV series *Jungle Jim*.

Next came an offer of a role in RKO's *Androcles and the Lion*, in which Strode was dressed as the lion for $500 a week for eight weeks. Afterward he was bragging to stuntmen that he had earned such a big amount for doing so little. One stuntman told him the job was worth $2,500 a week, and the stuntmen wouldn't take the job for anything less. Soon after, Strode hit the big time when he was offered a role in Cecil B. DeMille's *Ten Commandments* alongside Charlton Heston. He played the king of Ethiopia, a job that lasted a week. Just when he thought he was through, he was asked to appear as a slave in the movie, but DeMille warned him, "Son, don't you ever tell anyone you got two roles in my picture." Strode ended up with fifteen weeks of work.

Another change was in the works. In 1958 Strode was offered a role in *Tarzan's Fight for Life*, for which he was asked to shave his head. Strode was still wrestling, and he wanted to have "beautiful hair and locks and [look] as good as I could." Strode told the producers, "You got to be crazy." They offered him $500 a week for eight weeks. Again he told the producer he was crazy, but "then I asked where the pluckers were." Strode was so embarrassed about being bald that he wore a hat. "I looked like a robot. All my bone structure was sticking out. My cheek bones were jumping off my face. But everybody said, 'Magnificent.' And when I went to interview for my next picture, *Pork Chop Hill* [starring Gregory Peck] with director Lewis Milestone, he said, 'The bald head's perfect.'" Strode rarely let his hair grow out again.

Strode's next big role was in *Spartacus* with Kirk Douglas, a role that earned him a Golden Globe nomination in 1960. Strode called his seven-minute fight sequence in the film "probably my most famous moment on the screen." Movie buffs still remember that scene years later. It may have been the most famous fight in film history up to that point. In that segment after his battle with Douglas, Strode had to scale a twelve-foot-high wall to kill the emperor (played by Laurence Olivier). "I would have lost that role if I hadn't been in shape, and if I hadn't had a lot of experience as a wrestler," he said. "It took skill to do that fight scene without actually hurting myself or hurting Douglas." Strode was forty-five years old at the time, and "I was about the only actor in the world who could do that stunt." Peter Ustinov, who won an Academy Award as best supporting actor in the film, called Strode "frightfully athletic" because he could throw the twenty-five pound trident in the fight scene.

"For the first five or six years I was acting, I never saw my motion pictures," Strode recalled. "I wouldn't go to the theater. I was embarrassed. I was in a glamorous business, and I wasn't prepared to be glamorous. I had more of the Joe Louis attitude, and I was confident I had the ability to do anything asked of me."

Spartacus was followed by *The Last Voyage* (with Robert Stack) and the leading role in *Sergeant Rutledge*. All four pictures were released in 1960. Strode was now a recognized figure on the silver screen.

When Strode returned home from filming *The Last Voyage* in Japan, he was summoned to be reunited with famed movie director John Ford, whom he had met in Hawaii when he played football there. Ford wanted Strode to portray Sergeant Rutledge, who was a Buffalo Soldier, one in a troop of all black soldiers. Ford told Strode that he wanted to produce a movie that showed how blacks had helped build the American West. "Way before anybody started to march or decided to do anything, he [Ford] just did it on his own," Strode said. "And they weren't ready for 'Sergeant Rutledge.'" In the film, set in the 1860s, Rutledge was accused of murdering his post commander and raping and killing his daughter. "The sergeant would have been a cinch to die in that generation," Strode said. But he was exonerated. Ford's studio, Warner Brothers, wanted Harry Belafonte or Sidney Poitier to play Rutledge, but Ford insisted on Strode. "They aren't tough enough," Ford argued. But Ford didn't think Strode looked black enough. Strode admitted he looked too Indian. Ford ordered Strode to take his hat off in the hot Arizona sun "so I could get as dark as possible." "I never did get black enough, but I did get a nice dark, dark, dark."

Ford was famous for insulting his actors as a way of motivation. (John Wayne used to take a great deal of abuse from Ford.) Strode was no exception. Ford laced racial epithets on him while shooting *Sergeant Rutledge*, though Strode treated them as a motivational technique. The movie became Strode's favorite because he thought he had finally arrived as an actor. But it was a disappointment at the box office, particularly in the South. Ford was somewhat discouraged. "I can't just make black pictures," he told Strode. "Do you have any Indian in you?" Ford told Strode he thought the actor should have received an Academy Award nomination for his role in the movie, but Strode said awards meant nothing to him. "All I want to know is that the next time they need somebody, they'd go to get Woody because he's a good worker," Strode said. "He knows how to do the stuff we need."

Ebony, a magazine predominantly for black readers, was touting Strode as the next big movie star right up there with Belafonte and Poitier. It called Strode the "most promising of them all, the fastest rusher toward the wonderful state of stardom." *Sergeant Rutledge* was the start of a long and warm relationship between Ford and Strode. The actor was one of the few people in Ford's life who was allowed to call him "Papa." It turned into a father-and-son relationship, particularly after Ford almost died and Strode spent four months in his house, sleeping on a mat in the director's room while he recovered. "He treated me like a son," Strode stated. "I had a certain amount of crudeness that went back a hundred years, and that's what he liked."

Ford's biographer Joseph McBride wrote that Strode "was the last great love of John Ford's life." Ford and Strode worked together on two more films, *Two Rode Together* (starring Richard Widmark and Jimmy Stewart) and *Who Shot Liberty Valance?* (featuring John Wayne, Lee Marvin, and Stewart). Strode played a subservient role as Wayne's right-hand man. In the movie Strode accompanies Wayne into a saloon where Wayne orders a drink. The bartender serves it up and tells Strode that he cannot serve him a drink because he is a Negro. Strode says he understands and stands alongside Wayne while he drinks.

It turned out Strode wasn't through with wrestling. In 1962 a promoter offered him $2,500 for five nights to get into the ring again. He couldn't turn it down. "That was almost twice what I was making in the movies, so I had to accept." But at age forty-eight he couldn't do it any more, particularly against the likes of Bobo Brazil, a 300-pound, 6-foot-7 black wrestler.

In a movie with Charlton Heston, *Major Dundee*, Strode played a soldier who was to polish a white officer's shoes. Heston had a hard time calling him a "nigger." Director Sam Peckinpah told Strode, "You've got to shine this white officer's shoes and he's got to call you a nigger. But the problem I'm having is that you aren't really a Negro. You're a mongrel." Strode said that was Peckinpah's way of telling him he wasn't dark enough for the role. Strode responded, "Mr. Peckinpah, after four hundred years we're either half-white or half-Indian. That's the American Negro. We have no control over that."

Strode said that after Peckinpah called him a mongrel, he was insulted and was going to quit making movies. When he told his agent, Sid Gold, his plans, Gold dragged him into his office and growled, "You don't have the guts to stick it out." Then Strode received a call from Columbia Pictures producer Mike Frankovich, who had played football at UCLA in the seasons just before Strode. Frankovich got him to agree to play a Chinese in the movie *Genghis Khan* (with Omar Sharif). He was made to look Chinese, with slanted eyes and a long pigtail. One Chinese who was working on the film noted, "Woody, you look more Chinese than we do."

As Strode was obtaining better and better roles in movies, he was seeing a brighter future for African American actors. In an interview with the *Chicago Defender* Strode remarked, "Negro actors, in traditional or non-traditional movie roles, can become better actors, because as a minority, we can reach back into our mental file cards, and come up with joy, sadness, hope, and every other emotion needed for an acting role."

Strode decided in 1966 to head up an independent production of the Buffalo Soldiers, to be called *The Saga of the Tenth Cavalry*, in hopes of spurring more integration in movies. "The film will show the world that the American Negro did a lot more than toil in the cotton fields," Strode said. He hired forty urban black actors for the roles. But the film was never made, and Strode became somewhat disillusioned with Hollywood. The recreated Tenth Cavalry unit, however, appeared in several parades, state fairs, and television shows—including a full 1966 episode of *High Chaparral.*

One of Strode's most popular movies was *The Professionals* (featuring Lee Marvin, Robert Ryan, and Burt Lancaster), about an oil tycoon who hires four "professionals" to rescue his kidnapped wife in Mexico. Strode was delighted to receive top billing over Lancaster, following Marvin and Ryan, though Lancaster reportedly earned $350,000 while Strode took home $20,000. Strode was thrilled with his role. "I was a million to one shot, getting this role," he noted. "There's a tremendous cast all around me, and I'm very thankful for it. I'm hungry looking and maybe this paid off for me."

Once on the movie set, as the story goes, Strode and Lancaster, who had a reputation as a very physically strong man, often undertook contests of strength, which Strode won, allegedly sending Lancaster into despondency. Frank O'Rourke, who wrote a book about the movie in 1987 noted, "These men [Marvin, Lancaster, Ryan, and Strode] were innocent of prejudice, not because they were morally pure, or because prejudice did not exist in their world, but they lived in and with the peoples of that world in a natural way, so intent on the spending of their lives under any and all conditions that they had no time for the useless idiocy of weighing the comparative value of one man's skin against another's on the bigot's scale. They lived with people, not beside them."

Strode was feeling the heat from the civil rights movement in the mid-1960s into the 1970s. Some African Americans thought he should be more outspoken for equal rights for blacks, but Strode would have no part of it. He said he was not a black actor or a white actor, just a cowboy trying to make a living. He seemed oblivious to the struggle against racism. At one point in 1972 he exclaimed, "I'm tired of this black, black, black business. Me, I don't care. If the money is right, I'll play Mickey Mouse." That didn't go over well with the most militant black activists. What Strode was really trying to do was end prejudice by setting an example of succeeding in his chosen field.

Strode found difficulty with some of the tactics of civil rights activists . "Most of my life people have been trying to get me to sign up with the various black groups, including militants," Strode observed. "Not me. I'm sick of talking about race in this country. I don't want anybody calling me 'brother' either. I live my own life. I go my way and nobody stops me. Color means nothing to me, my children or neighbors. I'm no Uncle Tom. I'm me."

Frank Manchel in his book *Every Step a Struggle* accused the author of Strode's memoir of the oversimplification "of Strode's confusion, anger, and ostracism by a younger generation of black progressives." Manchel wrote that it was "disappointing that there is no thoughtful analysis of the culture shock that [Strode] experienced from the 1965 Watts riots in Los Angeles or his professional crisis during the changing racial scene in California." Regarding the Mickey Mouse quote, Manchel added, "It was not that Strode was a mercenary; rather, he believed the way to break down prejudice was to demonstrate your ability and not depend upon someone's else's good will."

Strode's disenchantment with the sixties' generation of activists was one of the reasons he decided to turn down roles in "blacksploitation" movies and go to Europe to chase fame and fortune. Said his nephew Tollie Strode Jr., "He could have gone the way of Super Fly. He could have played pimps, hustlers, and shoot 'em up roles. He chose the path of honorable roles."

From 1969 to 1971 Strode lived in Rome, where he starred in several spaghetti westerns that raised his popularity in Europe, whose people cared little about a person's race. Strode discovered in Italy that "I could just live completely with white people. I was like a zebra with a bunch of lions, and I went right to the trough with them." He learned that he could live anywhere in the world. "Race is not a factor in the world market," he said. "I once played a part of an Irish prize fighter. I've done everything but play an Anglo-Saxon. I'd do that if I could. I'd play a Viking with blue contact lens and a blond wig if I could. My dream is to play a Mexican bandit in the international market."

It was in Europe that Strode said that for the first time he made "real money." After earning salaries in the low four figures, Strode pulled down as much as $75,000 a picture in Italy. "I'd been in some classic pictures and never made a dime," Strode commented. "I was never in a position to bargain. Where else was I to go? I was unique doing just what I had been doing: throwing the spear, playing Indians, slanting my eyes, putting on pigtails. They probably thought they were doing me a favor."

Strode next starred in the British-produced *Black Jesus*, a 1971 movie that bombed at the box office but earned rave reviews for Strode's acting. According to Manchel, "For him the picture meant a chance for Americans to see on screen how blacks are willing to sacrifice their lives for a cause." *Black Jesus* was a thinly disguised story of the African idealist Patrice Lumumba. The *New York Times* wrote the following:

> Woody Strode? Yes, yes, a thousand times yes. "Black Jesus?" No. It was a thrill yesterday to see the name of this exceptionally fine Negro actor elevated to solo star billing, after propping up many a film for years. Sadly, neither this Italian-made picture nor the role itself, primarily a matter of saintly symbolism, is up to him. Mr. Strode, with his keen, lidded eyes and strong, gaunt face, does a perfectly respectable job of portraying an imprisoned, tortured and executed visionary leader in an African country. His gentle spirit of nonviolence and agonized endurance under pressure are painfully real. The rest is not. The film is a shadow play, hardly a movie at all.

Strode made one more Hollywood film before heading back to Italy, *The Revengers* (also starring William Holden, Ernest Borgnine, and Susan Hayward). Strode was given top billing, one of the first times he had been given an advertised starring role in an American picture. "That's how the Italians and 'Black Jesus' had inflated my value in this country," he said.

Strode returned to Italy for two more years, coming home only when John Ford was on his death bed, suffering from cancer. Strode sat by the side of Ford's bed, holding his hand for six hours before Ford slipped into a coma and died soon after. "He was so tough I didn't believe he could die," Strode recalled.

In 1980 Strode's wife Luana died from complications of Parkinson's disease after struggling four years with the ailment. She was sixty-four, Strode sixty-six. A year later he noted that he was sixty-seven and "just a kid." He attributed his good health to eating everything. "I'm a meat eater. I eat like a Mexican—chilies for breakfast, lunch, and dinner." Two years after his wife's death Strode married thirty-five year-old Tina Tompson, the daughter of a Las Vegas minister.

Age was catching up with Strode. At age seventy-four he recalled that the last three pictures in which he had acted had been too hard for him. "But I always stay in shape. I don't go to a job out of shape because the man looks at me and wonders, 'Can he still do the job?' My camouflage is close fitting T shirts, and I parade in them like an old race horse. I can still attract attention stepping off a plane anywhere in the world. I can still half-ass fight. I can do all that ballet stuff; the only thing I can't do is fall off the horses."

In all Strode acted in fifty-seven movies, three TV movies, and thirteen TV series, including *Rawhide* (with Clint Eastwood). He acted in films directed by DeMille, Ford, Richard Brooks, Budd Boetticher, and Stanley Kubrick. The *San Francisco Chronicle* noted after his death in 1994 that Strode was never reduced "to eye-rolling and shuckin' and jivin' to make a living in Hollywood. With rare exception he was powerful yet quietly profound. Regardless of his dialog, Strode's magnificent face always made apparent the brain behind the brawn."

"You know what they saw in me?" Strode asked.

They saw what I had, and they pulled it out of me. They didn't see a black man. They gave me the part because I was the man. . . . It wasn't a black thing. You had to have the ability to sit on the horse and not be doubled, do the little bit of fighting that I had to do in it, and get off the screen, and hold up the part. Make it believable. And every time they selected me, [it] was because I could make a part believable, whether I starred in it or not. This is the most important thing when your star is there, the character actor has got to be believable. Otherwise the whole picture is weakened.

Toward the end of his life Strode was being honored for his long service in the entertainment business. He received the Cauliflower Alley Club's Iron Mike Mazurki Award, wrestling's top honor in 1992, the first year it was given. He also was inducted into the UCLA Athletic Hall of Fame in 1992. He was inducted posthumously into the National Multicultural Western Heritage Museum and Hall of Fame in 2012–13.

Strode died on December 31, 1994, at eighty-eight after suffering from lung cancer for two years. He was buried with full military honors at the national cemetery in Riverside, California. His achievements inspired California Assembly member Cheryl Brown in 2015 to campaign for his inclusion into the California Hall of Fame. It honors those "who embody California's innovative spirit and have made their mark on history." Backers include Clint Eastwood and Kirk Douglas.

23

A Promotion Earned

[Robinson] was the only player I ever saw who could
completely turn a game around by himself."

—Hall of Famer Ralph Kiner

Jackie and Rachel Robinson left Montreal in 1946, he to go on a barnstorming trip and she to stay with her mother in California, awaiting the birth of their first child. They still had not been told whether Jackie was moving up to Brooklyn in the spring.

Robinson's barnstorming trip proved disastrous as most of the $3,500 in checks he received for playing bounced. The Robinsons were low on cash. When Jackie arrived in Los Angeles, he decided to play pro basketball for $50 a game for the Los Angeles Red Devils. He joined two other black players on the team, which won eight of its first nine games. One white player, Irv Noren, had played at Pasadena Junior College and in the Major Leagues for eleven years. He was almost six years younger than Robinson and signed with the Dodgers the same year as Robinson, although he never played for Brooklyn.

Robinson averaged just fewer than ten points a game. "But scoring is the least of the dusky marvel's accomplishments," the *Chicago Defender* wrote. "A lightning dribbler and glue-fingered ball handler, his terrific speed makes it impossible for one man to hold him in check." Robinson's last game came January 3, 1947, after seven games. The Red Devils had won six. His departure may have coincided with Branch Rickey's visit to Los Angeles for a series of base-ball meetings. Conjecture was that Rickey urged him to halt his play.

If Robinson had wanted to pursue pro basketball, he would have had to wait two more years, when the barrier was broken in 1948 in the pre-NBA years by the Dayton Rens of the National Basketball League. The NBA was integrated in 1950. But Robinson couldn't have predicted that. Over the years pro basketball officials tried to get Robinson to switch sports. Abe Saperstein of the Harlem Globe-trotters offered Robinson $10,000 to play with the team at a time when the Major League minimum for rookies was $5,000. Robinson turned him down. Robinson also got a pro basketball offer from the Canton Cushites, an all-black team that featured future Pro Football Hall of Fame member Marion Motley, who along with Washington and Strode broke the NFL color barrier, and Larry Doby, who would become the second African American in Major League Baseball and the first in the American League. Robinson declined that offer too.

Robinson's fate with the Dodgers was in limbo. Nine of the top ten hitters in the International League in 1946 had been called up, and Robinson was still waiting to hear. Rickey was in no hurry. "I have made every move with great deliberation," he told a reporter. "If Robinson merits being with the Dodgers, I'd prefer to have the players want him, rather than force him on the players. I want Robinson to have the fairest chance in the world without the slightest bit of prejudice."

To ensure that Robinson would avoid the racism during spring training that he had come under in the spring of 1946, Rickey decided to work out the Royals and the Dodgers away from the South. The Dodgers prepared for the season with seven games against Montreal in Havana and three in Panama, finishing up with three exhibition games against the New York Yankees in Ebbets Field. Even in Havana, however, Robinson and three other black players were relegated to a third-tier hotel that had no restaurant. One of the players, a future Dodger star, Don Newcombe, called the hotel a place only a cockroach could love. The food in Havana restaurants was abysmal, and Robinson became ill, probably with colitis, which caused him to miss games. The black players were about to complain to Rickey about the accommodations when they discovered he had placed them there to avoid problems with the white players, who were ensconced in a luxury hotel.

Before Rickey made a decision on Robinson's future, he wanted to take strides to make the path smoother. He met with black leaders in Brooklyn out of concern that the black community might go overboard in welcoming Robinson as he broke the color barrier. He also was concerned that white fans might stay away from the ballpark if blacks became too rowdy in celebrating their new hero. Some black leaders felt insulted by Rickey's concerns, but most agreed to try to keep blacks under control. One slogan they adopted was "Don't spoil Jackie's chances."

An informal poll of reporters covering spring training thought that Robinson would not be in the starting lineup. They reasoned that there was no place for Robinson to play because Pee Wee Reese was a fixture at shortstop and Eddie Stanky was holding down second base.

After leaving Havana, Robinson was asked to play first base, an indication that he was too good to keep out of the lineup. Like most athletic endeavors in which Robinson competed, his moving into a new position proved no problem. But he wasn't happy about it. He wondered whether Rickey was trying to undermine his chances of playing in the big leagues, at least that year. Robinson felt he was under enough stress without learning a new position. Rickey, however, had greater concerns. Stanky may have been the best second baseman in the league. In addition, Rickey didn't want it to look as if a black man was taking a white man's job. He also thought that Robinson stood less chance of being intentionally spiked at first base than at second.

Rickey told Robinson that he had to prove his worth to the Dodgers during a series of upcoming exhibition games:

> I want you to be a whirling demon against the Dodgers. I want you to concentrate, to hit that ball, to get on base by any means necessary. I want you to run wild, to steal the pants off them, to be the most conspicuous player on the field—but conspicuous only

because of the kind of baseball you're playing. Not only will you impress the Dodger players, but the stories that the newspapermen send back to the Brooklyn and New York newspapers will help create demand on the part of the fans that you be brought up to the majors.

In the seven games he played Robinson batted .625 and stole seven bases. Still no word.

If Robinson was anxious over the decision, he didn't let on. He told white sportswriters that he wanted to play for the Dodgers only if the players wanted him. "I wouldn't want to feel that I was doing anything that would keep them from winning," he said. And that was indeed a problem. A *New York Sun* reporter wrote, "The only thing keeping Robinson off the Dodgers now plainly is the attitude of the players." Another reporter wrote for the *New York Post* that "among the majority of Dodgers there is a positive feeling of antipathy towards Robinson as a possible teammate."

Unbeknown to any of the Dodger coaches or brass, several players were passing around a petition to protest playing with a black man. Leading the uprising among the Southerners were Dixie Walker, who was Brooklyn's best player; Kirby Higbe, the Dodgers' best pitcher; Bobby Bragan, a third-string catcher (he later became the manager of three Major League teams, all of which had black players, including Roberto Clemente, Larry Doby, and Hank Aaron); and pitcher Hugh Casey. A Northerner, outfield Carl Furillo, also joined the protest. Team captain Pee Wee Reese, who grew up in Louisville, Kentucky, refused to sign the petition, even though Robinson might be trying to take his job. "If he's man enough to take my job, he deserves it," Reese said. Reese's friends in Kentucky told him that a "good Southern boy" should refrain from playing with a black player. Reese decided they were wrong and remarked that there was "room enough in baseball for both of us." Apparently Higbe had had a few too many beers when he agreed to sign the petition and began to feel uncomfortable with the protest. He leaked word of the petition to Dodger officials. Said Reese: "You can hate a man for many reasons. Color is not one of them."

The team was in Panama when the Dodgers' bantam rooster manager, Leo Durocher, got wind of the protest. Durocher called a late-night team meeting during which he laid into his players. "I don't care if this guy is white, black, green, or has stripes like a fucking zebra," he bellowed at his players. "If I say he plays, he plays. He can put an awful lot of fucking money in our pockets. Take your petition and shove it up your ass. This guy can take us to the World Series, and so far we haven't won dick." Rickey also called the dissenting players into his office and told them straight on that if any one of them objected to playing with a black man, he would be traded. He told Furillo that if he didn't want to play with Robinson, he could "go back to pounding railroad ties in Pennsylvania." Furillo chose playing. Durocher knew Robinson's value to the team. He later remarked, "You want a guy that comes to play. But [Robinson] didn't just come to play. He came to beat you. He came to stuff the damn bat right up your ass."

While Rickey was preparing to announce that Robinson would be joining the Dodgers, he received a shock when Commissioner Chandler announced that Durocher, one of Robinson's biggest boosters, was being suspended for a year for hanging around with gamblers and other "unsavory" characters. While the suspension left Rickey without a manager, he also realized the hubbub over Durocher would take some of the attention away from Robinson.

The announcement about Robinson's promotion came in the middle of an exhibition game between the Dodgers and Montreal in Ebbets Field, which was packed with thousands of African Americans. Outside the ballpark vendors sold souvenirs that said, "I'm for Robinson."

Still the move created a furor. No sooner had Robinson's promotion to the Dodgers become public than hate mail and threats began pouring in. "Get out of the game or be killed," threatened one. Another claimed, "Get out or your wife will die."

24

Blending In

"When they start talking about me . . . as a Negro, they
are certainly not intending to flatter me, but they are
patting me on the back, as far as I'm concerned."

—Jackie Robinson

The Dodgers were facing a number of questions about their chances for the upcoming season, none bigger than what to do about Robinson. His fate "is as easy to handle as a fistful of fish hooks," wrote Arthur Daley in the *New York Times*. That was soon to be resolved.

The twenty-eight year-old rookie would be playing first base for the improving Dodgers. Robinson's teammates were comprised 60 percent of Southerners. The *New York Times* ran a photo of Robinson with two Dodgers on either side of him. Only one was a player; the rest were coaches. Robinson can be seen smiling at interim manager Clyde Sukeforth. The lone player was 6-foot-6 Howie "Stretch" Schultz, who lost his first base job to Robinson.

In his first game at first base, an exhibition, Robinson was hitless but drove in three runs and played flawlessly in the field. The Dodgers won 14-6. The next day Robinson drove in the Dodgers' only run with a single in an 8-1 Yankee victory. Robinson singled in the third game, a loss to the Yankees 10-9. Those were the only two hits he managed during the three-game series. The series drew almost eighty thousand fans, an all-time exhibition high, thanks in part to the large turnout of black fans.

Robinson was unsure what to expect once the season began. He vowed to keep his promise to Rickey by turning the other cheek to any racial baiting he might receive. The atmosphere had been somewhat defused by the three preceding games against the Yankees. If anything, his regular-season debut was almost anticlimactic. Rickey's charge now was to find a manager to take over the season in the wake of Durocher's suspension. Two games into the season, both of which the Dodgers won under Sukeforth, Rickey summoned Burt Shotton, a sixty-two-year-old retired manager from Florida, to take the Dodgers' reins.

Shotton was perfect for the job, although he was in direct contrast to Durocher. His character and integrity were beyond reproach. His calm demeanor fit well considering the upheaval going on in the organization and on the field. Said Reese about Shotton, "I know where he is. . . . He is in the dugout in full charge. The fans may not see him, but we see him. We know he is there." As for Robinson's presence on the team, Red Barber, the Dodgers' radio announcer, noted that Shotton "saw to it that serious internal trouble didn't break loose."

A less than capacity crowd of 26,623 fans, 60 percent of them black, turned out to see the Dodgers and Boston Braves play on Opening Day, April 15, 1947. That was two thousand fewer than in the inaugural game the year before. "This is my first ballgame in ten years," said Norman Hazzard, a firefighter from Connecticut. "I came out to look at the Negro boy play." In the past only 5–10 percent of the crowd had consisted of black fans. Now with such a large percentage of blacks it was evident that white fans had stayed away, unaccustomed as they were to being surrounded by African Americans. (Brooklyn's total in National League attendance declined from 20.18 percent in 1946 to 17.4 percent in 1947 despite a more successful year.)

In the dugout Robinson's teammates kept their distance. Many had never shaken hands with or showered with a black man. Sportswriter Jimmy Cannon of the *New York Post* wrote, "The Dodgers are polite and courteous with him, but it is obvious he is isolated by those with whom he plays. I have never heard remarks made against him or detected any rudeness where he was concerned. But the silence is loud and Robinson never is part of the jovial and aimless banter of the locker room. Robinson is the loneliest man I have ever seen in sports." A teammate told a *New York Times* reporter, "Having Jackie on the team is a little strange, just like anything else that's new. We just don't know how to act with him. But he'll be accepted in time. You can be sure of that. Other sports have had Negroes. Why not baseball? I'm for it if he can win games. That's the only test I ask."

As Robinson took the field, the Dodgers' radio announcer, Red Barber, born and raised in the south, reportedly broadcast that "Jackie is very definitely a brunette." Robinson got off to a horrible start. In four at bats, he grounded out to third, flied out to left, bounced into a double play, and was safe on an error. "Too bad about that double-play," said a fan, "but that colored fellow is just under terrific pressure." Robinson called it "just another ball game and that's the way they're all going to be. If I make good—well that will be perfectly wonderful." All spring Branch Rickey kept an optimistic tone. "You haven't seen the real Robinson yet. Just wait."

After the first eight days Robinson began to settle down, and he became more focused. His batting average rose to a lofty .444. Then he went into a spiral that saw his average plummet to .225 after he went hitless in twenty at bats over a week's period. He was nursing an old college football injury to his right shoulder, and it led to talk that he should be benched. "He should be given a rest in view of his ailing right arm and slump-pressing at the plate," Dick Young wrote in *New York Daily News*, "but the Dodger powers appear reluctant to bench him for attendance and possible public relations reasons." Nonetheless, his faithful African American fans cheered his every move.

Robinson also was adjusting to racial epithets, attempts to maim him with cleats, pitchers trying to hit him, catchers spitting on his shoes, and death threats. Police took the death threats seriously. "Two of the notes were so vicious that I felt they should be investigated," Rickey said. Robinson wasn't too worried, or at least he didn't let on that he was. Robinson wrote in the *Pittsburgh Courier*, a black weekly, that "the way they were written I would say they're from scatterbrained people who just want something to yelp about."

Then just as slumps come, they go. Robinson set out on a fourteen-game hitting streak that raised his average to .299. On top of that, despite the slump, no one faulted his play at first base. After a brief learning period Robinson picked up the nuances and was playing stellar defense. "They just handed him a first baseman's glove," said teammate Rex Barney, a pitcher. "And he had never played first base. He took it, and never said a word, never complained."

Pee Wee Reese knew the slump would end. "The guy has too much talent and too much guts," he said. Said Barney, "You'd look at him and you knew he was pressing and pushing. He had all that other stuff on his mind. He worked hard to break out of that slump. If we had a night game at eight o'clock, Jackie would be at the ball-park at 10 the next morning to take batting practice. If a pitcher got him out on a slow curve, he would have Sukeforth throw him slow curves until Jackie's hands blistered. I saw this. He just worked so hard. He could not let himself down. He could not let his race down. He couldn't let anybody down."

One of the most vicious attacks on Robinson occurred on a road trip to Philadelphia for a three-game series against the Phillies. It all started when Phillies general manager Herb Pennock, who was inducted into the Hall of Fame in 1948 for his playing days, called Rickey to tell him, "You just can't bring the Nigger here with the rest of your team. We're just not ready for that sort of thing yet. We won't be able to take the field against your Brooklyn team if that boy Robinson is in uniform." Rickey told Pennock that he would be happy if the Phillies forfeited the games because the Dodgers would pick up three victories. End of threat.

The Dodgers took a train to Philadelphia and then a bus to the Ben Franklin Hotel, but before they could even unload, they were told they weren't welcome to stay there. "And don't bring your team back here while you have any Nigras with you," they were told. The white players wound up staying there, but Robinson had to move to the Attucks, an all-black hotel.

It was in games against the Phillies that Robinson suffered the greatest anguish and humiliation. When the Phillies visited Ebbets Field for the first time that year, Phillies manager Ben Chapman and his players unleashed a vicious tirade against him, voicing epithets like, "Hey, nigger, why don't you go back to the cotton field where you belong?" and "They're waiting for you in the jungles, black boy," and "Hey, snowflake, which one of those white boys' wives are you dating tonight?" As a player, Chapman had been traded from the New York Yankees in 1938 for his continual taunting of Jewish spectators at Yankee Stadium, giving Nazi salutes and shouting anti-Semitic epithets.

"I have to admit that this day [in a game against the Phillies], of all the unpleasant days in my life, brought me nearer to cracking up than I had ever been," Robinson recounted in 1972. Chapman yelled at Robinson's teammates that they would get diseases and sores if they touched his combs or towels. The Phillies held up their bats like guns to pretend they were shooting him. Robinson almost broke his promise to Rickey. He thought about attacking Chapman, quitting baseball, and returning to California. All of a sudden "for one wild and rage-crazed minute I thought, 'To hell with Mr. Rickey's noble experiment. . . . To hell with the image of the patient black freak I was supposed to create.' I could throw down my bat, stride over to that Phillies dugout, grab one of those white sons of bitches and smash his teeth in with my despised black fist. Then I could walk away from it all." Robinson backed off when he thought twice about the promises he had made to Rickey and what he would have to tell his son one day.

Yankee Hall of Famer Mickey Mantle found it hard to believe that Robinson could keep it together in light of what he went through his first year. "When you think of Jackie's natural personality—he liked action, arguments, yelling, and taking charge—you wonder how he was ever able to control himself that first year." Mantle called him one of the best players he ever saw.

The Brooklyn players began rallying around Robinson after the attacks by Chapman and the Phillies players. Their taunts may have backfired on them. Rickey said Chapman helped to unite the Dodgers. "When he poured out that string of unconscionable abuse, he solidified and unified thirty men, not one of who[m] was willing to sit by and see someone kick around a man who had his hands tied behind his back. Chapman made Jackie a real member of the Dodgers." After the Dodgers and Phillies played their third game, Stanky screamed at the Phillies, "Listen, you yellow-bellied cowards, why don't you yell at someone who can answer back?" At that moment, Robinson began to feel better about his teammates. The press came to his rescue as well. Dan Parker, sports editor of the *New York Daily Mirror*, praised Robinson for ignoring "the guttersnipe language coming from the Phillies' dugout, thus stamping himself as the only gentleman among those involved in the incident."

Public reaction against Chapman was so severe that Rickey asked Robinson to pose for a photo with Chapman the next time the two teams met in the hope that it would save [Chapman's] job. Robinson agreed. Chapman refused to shake hands with Robinson, quietly telling him, "Jackie, you know, you're a good ballplayer, but you're still a nigger to me." But together they held a bat up between them. "I have to admit, though, that . . . was one of the most difficult things I had to make myself do," Robinson said.

Dixie Walker, who was a friend of Chapman's, was astonished. "I swear, I never thought I'd see Ol' Ben eat shit like that." Most of Walker's disdain for Robinson was for show because he fretted that if he became too chummy with the Dodger's new star, he would be chastised by friends in his Alabama hometown and that it might hurt his sporting goods and hardware store. Robinson went along with Walker's cover by avoiding shaking hands with Walker in one of baseball's rituals after he hit a home run.

Howie Schultz, who was traded to the Phillies in May, remembered asking Robinson how he could "handle this crap." Robinson replied, "Oh, I'll have my day." Schultz recalled, "That's all he said. And, of course, he did."

Chapman apparently had some regrets about his behavior years later. "A man learns about things and mellows as he grows older," he began. "I think maybe I've mellowed. Maybe I went too far in those days, when I thought it was OK to try to throw guys off-balance and upset them with jockeying. I'm sorry for many of the things I said. I guess the world changes and maybe I've changed, too."

Robinson was greeted in each ballpark in different ways, mostly with outright hatred because of his skin color. Before a game against Cincinnati a letter signed "The Travelers" threatened, "We have already got rid of several like you. One was found in a river just recently. Robinson, we are going to kill you if you attempt to enter a ballgame at Crosley Field." Robinson played, hitting a home run in the Dodgers' sweep of Cincinnati.

When Robinson took the field in Cincinnati, he was pummeled again and again with racial taunts. Pee Wee Reese had had enough. He walked over to Robinson and put his arm around him in a show of support. The crowd let out a gasp. Robinson said he and Reese talked at that moment, but "neither one of us . . . remembers what we were talking about. We do know what we were saying to the agitators and to the world." Robinson also said, "After than happened, I never felt alone on a ball field again." Robinson's wife, Rachel, recalled that she wanted to hug Reese. "What it did was change the dynamics of the whole team, showing them they had something dramatic to deal with. . . . Jackie felt very close to Pee Wee the rest of his life. Each of them had a strong sense of their impact on social change." Reese draped his arm around Robinson once again in a game in Boston against the Braves to show that the first time had been no accident. (In 1996 the Jackie Robinson and Pee Wee Reese Monument, which captures that watershed moment, was unveiled in Brooklyn.)

Early in the season the St. Louis Cardinals were threatening to conduct a protest strike that they hoped would spread throughout the league in an effort to keep baseball white. (Dick Gephardt, the longtime leader of the U.S. House of Representatives, recalled as a boy that he heard fans' extreme profanity and vulgarity toward Robinson while watching the Dodgers and Cardinals play in St. Louis.) National League president Ford Frick quickly put an end to any strike by threatening to suspend players who participated.

"I don't care if it wrecks the National League for five years," Frick said. "This is the United States of America, and one citizen has as much right to play as another."

Robinson still had trouble with some teammates, opposing players rode him unmercifully, and he ducked too many fastballs aimed at his head. Robinson kept his cool outwardly, although inside he was boiling mad. One of the toughest times he had controlling himself was at a game against the Cardinals at Ebbets Field. Outfielder Enos "Country" Slaughter, from Rexboro, North Carolina, and a future Hall of Famer, spiked Robinson while crossing first base, opening a sizable gash on his leg. Several of Robinson's teammates rushed onto the field to protest Slaughter's action. "I started the season as a lonely man, often feeling like a black Don Quixote tilting at a lot of white windmills," Robinson said. "I ended it feeling like a member of a solid team." The next inning, when Robinson got on first, he laid into first baseman Stan Musial, saying he'd like to rip Slaughter apart. "I don't blame you," Musial said quietly.

Musial was one of two significant players to support Robinson. The other was future Hall of Famer Hank Greenberg, a Jew who faced his own nightmare of bigotry. "You're a good ballplayer, and you'll do all right," Greenberg said. "Just stay in there . . . and always keep your head up. A lot of people are pulling for you to make good," Greenberg stressed. "Don't ever forget it." Musial gave Robinson encouragement and a tip or two about how to shift his feet when taking throws at first base.

Of course Robinson had the support of tens of thousands of black fans across the nation. Vernon Jordan, who had been a president of the Urban League and later a legal and political powerhouse in Washington DC, remembered seeing Robinson play in a preseason game in Atlanta. He was joined by several hundred other blacks who had been bused in to see the game from Robinson's hometown of Cairo, Georgia. "We blacks were cheering as if he had won something for us," Jordan recalled. "And, of course, he had. . . . It is literally impossible to overstate what he meant to me, to all of us, to the country. It is as instructive and inspiring a story of courage as you can find."

African Americans loved Robinson. When they couldn't go to the ballpark, they would listen on the radio or follow him in newspapers. Sportswriter Sam Lacy of the Washington DC *Afro-American* wrote, "No matter what the nature of the gathering, a horse race, a church meeting, a ball game, the universal question is: 'How'd Jackie make out today?'" Often when the Dodgers' train pulled into a city, hundreds of fans, nearly all black, would greet Robinson at the depot. Once at a game in Cincinnati Robinson had popped up, and when he returned to the dugout, black fans were "screaming and shrieking," pitcher Ralph Branca said. "He [Robinson] said, 'Be quiet. Behave yourselves. I only popped out.'"

Robinson was starting to relax and play the kind of ball the Dodgers expected. "Until today we just couldn't get him to take a normal cut at the cripples they were getting him out on," Shotton said. "Time after time we gave him signals to hit the three-and-one pitch, but very often he didn't even swing. Guess he had too much on his mind."

In midseason teams were getting a taste of what it was like to play against Robinson, especially the Phillies. Catcher Andy Seminick remarked, "Something about certain players: Get 'em mad and they'd hurt you. Jackie Robinson was definitely one of 'em. He rose to the occasion and clobbered the tar out of us. He beat us everywhere—at bat, on the bases, in the field. Finally Ben Chapman said, 'Let's lay off him. [Racial taunts are] not doing any good.'"

Robinson ran away with the Rookie of the Year award at season's end, after compiling a batting average of .297. He had 175 hits in 151 games, including 12 home runs. He led the league in stolen bases with 29 and was second in runs scored with 125. He walked 74 times and led the league in sacrifices. On defense he committed 16 errors at first base—the second highest in the league—while handling 1,031 chances. Considering that it was his first season in the position, such results were adequate. He finished fifth in the National League's MVP voting.

After Jackie won the Rookie of the Year award, he went home to Southern California for a dinner honoring him. Few whites were in attendance. Not much had changed in Pasadena.

In the World Series the Dodgers fell to the Yankees in seven games in one of the great Series up to that time. Robinson played below average during the Series, hitting .259 with 2 doubles and 3 RBIs. He stole 2 bases and walked twice. One of the most vivid memories Robinson had of the Series was what he called "a completely new emotion." That was when the national anthem was played and he felt he belonged. "This time, I thought, it is being played for me, as much as for anyone else. This is organized major-league base-ball, and I am standing here with all the others; and everything that takes place includes me."

Even one of Robinson's most severe critics, Dixie Walker, admit-ted that he "is everything Branch Rickey said he was when he came up from Montreal." Although there were scattered incidents of racial tension toward the end of the year, integration seemed to be mov-ing along successfully. Soon more African Americans joined teams, including Larry Doby with the Cleveland Indians and Roy Cam-panella with the Dodgers. Robinson and Doby, who were dealing with the same racial problems, would talk to each other on the tele-phone to share their experiences.

By any standards the Dodgers' season had to be considered a suc-cess, even while they lost the World Series. The nucleus of a strong team was in the making, one that would dominate the National League for the next decade. And it showed in attendance, in Brook-lyn as well as in other ballparks where fans turned out to see Rob-inson. Brooklyn's attendance at home and on the road rose by only eleven thousand over 1946, but the Dodgers still led the league in attendance. Overall attendance in the National League increased by 1.5 million, a record that stood until 1960. Almost 10.4 million fans passed through the turnstiles. Wendell Smith, a reporter for the *Pittsburgh Courier*, wrote, "Jackie's nimble/ Jackie's quick/ Jack-ie's making the turnstiles click." According to a poll conducted in 1947, Robinson was the second most popular man in the country, behind Bing Crosby.

Robinson received a pay raise, to $12,500, for the 1948 season, an amount less than he earned during the offseason, when he went on a vaudeville and speaking tour in the South, where he would answer pre-set questions about his life.

In spring training he received the welcome news that he was moving over to second base after the Dodgers traded Stanky to the Boston Braves. Robinson was delighted; he had never felt comfortable at first base. The Dodgers had to keep Gil Hodges and his bat in the lineup while making room for Roy Campanella behind the plate. Hodges moved from catcher to first base, a position he occupied for fifteen years with the Dodgers. (Hodges was a good fielder, and he would go on to average 32 home runs a season from 1949 to 1955. Many think he should be in the Baseball Hall of Fame.) Reese and Robinson turned into a formidable double-play combination for several years.

Despite showing up at spring training twenty-five pounds overweight in 1948, Robinson had a solid season. He led the National League in fielding percentage, batted .296, and had 85 RBIs, although the Dodgers finished in third place. He was hit by pitches 7 times, a league high. (Joe DiMaggio led the American League with 8.) Players were hit far less often than in today's game. For example, Anthony Rizzo of the Chicago Cubs was hit 30 times in 2015.

Joining Robinson on the Dodgers' squad was a twenty-one-year-old rookie pitcher, Carl Erskine. They would play together for nine years, so Erskine got a good look at Robinson. Erskine recalled in 1997 that no one could help Robinson on the field, not Rickey, not Rachel, not his mother. "When the ball was hit, he had to field it," Erskine said. "Jackie hit it; he threw it; he outran it; and he proved it. That's why he was accepted so quickly in baseball. The social side took a lot longer. And I have a feeling it's not there yet."

The year 1949 was a turning point for Robinson. He was going to be off his short leash. Rickey called him into his office and told him, "Jackie, you're on your own now. You can be yourself now." In referring to his action years later, Rickey explained it as follows:

> I could see how the tensions had built up in two years and that this young man had come through with courage far beyond what I

asked, yet, I knew that burning inside him was the same pride and determination that burned inside those Negro slaves a century earlier. Robinson knew that he had been considered a martyred hero but the minute the muzzle was off he would be considered an uppity nigger. When a white player did it, he had spirit. When a black player did it, he was ungrateful, an upstart, a sore head.

Such charges would hang over Robinson's head until the day he retired.

Now that Robinson was released from his two-year commitment to turn the other cheek, what better place to try it out than in Atlanta, Georgia, playing a Minor League team with the improbable name of the Crackers. Robinson made his first Atlanta appearance with the Dodgers April 8–10, 1949. Before the first game the Ku Klux Klan Grand Dragon announced that ten thousand people had signed a petition to boycott Crackers' games if any black players appeared on the field with whites. Not deterred, more than fifteen thousand fans, one-third of them black, overflowed the stands for the first game. Hundreds watched from a roped-off area in the outfield, while hundreds outside the park found vantage points. The fans cheered Robinson and Campanella throughout the game. Almost nine thousand turned out for the Saturday afternoon game, won by Atlanta 9–1. On Sunday more than twenty-five thousand fans attended, of whom almost fourteen thousand were black. The three games went on with no fights, riots, or disturbances of any kind.

Pitcher Don Newcombe, the Dodgers' third black player, arrived the season that Robinson was free to be himself. He remembered Robinson's leadership years later: "He not only showed Negro players that we could fight for our rights without fear of reprisal; he showed white players he was going to do the same doggone things they did when they thought they were right, even if it meant getting put out of the game."

Five years later Robinson found himself sitting side by side on an airplane flight with an umpire who knew him from when he had played for Montreal. The umpire asked, "What's made you change your attitude, Jackie? I liked you much better when you were less aggressive." Robinson was quick to retort, "I'm not concerned with you liking or disliking me. All I ask is that you respect me as a human being.... Your dislike of my aggressiveness has no effect on me. I'm after something much more important than your favor or disfavor. You should at least admit that you respect me as a man who stands up for what he believes in. I am not an Uncle Tom. I am in this fight to stay." Yankee great Mickey Mantle once observed the following:

> There's an odd thing about Jackie Robinson. I myself was never very friendly with him, and I have found that a lot of people who knew him in and out of baseball really disliked him. He's a hard man for some people to like because he isn't soft and smooth-talking and syrupy. He is tough and independent and he says what he thinks, and he rubs people the wrong way. But I have never heard of anyone who knew Jackie Robinson, whether they liked him or disliked him, who didn't respect and admire him. That might be more important than being liked.

That was all Robinson could ask.

It was more than coincidental that with Robinson feeling free to be himself, he also had his best year on the field as he set career highs in games played, hits, batting average, slugging, RBIs, and stolen bases as the Dodgers won the National League pennant. He won the batting title with a .342 mark and his Major league–Leading 37 steals were the highest total in the National League in nineteen years. He finished second in the league in RBIs (124), hits (203), and on-base percentage (.432), and he was third in slugging average (.528), runs scored (122), doubles (38), and triples (12). He was named the National League MVP. He was handsomely rewarded with a $35,000 contract for 1950, a far cry from the $5,000 he had received three years earlier.

Robinson was happy to win the MVP award, of course, but being a good teammate and fighting for racial equality meant more to him. He was particularly upset with Campanella, who often stated, "I'm no crusader."

In 1950 Robinson turned movie star, joining the likes of Kenny Washington and Woody Strode, but he played himself "and quite well indeed" in *The Jackie Robinson Story*, which was called "one of the best and most convincing baseball biopics every filmed." The movie's main asset, a reviewer commented, was that Robinson played himself. "I'm sure he felt that even a 'B' film heightened the awareness of the general public to his struggle," said his wife Rachel.

In the middle of the season Robinson was one of several blacks called to testify before the House Un-American Activities Committee about his views on a statement by Paul Robeson, the noted black singer and civil rights activist. Robeson had said that American Negroes would not fight for America if war broke out with Russia, and he was accused of leaning toward communism. In an eloquent speech Robinson concluded that although he could not speak for fifteen million African Americans,

> I know that I've got too much invested for my wife and child and myself in the future of this country, and I and other Americans of many races and faiths have too much invested in our country's welfare, for any of us to throw it away because of a siren song sung in bass. I am a religious man. Therefore I cherish America where I am free to worship as I please, a privilege which some countries do not give. And I suspect that nine hundred and ninety-nine out of almost any thousand colored Americans you meet will tell you the same thing. But that doesn't mean that we're going to stop fighting race discrimination in this country until we've got it licked. It means that we're going to fight it all the harder because our stake in the future is so big.

Robinson was growing disenchanted with the Dodgers organization. He disliked new owner Walter O'Malley, who drove Branch Rickey out of the Brooklyn front office in 1950. Robinson took Rickey's departure hard. O'Malley knew that Robinson felt deeply about Rickey, and "I became the target of his insecurity." He said O'Malley's attitude toward him turned "viciously antagonistic." O'Malley called Robinson a prima donna. "To put it bluntly, I was one of those 'uppity niggers' in O'Malley's book."

Robinson wrote a letter to Rickey in November after his mentor left the Dodgers. "It has been the finest experience I have had being associated with you and I want to thank you very much for all you have meant not only to me and my family but to the entire country and particularly the members of our race," he wrote. Despite Robinson's despair, he went on to have one of his best seasons in 1951. It no doubt helped that he was free of restraints on the field.

Dodger center fielder Duke Snider gave one example of what Robinson had brought to Brooklyn's success. He remembered a game against the Chicago Cubs in the top of the ninth inning with the score 2–2. "Sad" Sam Jones, known for his blazing fastball, was on the mound for the Cubs. (In 1955 Jones became the first African American to pitch a no-hitter.) Snider was at bat when Robinson, who was in the on-deck circle, began yelling at Jones so loudly that one could hear it almost all over Wrigley Field. "Sam, you're no good. Sam, I'm gonna beat you. You got no guts." Snider flew out, and Robinson stepped into the batter's box. He still was yelling at Jones "until you can tell that Jones is madder'n hell." Snider continues:

> Jones is so mad he hits Robinson with a pitch and puts him on first base. Now Jones . . . is in real trouble, because Robbie is dancing off the bag and yelling and Sam keeps throwing over there, trying to keep him on the bag. It gets to Jones, and this time he tosses the ball at Robinson instead of the first baseman. [Robinson ducked and the ball sailed down to the Dodgers' bullpen, and he scampered all the way to third base.] Sam is beside himself, and Jackie's still yelling and laughing and dancing up the line on every pitch and screaming, 'Sam, I'm gonna beat you. You got no guts.' By now Sam is looking at Jackie and cursing and paying him more attention than the batter, and he throws the next pitch into the dirt. It's a short [wild pitch], and here comes Jackie with the winning run. . . . That Robinson was something else.

In 1950 and 1951 Robinson batted .328 and .338 and finished second and third respectively in the batting race. Both years the Dodgers lost the pennant on the last day of the season. The Dodgers returned to the top of the National League standings in 1952 as Robinson hit .308, scored 104 runs, stole 24 bases, and belted 19 homers.

Five years had passed since Robinson had broken into the Majors, and while the harassment he had initially endured had tapered off, it was still there to a great extent. Some would never accept an African American in the country's national pastime. Robinson received a letter before a game in St. Louis in 1953 that warned, "Robinson, you die, no use crying for the cops. You will be executed gangland-style in Busch Stadium." That caused Pee Wee Reese to wisecrack during warm-up drills, "Not so close, Jack, please."

In 1952 an African American pitcher, Joe Black, joined the team. It didn't take long for Robinson to get in his ear.

"Can you fight?"

"Yeah, I can fight," Black said.

"Good. This thing's [integration] not over."

For the 1953 season, a top-notch second baseman, Junior Gilliam, was ready to advance to the Majors, so Robinson agreed to change positions if it would help the team. At age thirty-four he wound up playing 77 games in the outfield, 44 at third base, 9 at second base, and 6 at first base. He still hit .329, drove in 95 runs, and scored 109 times. Gilliam was selected the National League Rookie of the Year.

For his good work on the field the Dodgers made Robinson the highest paid player on the team. But nobody was complaining. He earned $39,000 in 1953, $1,000 more than the runner-up. Owner Walter O'Malley made sure that Robinson was the best paid player on the Dodgers as long as he was on the field.

Age was beginning to take its toll on Robinson. His statistics started to slide, although they remained solid in 1954. He continued to play left field and third base and batted .311, but he stole only 7 bases and missed 38 games. The Dodgers fell short of the World Series.

In 1954 the Robinson family decided to move out of Brooklyn and began looking for land to build a house in Westchester County, New York. Jackie and Rachel found a piece they liked, and they offered the owner full price. They waited a "long time" and then were told the price had been raised $5,000. They agreed to pay that. More time passed, and then the owner told the Robinsons the property had been sold to someone else. "Everywhere we went it was like that," Robinson said. They eventually found a house in North Stamford, Connecticut.

In 1955 the Dodgers would win their first World Series, although Robinson's contribution diminished even more from the previous season. Statistically Robinson had the worst season of his outstanding career. He missed 57 games and batted .256 with 12 stolen bases. In the Dodgers' World Series win, Robinson played in six of the seven games. He hit only .182 with 4 hits, but he scored 5 times, including a steal of home in the eighth inning of a losing cause in the first game. "It was not the best baseball strategy to steal home with our team two runs behind, but I just took off and did it," Robinson admitted. "I really didn't care whether I made it or not—I was just tired of waiting. . . . Whether it was because of my stealing home or not, the team had new fire." The Dodgers went on to beat the Yankees in the seventh game behind Johnny Podres's shutout.

During the offseason Robinson began thinking of retiring and what his next job would be. He had hoped at one time to work in the Dodgers' organization, but his run-in with O'Malley and his dislike of manager Walter Alston made that unlikely. He had hoped that he could become the manager of the Montreal Royals but knew that wouldn't happen under O'Malley's reign. In 1956 there was talk that Robinson might become a manager in the PCL, a Triple A league, after he retired. Robinson met the talk head on. He told a newspaper reporter that he had no doubt he could manage in the Major Leagues. "The doors of the big leagues are opened wide now for any man who is qualified for any job that has to be filled," he said. "With pride I say I had a hand in that. With pride, too, I say I can manage the majors." He never got the chance. And he wasn't any more hopeful other blacks would become managers either. "Negro players play their hearts out," he wrote. "But when their popularity or their best playing days are over, there is just no room for them in the executive suite." It was talk like that led to Robinson's being called "the most hated man in baseball."

Not surprisingly as early as 1950 Branch Rickey thought that Robinson could do well as a big league manager. "I do not know of any player in the game today who could, in my judgment, manage a major league club better than yourself," he wrote in a letter to Robinson. He wrote that he had suggested that to several sportswriters in the past, but they had ignored him.

In 1960 Bill Veeck, who brought the second black player to the big leagues in Larry Doby, had doubts whether Robinson would have made a good manager. "I'm not sure that his temperament would be that of a basically successful major league manager." Robinson said he had no interest in becoming a manager, "so the question of my qualifications or 'temperament' as a manager isn't at all important." He pointed to two white managers who had volatile temperaments and had succeeded—Leo Durocher and Casey Stengel. "None of these gentlemen could be accused of 'lack of temperament' and none could 'prove' a 'particularly subdued personality.'"

Robinson never let up on his crusade to move more blacks into the baseball hierarchy. "Baseball moguls and their top advisers seem to earnestly believe that the bodies, the physical stamina, the easy reflexes of black stars, make them highly desirable but that, somehow, they are lacking in the gray matter that it supposedly takes to serve as managers, officials, and executives in policy-making positions."

In 2009 ten African Americans or Latinos were managing Major League teams. By 2015 the only black manager left in the Major Leagues, Lloyd McClendon, was fired by the Seattle Mariners. Not long after, however, the Washington Nationals hired longtime baseball manager Dusty Baker. A month later the Dodgers picked Dave Roberts as their first minority manager. A Latino, Fredi Gonzalez, managed the Miami Marlins and the Atlanta Braves between 2007 and 2016. McClendon won 499 games and lost 607 over seven years of managing the Pittsburgh Pirates and the Mariners. He had one winning season. The first black manager, Frank Robinson, managed sixteen years and finished with a record of 1,065 wins and 1,176 losses. He was the American League's Manager of the Year in 1989 while with the Baltimore Orioles. He never won a division championship, finishing second twice. Bill White, who played for three teams in twelve seasons, was National League president from 1989 to 1994.

The year 1956 was somewhat better on the field for Robinson. He hit .275 in 117 games in what was to be his last season. In the Dodgers' seven-game World Series loss to the Yankees, Jackie drew 5 walks, scored 5 times, and blasted a home run. He hit .250. For the six World Series in which he appeared, Robinson's batting average was .234.

Robinson knew he wasn't playing as well and that injuries were coming more often. In addition, with his integrity intact after nine years with the Dodgers, he began to assert himself on racial issues on and off the field. The Dodgers hoped Robinson would retire, but no announcement was forthcoming. The Dodgers' front office then traded him to the New York Giants on December 13, 1956, for a journeyman pitcher and $30,000 in cash. "I'm shocked to the core," said one Robinson fan. "This is like selling the Brooklyn-Battery Tunnel. Jack Robinson is a synonym for the Dodgers. They can't do this to us."

Robinson had decided to retire before the trade, but he had made an exclusive deal to make the announcement in *Look* magazine. (In the article he criticized the remaining segregated teams in the Majors.) He was being paid $50,000 to announce his retirement in the magazine. The Giants reportedly offered him $60,000 to stay, and the prospect of playing alongside Willie Mays definitely had some appeal. "There was so much pressure from fans and youngsters for me to remain in the game that I did have some vague second thoughts." When Brooklyn general manager Buzzy Bavasi publicly implied that Robinson was just trying to use the magazine article to get a better contract, Robinson decided to prove the Dodgers wrong and declined the Giants' offer. Besides, he wrote in *Look*, "My legs are gone and I know it . . . . [The Giants] ballclub needs . . . rcbuilding. It needs youth. It doesn't need me. It would be unfair to the Giant owners to take their money."

Robinson said he would miss the game. "I love baseball, and I'll miss playing the game. Every inning is a new adventure in baseball. I'll miss that kind of fun. I'll even miss my rhubarbs with the umpires. I'll miss some of the players I've known, but I'll miss the game more. You play baseball for pleasure and for money—not to make friends. I don't regret any part of the last ten years."

For his career Robinson batted .311 while leading the Dodgers to six National League pennants and a World Series championship. He stole 197 bases, including 19 of home plate—Ty Cobb holds the Major League record with 54—and hit 137 home runs. Robinson was one of only two players during the span of 1947–56 to accumulate at least 125 steals while registering a slugging percentage over .425. He walked 740 times while striking out only 291 times. That he put up such terrific numbers is testimony again to what an outstanding athlete he was, perhaps the best all-around athlete in U.S. sports history. Nor can one dismiss the fact that Robinson had all the motivation he needed to succeed, for if he failed, black athletes would be set back for years, perhaps decades, in making further strides toward integrating baseball.

"Baseball was just a part of my life," Robinson would say. "Thank God that I didn't allow a sport or a business or any part of my life to dominate me completely. . . . I felt that I had my time in athletics and that was it." It was time to move on.

25

Changing Los Angeles

"As well as anybody could say that they are colorblind,
I really believe that is a fact of my life."

—Tom Bradley

With his election Bradley was not only the first African American mayor of Los Angeles, but he also was the mayor of the largest city in the country with an overwhelming white population. He would serve twenty years during a time of vast growth in the Southern California city. As the dominating figure in Los Angeles politics, he helped bring consensus toward improving the city. These accomplishments overshadowed problems that arose toward the end of his administration.

"He came from the liberal reform section of the Democratic Party.... He built bridges to whites and to other groups. He reached into other worlds, but he did it without ever losing his commitment to the black community," said Raphael J. Sonenshein, a political scientist at California State University, Fullerton.

As he had throughout most of his life, Bradley continued to bridge racial barriers during his five terms as mayor. His administration thrived on building coalitions between blacks and Jews. For example, during the 1973 mayoral campaign Bradley attended the meeting of a key Jewish group that he was courting. A staffer, Blair Levin, noticed that many of the men were wearing yarmulkes. Levin had one in his jacket and offered it to Bradley. The candidate stuffed it into his pocket. During the event, his opponent, Sam Yorty, was offered a yarmulke, and he put it on. When Bradley was called to speak before the group, he too was offered a yarmulke, but he said, "I have my own," and he donned it. The room broke out in laughter. "It sent a message not of pandering—'I am one of you'—but rather, 'We are all in this together,'" Levin recalled.

The *Los Angeles Times* wrote upon Bradley's death that he had been "key to the racial peace that the rapidly diversifying city enjoyed during most of his hold on the mayor's office. He opened doors for minorities and women to serve on city commissions, to rise in the ranks of City Hall employees and to share in city contracts." The *Times* described Bradley as "a tall, dignified figure with a quiet, sometimes nearly expressionless demeanor [and] never a firebrand. He preferred to work quietly behind the scenes." That demeanor led to unflattering nicknames such as "the Sphinx of City Hall" and "Mayor Automaton" that did not sit well with his backers.

One colleague remarked, "Some people make the mistake of underestimating [Bradley] in this area; they confuse his quiet approach with indecisiveness and think that he can be molded to fit others' expectations, but that is not Tom Bradley." He was a listener, another one said. "He is able to grasp more of the detail and the context of the problem than most people." A staff member commented that after reading a long list of items that needed attention, Bradley sat in silence. Finally the staff member got up to leave. Bradley stopped him and asked, "Don't you want to know my response to your list?" The staffer recalled, "That is how he is at times; you don't know if he is paying attention, when all along he is right with you and afterwards gives you a response that not only answers your questions, but raises others."

The first obstacle Bradley had to overcome was the opposition of powerful business owners, but he pushed through a redevelopment plan within a year that wooed them to his side. The plan called for construction of several skyscrapers in the downtown financial district. Bradley's leadership also contributed to the establishment of the outlying Century City on the city's west side and the Warner Center in San Fernando Valley, both of which proved to be huge financial successes. Bradley was in the forefront of developing the Los Angeles light rail system and the expansion of Los Angeles International Airport (LAX).

Under Bradley's administration strong efforts were undertaken to improve the black community. A shopping center was built in Watts, the first since the area had been largely abandoned by businesses after the 1965 riots. Bradley persuaded the Produce Market to stay in the city, and he succeeded in saving shopping centers in two inner-city areas threatened with decay—the Slauson-Vermont neighborhood and the Crenshaw district. Bradley's experience in the LAPD also helped him deal with the tumultuous times during the tenures of controversial police chiefs Edward M. Davis and Daryl Gates. During Bradley's administration Los Angeles saw its first homosexual rights law in 1979 and efforts that led to the discovery of AIDS in 1981.

Despite his high approval rating, Bradley was going to get a familiar challenger as he sought to retain his mayoral position in 1981. Former mayor Sam Yorty announced he would seek a return to the mayor's office, and the racial innuendos began all over again. For example, Yorty told a Chamber of Commerce meeting that "black people are really racist [because] they vote for black people because they are black." He also attacked Bradley for allegedly supporting the mandatory busing of children as an answer to segregation despite Bradley's consistently being on record as opposing busing.

During the campaign a *Los Angeles Times* poll gauged Bradley's popularity statewide if Bradley were to run for governor in 1982. The poll found that he had the support of 85 percent of the respondents. Those who didn't back Bradley were mostly "law-and-order oriented voters who are pro-police, anti-gun control, pro-death penalty and who are hostile to the courts." The *Times* analysis also suggested that a candidate "capable of mounting a major law-and-order campaign" could cause Bradley trouble. It also suggested that race could play a part in voter preference. "Political strategists have speculated [that] the fact that Bradley is black with a reputation as a Democratic liberal could hurt him in a statewide race against a well-financed conservative Republican candidate." The poll turned out to be quite prophetic.

Bradley handily won the race for mayor, earning 64 percent of the vote in the primary, thereby putting aside any need for a run-off. It was by far his biggest margin since he was elected in 1973. With popularity like that it took little for Bradley to set his sights on the state capital, Sacramento, even though publicly he was only a "possible" candidate. Then in January 1982 Bradley jumped into the gubernatorial race. "I want to revive the promise and opportunity of the American Dream," Bradley said.

Bradley easily captured the Democratic nomination for governor with 67 percent of the vote; the next closest candidate gained 24 percent. He was the first and only African American to head the gubernatorial ticket in California. Bradley's Republican opponent in the general election was California attorney general George Deukmejian, who had squeaked by Lieutenant Governor Mike Curb. Curb charged Deukmejian with smear tactics in the last week of the election that pushed him over the top. Such tactics would prove to play a dominant role in deciding the general election race.

A day after the primary Bradley proposed that the two opponents sign a "fair campaign code," but Deukmejian quickly rejected the proposal. It was going to be a gloves-off election. While Bradley's campaign focused on what he planned to do as governor, Deukmejian kept up a steady stream of negative tactics. Bradley appeared unconcerned about the race issue because he had successfully fended it off in earlier elections. Deukmejian's campaign manager claimed Bradley's race would not be an issue, thereby reminding or informing voters that Bradley was an African American.

A Bradley staff member charged that the Deukmejian campaign had raised the topic of Bradley's race in an "effort to skirt discussion and debate on the real issues. . . . As long as they could keep the public and the journalists' minds off the real issues and the records, they could hope to benefit by playing to people's stereotypes and fears." The race issue, however, received no attention in the campaign until the final days.

The black community was upset that Bradley thought that the black vote was a sure thing and that he campaigned lightly for its votes. That was a mistake because there was a the weak minority vote in what turned out to be a tight race. Bradley focused on the voters outside Los Angeles for the most part, spreading his beliefs in the California Dream. "[For] people of every race, creed, and color—I want them to know if they work hard, they can achieve. They can look at Tom Bradley and say, 'If he can do it, so can I.'"

About a month before the election, when Bradley seemed to have a comfortable lead, Deukmejian's campaign manager, Bill Roberts, tried to explain why he was unconcerned that his candidate was behind in a California poll. Roberts believed 5 percent of the people who had been questioned had lied to the poll takers to conceal a racial bias that would keep them from voting for a black candidate. Once again race became the fodder of headlines throughout the state. Roberts told the press, "You will not get the truth from people regarding the race issue. . . . If we are down only five points or less in the polls by election time, we're going to win. . . . It's just a fact of life." Roberts said the polls couldn't be trusted because "if people are going to vote that way, they certainly are not going to announce it for a survey [poll] taker."

Bradley was stunned. "It's an insult—not to me, but to all the people of California—to suggest that in 1982 people will vote for governor based on something other than the merits of the candidates." To one backer it didn't matter what Roberts's motive was "because it is the effect that counts, and race is now an issue." Former U.S. senator John Tunney, a Democrat, responded similarly: "If you go up and down the state saying that something is not an issue, such as race, it finally becomes an issue in the public's mind." Former Democratic governor Pat Brown was blunter: "Let's make this perfectly clear. The whole thing was planned from the beginning by Roberts and Deukmejian." Deukmejian disclaimed that he might be seeking the anti-black vote, but he and the press continued to keep the issue alive, despite the plethora of bigger issues facing the state. Roberts resigned four days after he made his statement, but the damage was done.

Bradley had led the polls by 49 to 42 percent right up until election night. As one pollster put it, Bradley was "the kind of guy that a lot of whites who fear they might be prejudiced would like to vote for." A Bradley staff member put it this way about the Deukmejian campaign: "It was a subtle, effective racist campaign." That Bradley lost led to the so-called "Bradley effect," a theory concerning observed discrepancies between voter opinion polls and election outcomes in some U.S. government elections where a white candidate and a non-white candidate run against each other. In effect that is what Roberts had said.

Bradley came close to beating Deukmejian, losing by slight more than 50,000 votes of the 7.7 million votes cast, a margin of .67 percent, the narrowest margin in races for governor in California. If elected, he would have become the first black in the nation to win a gubernatorial election. The closeness of the race gave some credibility to Roberts's claim.

Bradley never had the chance to give the speech prepared in the event he won. In part it said, "Don't let anyone tell you that you cannot become anything you want to be in the world, don't let anyone tell you that something is impossible. Stay away from the drugs, study hard, work hard, do not ask for any favors, play by the rules and dare to dream. . . . Look at me the grandson of slaves and know that in California anything is possible. California is the place where impossible dreams can come true."

A disappointed Bradley tried to put the race behind him by returning to City Hall and focusing on his mayoral duties. One of the duties was to successfully lure the 1984 Summer Olympics to Los Angeles. Bradley called the securing of the Olympics the "highlight of my entire political career. . . . First of all, it was very difficult to get the Games. I had opposition from politicians and from the public in Los Angeles." The Olympics turned out to be a resounding success that produced a $250 million surplus for the city.

Bradley is credited with making Los Angeles "a Jewel of the Pacific." The ports of Los Angeles and Long Beach are among the busiest ports in the world. LAX became the third busiest airport in the nation. More than 60 million passengers annually passed through its gates. Because of his successes Bradley was gaining national attention. President Jimmy Carter sounded him out for secretary of Housing and Urban Development, a position that he turned down. Walter Mondale considered him as a vice presidential candidate when he ran for president against Ronald Reagan in 1984.

Bradley was not one to give up. He never took his eyes off the big prize—the governorship—because retreating was not in his nature. His daughter Loraine remembered glancing at a photo in Bradley's home office of him running the 440-yard dash while at UCLA. She remembered asking her father when she was a young girl why he had such a determined look in the picture. He told her, "Never give in, never give in, never, never, never—in nothing great or small, large or petty—never give in, except to convictions of honor and good sense."

In the 1986 election Deukmejian swamped Bradley by a margin of 24 percent. Bradley may have been dejected, but he showed the kind of sportsmanship in politics that he had shown in athletics. "I want you to know the indomitable spirit of this old warrior will never die," he told supporters after the election. A Deukmejian campaign official noted that Bradley lost because he had chosen to attack the governor, a stance that was "not credible with the electorate. It was out of sync with the mood of the voters." Bradley had the misfortune to run against an exceedingly popular governor. The year before the election the governor had a 73 percent approval rating. In addition, no sitting governor had been defeated in a reelection bid in the previous forty years. Deukmejian also outspent Bradley by a two-to-one ratio. Also Bradley was hurt by Deukmejian's claim that he was soft on crime.

Bradley was back at his job early the next day. He told reporters that he was delighted to still have "one of the best jobs in the world." He made it clear that despite having said he would serve only for two terms, he would seek a fifth term in 1989.

His resounding rejection by California voters in the 1986 gubernatorial race notwithstanding, Bradley was elected mayor for a fifth term. But his political mojo was waning. Environmental issues, his reluctance to condemn the Black Muslim leader Louis Farrakhan, and losses by key Bradley supporters in bids for reelection to the City

Council weakened his political strength. He also was embroiled in more than a dozen investigations of his finances based on a $42,000 fee he had accepted while serving as an adviser to two banks doing business with the city. He was exonerated of any wrongdoing.

One of Bradley's most difficult problems came during his last years in office when riots broke out in South Central Los Angeles on April 29, 1992, after a jury acquitted four Los Angeles policemen of excessive force in arresting a black man, Rodney King. More than fifty people had been killed in the rioting. At one point Bradley boarded a helicopter to survey the damage from the air. According to a bodyguard, Bradley was deeply shaken by what he saw. "Flying above the city in a helicopter, witnessing the city erupt in flames and in complete chaos, a city in which he loved and proudly served for fifty-one years, just tore him up deeply," the bodyguard said. "All that hard work comes down to this. I think he was saying to himself, 'My time as mayor has come to an end.' He was just too proud to cry."

Five months later Bradley admitted, "The April unrest tore at my heart, and I will not be at peace until we have healed our wounds and rebuilt our neighborhoods." Then he announced he would not seek a sixth term. "Let us all, every one of us, pledge to make Los Angeles a beacon of mutual respect, justice and tolerance from this day forward."

In 1993 Bradley stayed true to his promise and declined to seek a sixth term. Despite his many accomplishments, only 42 percent of respondents to a *Los Angeles Times* poll believed Bradley would be remembered as an "above average" mayor. At the age of seventy-six Bradley was showing no signs of slowing down. He went to work for the downtown law offices of Brobeck, Phleger and Harrison, specializing in international trade issues. As was his habit, he was usually the first to arrive in the morning and stayed late at night. Bradley didn't miss the media attention. "I had enough exposure in twenty years to last a lifetime. If my name was never printed again, it wouldn't bother me."

In March 1996 Bradley was stricken with a heart attack. Doctors performed triple bypass surgery, but less than a day after the surgery he suffered a stroke that left him unable to speak clearly for the rest of his life. Two years later he died of a heart attack at the age of eighty.

In a tribute to Bradley Richard Riordan, who was elected to replace Bradley when he retired, called him "a regal leader in appearance, word and deed. . . . [He was] the right leader at the right time for our city—a unifying force in bringing together diverse elements from throughout Los Angeles. Tom Bradley earned the confidence of leaders everywhere. His impact was felt throughout our city, our nation and the world." In a eulogy at Bradley's funeral Vice President Al Gore called him the Jackie Robinson "of public service—making history through his quiet dignity, his iron determination, and his ability to walk through doors that opened to his insistent knock."

Unemployed fifty-one year-old Leon Cheatham left his house at 7:00 a.m. and walked more than two miles to attend Bradley's funeral, but when he arrived at the church, it was already packed with people who had lined up starting at 6 a.m. to attend the 10:00 o'clock services. He and scores of others heard the services over loudspeakers outside. "I don't have the money to spare to catch buses and stuff," Cheatham said. "So, I walked. I just had to come to pay my respects. Mayor Bradley didn't have no color barrier or nothing. He just loved people and brought them together." Melvin Hill, who was just a boy when Bradley was elected mayor in 1973, also wanted to pay his respects but to make a few dollars too. Hill, thirty-four, sold T-shirts with a series of photographs depicting stages of Bradley's life, from his days as a UCLA track star through his years as mayor. "A lot of older black people are buying the shirt," Hill said. "They can relate best to his struggle from sharecropper to mayor of L.A. But if you think about it, what he did was incredible." The fronts of the shirts read, "Mr. Mayor, thanks for the memories."

26

The Civil Rights Years

"He did us proud but at a cost beyond paying."
—Author Roger Angell

Robinson wasn't about to fade into oblivion now that his baseball
career was over. Far from it. He had a sense of social responsibility
that led him to undertake an effort to change the world, which he
knew discriminated against all persons, not just African Americans.

Robinson joined the popular chain of Chock Full O'Nuts restaurants in New York City as a vice president. It seemed an unlikely
job for a former ballplayer, but he was intrigued that he would be
directing personnel matters for more than a thousand employees.
He was recruited by owner William H. Black, who was white. "From
what I've read about Jackie he was just about the best man for the
job," White said.

Robinson was amused to learn that Black was considered guilty
of discrimination against whites because most of the employees
were black. Racists called the company "Chock Full O'Niggers."
Apparently white people shunned restaurant counter jobs and blacks
needed jobs. Black didn't care what color a person's skin was as long
as he or she did the job.

A clincher was that Black gave full support to Robinson's request
to become chairman of the Freedom Fund Drive of the NAACP.
Robinson noted that Black "told me that if he were in my place
there wouldn't be enough he could do for the cause of freedom

for black people." He told Robinson he could use company time to travel, work, and speak for the NAACP as long as it didn't interfere with his job. To sweeten the job offer, Black donated $10,000 to the NAACP. Robinson helped raise more than $1 million in the first year of his tour.

Robinson was true to his word. He worked tirelessly for Chock Full O'Nuts right from the start. He was anything but a figurehead in a job that used his name to gain publicity for the company. Robinson jumped right in by studying wage scales, benefits, training, and mobility patterns. He would travel to restaurants throughout the city to gather information from employees in person. By 1961 Robinson was elected to the company's board of directors. During his years at Chock Full O'Nuts and long after, Robinson took any means necessary to seek equality, from writing letters to key political figures and prominent people to debating civil rights with Presidents John F. Kennedy and Richard M. Nixon, and the Reverend Martin Luther King Jr.

Not long after Robinson retired from baseball, June 7, 1957, Howard University in Washington DC awarded an honorary Doctor of Law degree to him and Reverend King, whom Robinson would join in civil rights protests in the years to come. The degree was the first of dozens of awards Robinson would receive while alive and posthumously. Six years later, on August 28, 1963, Robinson stood close by, looking on with his children when King gave his famous "I Have a Dream" speech on the steps of the Lincoln Memorial in Washington DC.

In 1957 Robinson was diagnosed with diabetes, a disease with which his brothers Edgar and Mack also were afflicted. He told a friend that his doctor said that for an athlete who abstained from smoking and drinking (as Jackie did), he had never seen a body in such bad shape. The Robinsons were shocked by the discovery, but as Rachel put it, "It was premature for us to be concerned with mortality—too premature and too frightening."

Robinson may have been the first insulin-dependent diabetic to play Major League Baseball, despite his claim that the illness hadn't been diagnosed while he was an active player. But former tennis great Bill Talbert, a close friend of Robinson's and the first famous athlete known to perform with diabetes, believed that Jackie became insulin dependent in midcareer. "I think Jackie felt it was a weakness. With all the publicity about blacks in baseball, he didn't want another thing to talk about," Talbert said after Robinson's death.

In 1959 Robinson signed on with the *New York Post*, which was considered a liberal newspaper, to write a column three times a week "on any subject that he [felt] strongly about." He had a ghostwriter, black playwright William Branch, to help him fashion his words. "As a Negro, I could hardly ignore this rare opportunity for one of us to speak to so wide an audience concerning just what we feel and think," Robinson wrote. "That this person happens to be me isn't important. The fact that it is happening is the thing." His columns covered the gamut from family to race relations, from politics to sports. Michael G. Long, who edited a book of Robinson's columns, commented, "Robinson wrote to prod and provoke, inflame and infuriate, and sway and persuade, as he sought to build his readership. Indeed, as Robinson played to win, he also strove to win the arguments of his day. . . . The whole story, as revealed by his commentary, is that Jackie Robinson had a heart full of passion and comparison."

The columns lasted until November 1960, when Robinson was fired, probably for supporting Richard Nixon for president over John Kennedy, although the editor denied that was so. One reason given for his dismissal was that his use of a ghostwriter failed to reflect Robinson's personality.

"No one will ever convince me that the *Post* acted in an honest manner," Robinson wrote in 1962 for his new newspaper, the weekly *Amsterdam News*, a black newspaper. "I believe the simple truth is that they became somewhat alarmed when they realized that I really meant to write what I believed." That column was written with a new ghostwriter, Alfred Duckett, a public relations expert who in 1972 would ghostwrite Robinson's autobiography *I Never Had It Made*. Each of Robinson's ghostwriters worked closely with Robinson to make sure they reflected his views. Nothing went out under Robinson's name without his approval. This time the column was on the editorial page and rarely covered sports. The column ran through 1968.

Robinson wholeheartedly kept up his work with the NAACP despite his illness. He traveled thousands of miles across the country giving speeches and raising money to boost the organization's treasury. In 1967, however, he had a falling out with Executive Director Roy Wilkins and resigned. He accused Wilkins of a dictatorial administration that had become reactionary and undemocratic. Robinson apparently was upset by Wilkins's old guard crushing the young turks in national board elections. Robinson later regretted his resignation, saying he should have tried to bring about change within the organization.

In the 1960s Robinson also found time to help establish the Freedom National Bank, for which he served as board chairman. It was a black-owned institution based in Harlem to provide loans and banking services for minority members who were largely being ignored by establishment banks in New York City. The bank operated until 1990, when it failed. He also wrote several autobiographical works.

Robinson continued to use his newspaper column to sound off on a myriad of subjects, with a great many focusing on his views of racial discrimination and politics. One column may have had a strong influence in combating racial discrimination in golf, his second favorite sport. In 1960 he took on the Professional Golf Association (PGA) for banning African Americans from membership—in particular Charlie Sifford. He pointed out that players [read: white players] worse than Sifford had been admitted as members and that crooner Bing Crosby and President Dwight Eisenhower were members of white-only golf clubs. In late March Robinson received a telephone call from an excited Sifford, who told him, "We did it!" Sifford said PGA officials had been influenced by Robinson's recent columns. "Robinson hit us pretty hard, didn't he?" an official told Sifford.

(For his contributions to golf, Sifford was inducted into the World Golf Hall of Fame. He was awarded the Presidential Medal of Freedom in 2014 and an honorary doctorate from the University of St. Andrews in Scotland, golf's birthplace. Pro golfer Lee Trevino said of Sifford, "You have to put him in the Jackie Robinson category." Tiger Woods referred to Sifford as "the Grandpa I never had" and that without Sifford, "I probably wouldn't be here. My dad would never have picked up the game. Who knows if the [white] clause would still exist or not? But he broke it down.")

Although Robinson was active in politics, he rejected reports that he planned to run for public office. He preferred to be free from the bounds of the politically correct positions of the time to speak his mind about any and all issues that stirred him. Robinson may have called himself a political independent and voted for Republicans and Democrats alike, but he tended to lean toward conservative issues except when it came to civil rights. He believed that through economic progress African Americans would improve their position in society.

Robinson supported several conservative issues, including the Vietnam War. (He once wrote to Martin Luther King Jr. to defend the Johnson administration's Vietnam policy.) He noted that the Republicans were the party of Lincoln. He let his views on the candidates be known and even surprised some by endorsing Richard Nixon over John Kennedy in 1960 because he felt Kennedy had not made it "his business to know colored people." Robinson later regretted his lack of support for Kennedy. "I do not consider my decision to back Richard Nixon over John F. Kennedy for the Presidency in 1960 one of my finer ones. It was a sincere one, however, at the time," Robinson wrote in his autobiography.

The turning point in Robinson's support of Nixon may have been Robinson's long-standing anger over the former vice president's refusal to show support for Reverend King when he was unjustly sentenced to four months in jail for taking part in a sit-in demonstration. Kennedy, however, intervened to persuade a local judge to release King. After Kennedy's assassination and Lyndon Johnson's ascent to the presidency, Robinson supported Johnson's efforts to secure passage of the Civil Rights Act of 1964. He was angered by the opposition of some Republicans to the legislation.

Robinson was more in line with the policies of New York governor Nelson Rockefeller, becoming one of six national directors for his presidential run in 1964. Robinson was dead set against Senator Barry Goldwater of Arizona, arguing that Goldwater reeked of prejudice and bigotry. In Robinson's autobiography he recalled the following of the 1964 GOP convention: "As I watched this steamroller operation in San Francisco, I had a better understanding of what it must have felt [like] to be a Jew in Hitler's Germany." In a column titled "I Would Love to Be a Republican but Barry Goldwater Is a Bigot," Robinson wrote that he shuddered "at the thought of the Goldwater–Bill Buckley conservatism being allowed to capture the Republican Party. The far-out, right-wing kooks, goons, and bigots who constitute a frightening segment of the pro-Goldwater offensive would sign the death warrant [of the party of Lincoln]. . . . I admit freely that I think, live, and breathe black first and foremost." He explained that was one of the reasons he was so committed to Rockefeller. When Goldwater won the Republican nomination for president, Robinson warned that the GOP was becoming a "white man's party" and supported Lyndon Johnson. In 1966 he became a special assistant for community affairs to Governor Rockefeller.

In the 1968 election Robinson called Nixon's nomination "signs of the sick and troubled times. [The nominating convention] was a white folks' affair and the once Grand Old Party's new caretakers, under Richard Nixon, leaned over backwards to give Dixie some Southern Comfort." He warned that if Nixon was elected, "we as Negroes are in serious trouble; we would, in my opinion, be going backward." He supported Hubert H. Humphrey for president.

Robinson couldn't have been happy when President Nixon's counsel in 1969 asked FBI director J. Edgar Hoover to look into Robinson's activities. Hoover responded that Robinson had associated with Communist fronts and had addressed a meeting of the Black Panthers. Nothing came of the investigation. History has proven that Hoover's political investigations often were tainted. It's probable that Robinson didn't even know about the investigation; Nixon's directive wasn't declassified until twelve years after his death.

In 1972 Robinson swung back to Nixon because of shortcomings he saw in his Democratic opponent for president, Senator George McGovern—basically that McGovern was weak in foreign policy. Robinson also tended to let bygones be bygones in his hopes of seeing improvement in African American chances of achieving the American Dream during a Nixon administration.

Five years after he retired, Robinson became eligible for selection to the Baseball Hall of Fame. Speculation ran high about whether he would be elected on the first ballot because, as he put it, his "fiery temper" made him a "much hated player." Robinson said he would be thrilled if he were selected, but "I'd like to make it perfectly clear that I do not think I deserve rejection either, simply because I directed my 'fiery temper' against violations of my personal dignity and civil rights and the civil rights of the people for whom I have such deep concern."

Sportswriters vote on Hall of Fame candidates, and Robinson needed 75 percent of those voting to get into the Hall. Robinson told sportswriters that when considering his candidacy, they should consider only his ability on the playing field. When the ballots were counted, he was four votes over the required minimum, the first player to be selected in the first year of eligibility since the inaugural players at the beginning of the Hall of Fame in 1936. It had been six years since the last player had been inducted. "I am so grateful," Robinson told the press. "I have had a lot of wonderful things happen to me in my life. . . . But to make the Hall of Fame on the first go-around, where do you put that on the list?" Among the crowd attending the induction was the five-member family of George Brown, a retired mail carrier. Brown had driven the family 240 miles from Boston. They slept in their car the night before the induction. "I was at Braves Field when Jackie played his first game there in 1947," Brown said. "Wheelchair and crutches couldn't have stopped this old mailman from being here today."

Robinson was selected along with former Cleveland pitching

great Bob Feller, who had once predicted that Jackie's "football shoulders" would keep him from hitting big league pitching. But Robinson held no grudges. He told Feller that he was pleased they were going into the Hall together.

At the induction Robinson set aside his bad memories and focused on the good ones. In his speech he said about his baseball career that "everything is complete." He went on to say that he would not be at Cooperstown without the help of his wife Rachel, his mother Mallie, and Branch Rickey, calling them "three of the most wonderful people that I know." Not long after the induction Robinson wrote to Rickey, telling him how inadequate he had felt expressing his feelings toward him. "I owe much to you, not because you brought me into baseball as the first—but because your life has been such an inspiration to me. I am a better man for having had the rich years of association with you."

Robinson's Hall of Fame plaque granted his wish that he be recognized only for his efforts on the field. It contained only his playing statistics. That plaque remained until 2008, when it was updated with the following to reflect his efforts to integrate baseball: "Displayed Tremendous Courage and Poise in 1947 When He Integrated the Modern Major Leagues in the Face of Intense Adversity." Jane Forbes Clark, board chairman of the Hall of Fame, remarked, "There's no person more central and more important to the history of baseball, for his pioneering ways, than Jackie Robinson. Today, his impact is not fully defined without mention of his extreme courage in crossing baseball's color line. We are proud of the changes we have made."

The next year Robinson and heavyweight boxer Floyd Patterson traveled to Birmingham, Alabama, to support demonstrators led by Reverend King seeking desegregation and an end to the brutality of Police Chief Bull Connor's forces. Robinson was shocked by what he saw and reflected that just a few short months ago he had been honored in Cooperstown, but in Birmingham he was "that negrah who pokes his nose into other peoples' pudding.'"

Between 1965 and 1972 Robinson dabbled in the sports world. He became an analyst for ABC's *Major League Game of the Week*, a first for an African American; he was hired as general manager of the soon-to-fail Brooklyn Dodgers of the Continental Football League; and he was a commentator on Montreal Expos telecasts. He also found time to start up a construction company to build housing for low-income families. "Jack finally found the business opportunity he had been searching for since leaving baseball a decade earlier," said his wife Rachel. After he died, Rachel took over as president of the corporation, which eventually saw the construction of more than sixteen hundred housing units.

Toward the end of his life, Robinson was heavily burdened by his troubled son, Jackie Robinson Jr., who had emotional problems as a youngster and was put in special education classes. He left high school without graduating to join the army and while in Vietnam was wounded on November 19, 1965. He came home with a deep drug addiction that led him to a treatment program that he successfully completed. He became a drug counselor after being clean for three years. On June 17, 1971, after working a long shift Jackie Jr. was killed in an auto accident on his way home. He was twenty-four years old. The tragic death was a setback for Robinson, who was in declining health. He had aged beyond his years, was almost blind, and was barely able to walk. He slowly began slipping away.

Robinson turned down requests to appear in old-timers' games or other ceremonies over the years, but he agreed to visit Dodger Stadium on June 4, 1972, the day his number was retired. It was difficult physically for Robinson to attend. He had suffered a recent heart attack, his diabetes was worsening, he was blind in one eye, and he was almost obese. He walked with a slow shuffle, like a man close to his nineties. But his mind and his passions were still strong.

The Dodgers could honor him by retiring his number, but if they expected him to return the favor, they were sadly mistaken, wrote sportswriter Ron Rapoport, who interviewed him that day. "Baseball and Jackie Robinson haven't had much to say to each other," Robinson told him. "I told Peter [O'Malley, Dodgers president and Walter O'Malley's son] I was disturbed at the way baseball treats its black players after their playing days are through. It's hard to look at a sport which black athletes have virtually saved and when a managerial job opens they give it to a guy who's failed in other areas because he's white." As for the retirement of his number Robinson remarked,

> [I] couldn't care less if someone is out there wearing 42 It is an honor, but I get more of a thrill knowing there are people in baseball who believe in advancement based on ability. I'm more concerned about what I think about myself than what other people think. I think if you look back at why people think of me the way they do it's because white America doesn't like a black guy who stands up for what he believes. I don't feel baseball owes me a thing and I don't owe baseball a thing. I am glad I haven't had to go to baseball on my knees.

Robinson made one final public appearance, on October 15, 1972. He threw out the first pitch before Game 2 of the World Series. He was presented with a plaque honoring the twenty-fifth anniversary of his integrating baseball. Nine days later, on October 24, Robinson was preparing to travel to Washington DC to lobby for a housing bill. He was going to tell Congress that integrated schools were fine, but if housing was bad, little was gained. Children were going to hang out on the streets and get in trouble, he believed. Just as he was ready to leave, Robinson suffered a fatal heart attack at his Stamford, Connecticut, home. He was fifty-three years old. Irving Rudd, one-time publicist for the Brooklyn Dodgers, said, "I am certain that Jackie's forced cool during those first seasons in Brooklyn cost him a couple of decades of his life."

More than twenty-five hundred people jammed into Riverside Church on Manhattan's Upper West Side for the funeral, and thousands more lined the streets to watch the passage of his mile-long funeral procession through Harlem and Bedford-Stuyvesant, predominantly black neighborhoods. Pallbearers were Boston Celtics star Bill Russell and Dodgers teammates Don Newcombe, Joe Black, Junior Gilliam, Pee Wee Reese, and Ralph Branca. Thirty-one-year-old Jesse Jackson gave the eulogy. In part he said, "When Jackie took the field, something within us reminded us of our birthright to be free. . . . In his last dash Jackie stole home and Jackie is safe." Robinson was buried in Cyprus Hill Cemetery in Brooklyn. His wife Rachel, son David, and daughter Sharon survived him.

Shortly after his death Robinson's ordeals and accomplishments were the subject of a Broadway musical, *The First*. In 1987, on the fortieth anniversary of his breaking of the color barrier, the Rookie of the Year Award was redesignated as the Jackie Robinson Award. On the fiftieth anniversary of his debut, his number 42 was permanently retired by all Major League teams, although current Major Leaguers already wearing the number were allowed to keep it for the remainder of their careers. The last player with that number, Mariano Rivera, retired after the 2013 season.

In a tribute to Robinson, *Sports Illustrated* writer Ralph Wiley wrote the following:

> Jackie Robinson's life was built around service to an idea, an ideal or a cause. He was always at the service of someone or something: UCLA, the U.S. Army, the Dodgers, the Republican Party, Branch Rickey, the NAACP. He was a champion that way to all people, not just blacks. He was a combination of the times he lived in and the fire that burned inside him. There has never been anyone quite like him. He burned with such intensity and needed a cause to direct it into. He was perfect for a cause. He needed to impact society through his efforts. He was addicted to competition and service, and I think it cost him his health. He was so driven to perform at a certain level to be a champion for his people. The lesson is that the brightest star often has the shortest life.

Their Legacy

"A life is not important except in the
impact it has on other lives."

—Carved on Jackie Robinson's gravestone

The common legacy of the five superb athletes and their remarkable lives is that they broke color barriers or improved racial relations or both. They accomplished these feats in the same way, with a "go along to get along" philosophy. Jackie Robinson was no exception, even though his turn-the-other-cheek approach lasted only two years. If he had disregarded Rickey's advice for the first two years in the Major Leagues, it seems unlikely he would have succeeded. As the *Los Angeles Times* put it in Tom Bradley's obituary, Bradley subscribed to his "membership in the generation of American blacks who cracked the color line and, in doing so, were counseled to hide their hurts and resentments from a hostile white world." Their black skin had to be thick.

To recap: Robinson integrated baseball; Washington took down barriers in football; Strode did likewise in football, wrestling, and film; and Bradley and Bartlett opened doors in politics and civic affairs. Dr. Martin Luther King once remarked that "the arc of the universe is long, but it bends toward justice." All five of these gentlemen surely lent their hands in bending that arc.

Jim Murray, the Pulitzer Prize–winning sportswriter of the *Los Angeles Times*, called Robinson, Washington, and Strode pioneers, "individuals who fought for African American rights in a day when it was a fight in the dark, when the support system was not forthcoming. They ministered to group esteem on the field and battled for it off the field. They made their country a better place. For everybody." The same held true for Bradley and Bartlett.

What would Robinson say about his legacy today if he were alive? He told *Los Angeles Times* sportswriter Ron Rapoport the following just before he died in 1972: "I honestly believe that baseball did set the stage for many things that are happening today and I'm proud to have played a part in it. But I'm not subservient to it."

Robinson's efforts on and off the field brought racial equality with changes broader than in just the political arena. Dr. King believed that Robinson was "a legend and a symbol in his own time" and that he had "challenged the dark skies of intolerance and frustration." According to historian Doris Kearns Goodwin, Robinson's "efforts were a monumental step in the civil-rights revolution in America. . . . Jackie's accomplishments allowed black and white Americans to be more respectful and open to one another and more appreciative of everyone's abilities." Lester Rodney, the longtime sportswriter for the *Daily Worker*, wrote that Robinson's breaking of the color barrier "has to be the single most heroic act ever performed in the history of sports in this country. I think I can say that. He made a real difference in America."

Robinson stressed that baseball was just part of his life and that he had other challenges to meet for a life fully lived. "If I had a room jammed with trophies, awards, and citations, and a child of mine came to me into that room and asked what I had done in defense of black people and decent whites fighting for freedom—and I had to tell that child I had kept quiet, that I had been timid, I would have to mark myself a total failure in the whole business of living." Close friends like Dodgers teammate Don Newcombe and civil rights activist Dr. King believed that Robinson helped start the civil rights movement. "In those days, there was no Civil Rights Movement. People like Martin Luther King were too young then," Newcombe said. King said Robinson forced people to confront the possibility of change: "Back in the days when integration wasn't fashionable, [Robinson] underwent the trauma and humiliation and the loneliness which comes with being a pilgrim walking the lonesome byways toward the high road of freedom."

Robinson changed issues, but he also changed lives. Dr. King told Newcombe, "Jackie Robinson made it possible for me in the first place. Without him, I would never have been able to do what I did." Red Barber, the sports broadcaster when Robinson debuted with the Dodgers, didn't grasp the idea of desegregation of baseball right away. A Southerner, Barber admitted the idea "tortured me. I set out to do self-examination. I attempted to find out who I was. I know that if have achieved any understanding and tolerance in my life . . . it all stems from this. I thank Jackie Robinson. He did far more for me than I did for him."

Perhaps a not so flattering legacy is that Robinson has been called the most hated man in baseball. *Bleacher Report*'s Brandon McClintock in 2011 named him one of the fifty most hated players, but if Robinson were alive today, he no doubt would not have cared. He wanted respect and didn't care whether he was liked. He was so hated because he integrated baseball and was outspoken on such issues as the failure of some teams to use black players or hire African Americans to manage teams and operate in executive offices. It goes without saying that he certainly wasn't hated by fans of his race but by the whites who rejected his place in baseball lore. Branch Rickey was right; too many white people thought he was an "uppity nigger."

After Robinson's death, his widow, Rachel, established the Jackie Robinson Foundation, of which she remains an officer as of 2015 at age ninety-three. Since it began in 1973, the foundation has granted $65 million in college scholarships to 1,450 minorities; their graduation rate has been 98 percent. Nearly four thousand high school seniors apply annually for the scholarships, which can be as much as $24,000 for four years. In addition, the foundation has in place a

forty-two-point strategy to help students succeed, a job and intern-
ment placement program, and a requirement of mandatory community service. The class of 2016 had fifty-seven scholars.

The foundation also has been working to build a museum devoted
to Robinson in New York City. The foundation's goal was to raise
$42 million to cover construction, opening costs, and an operat-
ing endowment. Fund raising, however, was slowed by recession,
and the opening has been delayed several times. Plans call for the
museum to occupy 18,500 square feet on two floors of One Hudson
Square in Lower Manhattan, just blocks from the Freedom Tower
and the 9/11 Memorial. The space will also house the foundation.
Two galleries, a seventy-five-seat theater, and interactive stations
for visitors are in the plans.

Robinson accumulated dozens of honors before and after his death.
The following are just a few of the most significant honors. In 1999
he was named by *Time* magazine on its list of the one hundred most
influential people of the twentieth century. He also ranked number
forty-four on *The Sporting News* list of baseball's one hundred greatest players. Robinson reaped dozens of honors outside of baseball as
well. In 1956 he was the first athlete to receive the NAACP's Spring-
arn Medal "in recognition of his superb sportsmanship, his pioneer
role in opening up a new field of endeavor for young Negroes, and
his civic consciousness." Posthumously Robinson was awarded the
Presidential Medal of Freedom by President Ronald Reagan on
March 26, 1984, and the Congressional Gold Medal by President
George W. Bush on March 2, 2005; the Congressional Gold Medal
is the highest civilian award bestowed by Congress.

Several buildings have been named in Robinson's honor. The
UCLA Bruins' baseball team plays in Jackie Robinson Stadium, which
features a memorial statue of Robinson. City Island Ballpark in
Daytona Beach, Florida, was renamed Jackie Robinson Ballpark in
1990, and a statue of Robinson with two children stands in front of
the ballpark. The New York public school system has named a middle school after Robinson. A ten-mile stretch of Georgia Highway

83 outside Robinson's hometown of Cairo has been renamed the Jackie Robinson Memorial Highway.

A tribute to Robinson plays a prominent role in the Smithsonian National Museum of African American History and Culture, which opened in the fall of 2016. The museum will feature a 5,500-square-foot sports exhibition with a baseball gallery. The gallery devotes space to Jackie Robinson and the importance of the integration of the game. Another section highlights game changers—people, places, and institutions that have transformed sports or the larger society or both. One of the seventeen game changers is Jackie Robinson. Within his display there are three story lines: his role in the integration of baseball, his civil rights activism, and an examination of how he may have been the most hated man in baseball by the time he retired. The exhibition has six life-sized statues, one of which will be of Robinson.

Often described as a man of quiet determination, Tom Bradley "spent a lifetime bridging racial barriers and used his skills to forge extraordinary coalitions, most notably between blacks and Jews and between labor and business," his legacy foundation at UCLA has written. "He presided over a period of enormous growth in Los Angeles, leaving the gleaming downtown skyline of Bunker Hill and the start of a subway and light-rail system as the most tangible of his legacies." California state historian emeritus Kevin Starr called Bradley "a very great public figure. I know of no one with a greater gift for reconciliation and healing. He was a prism through which we can see both the rise of Los Angeles as an international city and the reemergence of a vibrant black community that reaches back to the very beginnings of the Pueblo. . . . His mayoralty was a time in which Los Angeles reconfigured itself, redefined itself."

Although Bradley lost two races for governor when victories would have built even more onto his legacy, he will always be known for "the Bradley Effect," the theory of discrepancies between voter opinion polls and election outcomes when a white candidate and a non-white candidate run against each other.

Bradley's legacy helped set the pace for Barack Obama's election as president in 2008. Lyn Goldfarb, who co-wrote (with Alison Sotomayor) the documentary *Bridging the Divide*, noted that Bradley's career led to Obama's victory: "Tom Bradley laid the foundation for the kind of coalition politics that allowed President Obama to be elected. When he won [the mayoral election] in 1973, his victory enabled other candidates or potential candidates from around the country to see that, yes, it can be done." In 2005 Antonio Villaraigosa, the first Hispanic mayor in modern times, said during his victory celebration, "I am standing here on the shoulders of Tom Bradley."

In 1993 Bradley participated in the formation of the Tom Bradley Legacy Foundation, headquartered in a hall bearing his name on the UCLA campus. The foundation sponsors, encourages, and facilitates scholarships for disadvantaged youths, particularly those in the inner city. According to its website, "[The foundation] continues [Bradley's] vision to bring together individuals from all of the fragmented communities to work as one in continuing his vision for Los Angeles. The foundation focuses on the youth of today to help build the leadership for the future."

Woody Strode's legacy is locked solidly in the sports and entertainment worlds. While his impact may not have been as great as Robinson's or Bradley's, it is spread across a visible part of America's culture. Although his career in the NFL was an afterthought to Kenny Washington's and was short-lived, he left his mark on the league with his integration of it.

Here's how Strode saw his career: "See, I was always opening doors never knowing what I'd find on the other side. One hundred years from today they'll look at all this and say, 'Shit man, this guy did all this stuff before anybody did anything.' I never thought of it like that. I was just trying to make a living, just trying to survive in my generation."

Sports historians have overlooked the fact that Strode was one of the first popular African Americans to climb into the pro wrestling ring with the likes of Gorgeous George, who was considered to be the No. 1 villain in the golden age of the sport. Strode played the good guy, right down to his white trunks, who gets roughed up by the bad dude in this immensely popular event. Moreover, Strode's film roles were groundbreaking at a time when blacks played subservient roles like butlers or lackies whose main lines were "Okay boss" or "Yessuh." He was a good actor who brought more to the screen than his chiseled good looks and statuesque physique.

Author Terence Towles Canote described it best about Strode's acting:

> While Woody Strode spent much of his career playing bit parts and he never played a lead role in a Hollywood film, he was still a pioneer among African American actors. In the Fifties, when many African American actors were still playing somewhat stereotypical house servants, Woody Strode was playing the King of Ethiopia, a gladiator in the Roman Republic, and a private in the United States Army. Very few of the roles played by Woody Strode could be considered stereotypes. In fact, more often than not Mr. Strode played intelligent, strong willed, independent characters. And while many of his appearances in films could be measured only in minutes, he was obviously a talented actor. Even when his character was only on screen briefly, Woody Strode could deliver a strong performance. In playing roles that were not stereotypes and giving good performances while doing so, Woody Strode helped break down barriers in Hollywood. Quite simply, it was Woody Strode who paved the way for such African American action heroes as Wesley Snipes, Ving Rhames, and Samuel L. Jackson.

Strode was inducted into the Stuntmen's Hall of Fame despite not being a member of the Stuntmen's Association. "All the old-timers know the stuff I've done in the movies," Strode said. A California legislator, Cheryl Brown, was campaigning in 2015 to have Strode included in the State Hall of Fame. Backers include Clint Eastwood and Kirk Douglas.

Strode's son Kalai, a writer and scholar who died in 2014, once summed up Strode's life and legacy as follows:

He was sincere, honest, and optimistic. He was a good role model, not to me only, not to all African Americans only either, but to all Americans. He overcame more obstacles then we could imagine, and did it with grace and integrity. . . . I wish he could have lived long enough to see an African American elected as president of the United States. I believe his legacy laid a foundation for that, and for all other minorities who have tried to crack the glass ceiling of racial discrimination. He was a very good man.

Many have claimed that Kenny Washington could have been the best professional football player who ever lived, but by the time he integrated the NFL, his body was worn down by years on the gridiron. Yet he continued to perform admirably. Nonetheless, he has never received much support for induction into the Pro Football Hall of Fame. In 2011 Jim Tunney, former longtime referee and Lincoln High administrator in Los Angeles whose father once coached Washington there, noted, "[Washington] wasn't in the NFL long enough, so he just faded out of sight. And now nobody knows what to do with him." Said his granddaughter Kysa Washington, "You would think there should be some sort of shrine to him somewhere, but there's barely a mention of him anywhere."

Washington deserves to be in the Pro Football Hall of Fame not only because he integrated the NFL, but also for his performance on the field. His career included playing in the Pacific Coast Football League, and that should be considered. After all the Hall is not the NFL Hall of Fame, it's the *pro* Hall, and Washington dominated the Pacific Coast League for four years.

There's a movement afoot to gain Washington access to the Hall. Two of the four players who broke the barrier at the same time as Washington, Bill Willis and Marion Motley, are in the Hall. Their careers reflect that honor. (Strode was an afterthought in joining the Rams with Washington, and he played just a little more than a single season, although he also played in the coast league and in Canada.)

Adam Rank, an NFL media writer, has been a strong booster of

Washington's induction into the Hall of Fame. He wrote the following in 2014:

> There is some vague recollection of Washington throughout the
> league. Some might nod when they hear the name. Others might
> refer to him as the "Jackie Robinson of the NFL." Which is quite
> an amazing feat if you consider the fact that Washington broke
> the color barrier in the modern NFL a full year before Robin-
> son played for the Brooklyn Dodgers on April 15, 1947. And yet
> we don't honor Washington. The Rams haven't even retired his
> number. It is time for us to rectify that. It should start and finish
> with the Pro Football Hall of Fame. . . . Not only is Washington's
> exclusion in the Pro Football Hall of Fame egregious, it also goes
> against the core values of the Pro Football Hall of Fame itself.

Rank wrote that too often excellence is confused with statistics:

> But what Washington accomplished cannot be measured in yards
> and statistics. Washington played just three seasons for the Los
> Angeles Rams, but his legacy has stood for a lifetime. In fact, it
> still endures today. In a league where the overwhelming major-
> ity of players are African American, you can't deny what he has
> meant to the league. What he did can be measured in rushing titles
> and Pro Bowls bids, but not those in his name directly. Instead,
> his accomplishments come from those who are given an oppor-
> tunity today because of what Washington did years ago.

Being left out of the Hall of Fame doesn't take away from Washington's legacy in the least. His contribution to integrating the NFL
is beyond doubt. In many ways he was subjected to the same indignities on the field as Robinson, many of which were lost in the noise
and violence of the game. He always turned the other cheek throughout his brief career. What endures for Kenny Washington is what
came in his wake.

"He was a very proud man that worked extremely hard," his
grandson Kirk Washington said. "He was very competitive and
he wanted to make sure that his career meant something not only

from a football standpoint, but he wanted to conduct himself with integrity and high character and I think that in anything he did, he wanted to make sure people saw him that way. He was a hard-nosed guy, he was tough but he still had something about him where he wanted people to see a man setting an example by doing the right thing at all times."

The Kenny Washington Stadium Foundation was established in 2010 in an effort to help secure his place in history. The foundation is raising funds for a major renovation and improvement of the athletic facilities at Lincoln High, where Washington went to high school. It will be named in Washington's honor. The foundation also is stepping up efforts to get Washington into the Pro Football Hall of Fame. Lincoln High has given the football team's MVP award for him, even using the original trophy the Rams awarded Washington when he retired in 1949. His name also appears on a perpetual trophy given to the UCLA Bruin Offensive Player of the Year and also on an award presented annually by the National Football League Players Association.

Ray Bartlett's legacy may not be as strong as that of his teammates, but he also lived a truly extraordinary life that arose from humble beginnings. He is one of sixteen Pasadena Community College athletes whose likenesses are immortalized with bronze busts in the school's Court of Champions. Bartlett also is a member of the school's Sports Hall of Fame and the California Community College Athletic Association Hall of Fame. In addition, he has been chosen as one of the college's seventy-five Distinguished Alumni, simply as a "public servant." In 2008 Los Angeles County Supervisor Michael Antonovich called Bartlett "a friend and supporter who served our county and our nation with honor and integrity. He was a trailblazer in sports, law enforcement, the military and public service."

NOTES

Introduction

xi   "Three African American players": http://magazine.ucla.edu/depts /quicktakes/playing_for_posterity/, accessed November 22, 2015.

xii   "We have yet to find another single coach": *Chicago Defender*, December 16, 1939; cited in Demas, "On the Threshold," 97.

xii   "We were a tough group": Strode and Young, *Goal Dust*, 93.

xii   As Edwin Bancroft Henderson wrote: Excerpted in Wiggins and Miller, *The Unlevel Playing Field*, 188.

xii   UCLA sought the best players: Strode and Young, *Goal Dust*, 26, 31.

xiii   The USC Trojans didn't want them: Strode and Young, *Goal Dust*, 62.

xiii   "We couldn't play in Texas": B. J. Violett, "Teammates Recall Jackie Robinson's Legacy," UCLA *Today*, April 25, 1997.

xiii   "Whatever racial pressure was coming down": Strode and Young, *Goal Dust*, 35.

xiii   Said the Bruins' graduate manager Bill Ackerman: Ackerman, *My Fifty Year Love-in at* UCLA, 155.

xiii   They received lucrative benefits: Strode and Young, *Goal Dust*, 32.

xiii   Ralph Bunche: http://www.nobelprize.org/nobel_prizes/peace/laureates/1950 /bunche-bio.html, accessed February 15, 2013.

xiv   UCLA graduate James LuValle: http://www.blackpast.org/?q=aah/lu-valle -james-e-1912–1993, accessed June 15, 2013.

xiv   Perhaps none of these athletes: http://www.theatlantic.com/entertainment/archive/2013/04/the-real-story-of-baseballs-integration-that-you-wont -see-in-i-42-i/274886/, accessed August 17, 2013.

Prologue

1   "The Negroes who migrated": Strode and Young, *Goal Dust*, 10.

1   Undoubtedly they bought into the belief: Cited in Sides, *L.A. City Limits*, 11

1 **Such praise was coupled with comments:** http://www.blackpast.org /?q=aaw/edmonds-jefferson-l-1845-1914, accessed January 2, 2013. See also Flamming, *Bound for Freedom*, 51.

2 **In 1910 almost 36 percent:** Sides, *L.A. City Limits*, 16.

2 **"Only a few years ago":** Cited in Sides, *L.A. City Limits*, 11.

2 **As George Beavers Jr. put it:** Flamming, *Bound for Freedom*, 49.

2 **"The boomtown atmosphere of Los Angeles":** Sonenshein, *Politics in Black and White*, 26.

2 **In 1900 the black population made up 2.1 percent:** Census data cited in Sonenshein, *Politics in Black and White*, 22.

2 **Of the fifty thousand African Americans in Los Angeles:** *Los Angeles Times*, May 31, 1931.

3 **As a writer:** Federal Writers Project of the Works Progress Administration, *Los Angeles in the 1930s*, 4.

3 **White Southerners also were moving to Los Angeles:** Flamming, *Bound for Freedom*, 4–5.

3 **If attaining a good job:** *Los Angeles Times*, May 31, 1931.

3 **Eighty-seven percent of black women:** Sides, *L.A. City Limits*, 26.

3 **One bright spot:** Flamming, *Bound for Freedom*, 77.

3 **African Americans did find better schools:** *Los Angeles Times*, May 31, 1931.

4 **The growing African American population:** Sonenshein, *Politics in Black and White*, 26–27.

4 **Jackie Robinson's widow, Rachel:** R. Robinson with Daniels, *Jackie Robinson*, 24.

4 **During hot spells:** *Washington Post*, August 21, 1948.

4 **Although forbidden to do so by state law:** *Los Angeles Times*, May 31, 1931.

4 **Woody Strode called the racism "very subtle":** Strode and Young, *Goal Dust*, 11.

4 **"That's when our life was most vulnerable":** Strode and Young, *Goal Dust*, 21.

5 **The white population in Los Angeles:** Sonenshein, *Politics in Black and White*, 27.

5 **Communities like Inglewood:** Strode and Young, *Goal Dust*, 11.

5 **"Housing discrimination":** Sonenshein, *Politics in Black and White*, 28.

5 **And the Ku Klux Klan operated in the mid-1920s:** Strode and Young, *Goal Dust*, 10.

1. No Bed of Roses in Pasadena

7 **"If you poor Georgians":** Rowan with Robinson, *Wait Till Next Year*, 20.

7 **Mallie Robinson:** Jackie Robinson with Duckett, *I Never Had It Made*, 4.

7 **The Robinsons were living as sharecroppers:** Rampersad, *Jackie Robinson*, 11.

7 **Cairo was just "a day's hike":** Jackie Robinson with Duckett, *Baseball Has Done It*, 39.

7 **Robinson would later call living as a sharecropper**: Jackie Robinson with Duckett, *I Never Had It Made,* 3.

8 **But when Jerry left**: Rampersad, *Jackie Robinson,* 15.

8 **Then Mallie's half-brother**: Rowan with Robinson, *Wait Till Next Year,* 20.

8 **A family friend**: Rampersad, *Jackie Robinson,* 17.

8 **When Mallie and the others passed through**: Rampersad, *Jackie Robinson,* 18–19.

8 **"What my mother didn't know"**: Allen, *Jackie Robinson,* 19.

8 **Mallie and her children**: Rowan with Robinson, *Wait Till Next Year,* 21.

8 **Mallie then set out to look for a job**: Rampersad, *Jackie Robinson,* 18.

8 **After two years in Pasadena**: Rampersad, *Jackie Robinson,* 19.

9 **The Robinsons were among eleven hundred African Americans**: Rampersad, *Jackie Robinson,* 21.

9 **"Pasadena regarded us as intruders"**: Jackie Robinson with Duckett, *Baseball Has Done It,* 41.

9 **Pasadena residents also were concerned**: *California Eagle,* November 7, 1924; cited in Rampersad, *Jackie Robinson,* 22.

9 **Even though the Robinsons**: Jackie Robinson with Duckett, *I Never Had It Made,* 16–17.

9 **Years later his wife Rachel**: Long, *Beyond Home Plate,* 42.

9 **He recalled that he could**: *Washington Post,* August 23, 1949.

10 **As noted, at times the people Mallie worked for**: Jackie Robinson with Duckett, *Baseball Has Done It,* 41.

10 **"That's why I refused"**: Jackie Robinson with Duckett, *Baseball Has Done It,* 41.

10 **Brother Mack said**: Allen, *Jackie Robinson,* 23.

10 **There was little doubt**: Rampersad, *Jackie Robinson,* 23.

10 **Neighbors tried unsuccessfully**: Jackie Robinson with Duckett, *I Never Had It Made,* 4.

10 **Once Jack's brother Edgar**: Rowan with Robinson, *Wait Till Next Year,* 23.

10 **While Mallie was working**: Rowan with Robinson, *Wait Till Next Year,* 25.

11 **When it was time**: Allen, *Jackie Robinson,* 20, 26.

11 **He was a C student**: Mann, "Say Jack Robinson."

11 **When he was eight**: Jackie Robinson with Duckett, *Baseball Has Done It,* 42–43.

11 **"He was a special little boy"**: Rampersad, *Jackie Robinson,* 27.

11 **At twelve Jack moved**: Rampersad, *Jackie Robinson,* 26–27.

11 **Robinson's widow**: R. Robinson with Daniels, *Jackie Robinson,* 17

11 **They threw dirt clods**: Jackie Robinson with Duckett, *I Never Had It Made,* 6.

11 **"People used to ask"**: Allen, *Jackie Robinson,* 26.

12 **Robinson once confronted a quarterback**: Falkner, *Great Time Coming,* 42.

12 **During this time**: Jackie Robinson with Duckett, *I Never Had It Made,* 7.

12 **Robinson, Ray Bartlett, and their friends**: *Baseball Weekly,* February 26, 1997.

12 **"They weren't out to do trouble"**: Allen, *Jackie Robinson,* 22.

12 **Bartlett was born in Pasadena**: Pasadena City Directories, Pasadena Museum of History.

12 **When his mother told him**: *Los Angeles Times*, June 28, 2008.

12 **Robinson said his mother always maintained her composure**: Rampersad, *Jackie Robinson*, 23.

12 **Eventually the white neighbors began to accept the Robinsons**: Rampersad, *Jackie Robinson*, 24.

13 **Said Bartlett: "I can't think"**: *Baseball Weekly*, February 26, 1997.

13 **Robinson could have become a juvenile delinquent**: Jackie Robinson with Duckett, *I Never Had It Made*, 7.

13 **The other man was the Reverend Karl Downs**: Jackie Robinson with Duckett, *I Never Had It Made*, 7–8.

13 **Downs watched Robinson**: Jackie Robinson with Duckett, *Baseball Has Done It*, 42.

13 **Years later Rachel Robinson**: *Abilene, Texas, Reporter-News*, February 25, 2008.

13 **Strode was born in Los Angeles**: Strode and Young, *Goal Dust*, 1–3.

14 **"Well, I had to get rid of that title"**: Strode and Young, *Goal Dust*, 1.

14 **It was this upbringing**: Strode and Young, *Goal Dust*, 7, 12.

15 **Strode remembers playing in the Los Angeles River**: Strode and Young, *Goal Dust*, 18–19.

2. The Kingfish and Woody

16 **"The two finest football players"**: Strode and Young, *Goal Dust*, 59.

16 **Today Lincoln Heights**: http://projects.latimes.com/mapping-la/neighborhoods/neighborhood/lincoln-heights, accessed December 2, 2015.

16 **When Woody Strode met Kenny**: Strode and Young, *Goal Dust*, 50.

16 **Los Angeles Times sports columnist Jim Murray**: *Los Angeles Times*, August 6, 1961.

16 **Many of the men who lived in Lincoln Heights**: Strode and Young, *Goal Dust*, 51–53.

16 **Washington's grandparents**: Strode and Young, *Goal Dust*, 52.

17 **From 1919 to 1961**: http://www.imdb.com/name/nm0913405/bio, accessed December 1, 2015.

17 **Blue was making seventy-five dollars a day**: Strode and Young, *Goal Dust*, 53.

17 **He also earned a living boxing**: http://sabr.org/bioproj/person/b347deac, accessed June 10, 2014.

17 **Said Strode, "Athletically, Blue had the ability"**: Strode and Young, *Goal Dust*, 53.

18 **The Oregonian newspaper in Portland**: Cited in http://sabr.org/bioproj/person/b347deac.

18 **If grandmother Susie Washington was the woman**: Strode and Young, *Goal Dust*, 54–56.

18 **Rocky's wife, Hazel:** http://sabr.org/bioproj/person/b347deac, accessed January 16, 2016.

18 **The Washingtons lived:** http://www.si.com/nfl/2009/10/08/nfl-pioneers, accessed July 22, 2012.

18 **Strode called him the original "Crazylegs":** Strode, *Goal Dust*, 58.

18 **The *Los Angeles Times* described him:** *Los Angeles Times:* November 11, 1940.

19 **The grandson of slaves:** Payne and Ratzan, *Tom Bradley*, 2.

19 **The Bradleys worked:** *Los Angeles Times*, September 30, 1998.

19 **In 1921 the Bradleys gave up:** Payne and Ratzan, *Tom Bradley*, 6, and *Los Angeles Times*, October 18, 1982.

19 **In Somerton, Bradley developed a love of reading:** Payne and Ratzan, *Tom Bradley*, 7.

19 **His mother told him:** Payne and Ratzan, *Tom Bradley*, 8–9.

20 **"She made so many sacrifices":** Payne and Ratzan, *Tom Bradley*, 9.

20 **When Bradley was ten:** James Robinson, *Tom Bradley*, 29.

20 **Bradley's father helped out:** *Los Angeles Times*, October 18, 1982.

20 **As an adult:** Vice President Al Gore's eulogy, http://clinton4.nara.gov/WH/EOP/OVP/speeches/bradley.html, accessed December 2, 2015.

20 **The Bradleys desperately needed help:** *Los Angeles Times*, September 30, 1998.

20 **Although Bradley was close:** *Los Angeles Times*, June 3, 1973.

21 **One day his friend:** *Los Angeles Times*, October 21, 1982.

21 **To his good fortune:** *Los Angeles Times*, October 21, 1982.

21 **It was "one of my most depressing memories":** Payne and Ratzan, *Tom Bradley*, 11–13.

21 **To help with bills:** James Robinson, *Tom Bradley*, 39.

21 **In the junior high years:** Payne and Ratzan, *Tom Bradley*, 15.

22 **"So I quit my job":** *Los Angeles Times*, January 28, 1973.

3. The High School Years

23 **"Yeah, he's good enough":** Strode and Young, *Goal Dust*, 61.

23 **In 1935 Jackie Robinson enrolled:** Rampersad, *Jackie Robinson*, 36.

23 **The following fall:** Rampersad, *Jackie Robinson*, 37.

23 **In 1936 in the conference championship football game:** Jackie Robinson with Duckett, *Baseball Has Done It*, 44–45.

24 **Robinson was winning:** Rampersad, *Jackie Robinson*, 39.

24 **Robinson was getting a reputation:** Rowan with Robinson, *Wait Till Next Year*, 34–35.

24 **Robinson graduated at midyear:** Allen, *Jackie Robinson*, 37.

24 **In addition, Bartlett said:** "Jackie Robinson remembered by friends, family," www.eagleworldnews.com, March 27, 2007, accessed June 6 and 25, 2012.

24 **Across town:** Strode and Young, *Goal Dust*, 23.

25 **Strode sat on the bench:** Strode and Young, *Goal Dust*, 25.

25 **The *Los Angeles Examiner* reporters raved**: Cited in "The NFL's Jackie Robinson," http://www.si.com/vault/2009/10/12/105865272/the-nfls -jackie-robinson, accessed January 1, 2015.

25 **In the offseason**: Strode and Young, *Goal Dust*, 26.

25 **In his autobiography**: Strode and Young, *Goal Dust*, 26, 33.

26 **When Kenny Washington entered**: Strode and Young, *Goal Dust*, 61.

26 **In one game during the championship season**: *Los Angeles Times*, November 2, 1935.

26 **Before the championship game**: *Los Angeles Times*, November 11, 1935.

26 **Against Fremont High**: *Los Angeles Times*, November 26, 1935,

26 **Washington accounted for all but 4 yards**: *Los Angeles Times*, December 12, 1935.

26 **In the spring**: http://kwsfoundation.org/, accessed October 25, 2012.

27 **Washington knew**: Strode and Young, *Goal Dust*, 61–62.

27 **Tom Bradley was perhaps more ambitious**: *Payne and Ratzan, Tom Bradley*, 17.

27 **Nonetheless, he was somewhat of a loner**: James Robinson, *Tom Bradley*, 43.

27 **The other four athletes**: *Los Angeles Times*, June 28, 1973.

28 **He could have chosen**: Payne and Ratzan, *Tom Bradley*, 17–19.

28 **"At that time"**: Bradley, "The Impossible Dream," 25.

28 **Bradley had high expectations**: *Los Angeles Times*, April 24, 1998.

28 **While at Poly**: *Los Angeles Times*, June 3, 1973.

28 **Later Bradley broke another barrier**: Bradley, "The Impossible Dream," 27–28.

29 **"We never knew what Tom was doing"**: James Robinson, *Tom Bradley*, 43.

29 **After Bradley was admitted to Ephebians**: Payne and Ratzan, *Tom Bradley*, 23.

29 **At the same time Bradley was running track**: Bradley, "The Impossible Dream," 30.

29 **It started off by proclaiming**: *Los Angeles Times*, June 15, 1935.

4. The Little Brother

30 **"There is no question"**: Roberts and Bennett, UCLA *Football Vault*, 8

30 **UCLA football got its start**: Springer and Arkush, *60 Years of USC-UCLA Football*, 32–33.

30 **One class had a 17-to-1 ratio**: Ackerman, *My Fifty Year Love-in at UCLA*, 2.

30 **In 1924 the school**: Hamilton and Jackson, UCLA *on the Move*, 92.

30 **Nineteen diehards turned out**: Hamilton and Jackson, UCLA *on the Move*, 170.

31 **The *Los Angeles Times* reported**: Cited in Springer and Arkush, *60 Years of USC-UCLA Football*, 33

31 **In their first game**: Hamilton and Jackson, UCLA *on the Move*, 171–73.

32 **Its desire to shoot for the big time**: Cohane, *Great College Football Coaches*, 185, 188.

32 **At Western State**: http://www.wmubroncos.com/ViewArticle.dbml?
ATCLID=204948425, accessed February 11, 2015.

32 **In another instance**: http://kvm.kvcc.edu/info/museON/museographies
/RACE_issue.pdf, accessed February 11, 2015.

32 **Two years before Spaulding's arrival**: https://thesouthernbranch.wordpress
.com/2014/02/26/uclas-football-immortals-a-new-series-on-this-blog/,
accessed, February 11, 2015.

32 **As Southern Branch coach**: *Los Angeles Times*, May 24, 1925.

32 **He was soft-spoken**: Roberts and Bennett, *UCLA Football Vault*, 17.

33 **Writers for the Works Program**: Federal Writers Project of the Works Progress Administration, *Los Angeles in the 1930s*, 204.

33 **On the first day of practice**: Springer and Arkush, *60 Years of USC-UCLA Football*, 34–35.

33 **"Phew," said Spaulding, "What a track meet."**: Cohane, *Great College Football Coaches*, 186.

33 **The university's goal**: Roberts and Bennett, *UCLA Football Vault*, 17–18.

34 **Perhaps the lack of decent facilities**: Cohane, *Great College Football Coaches*, 184–87.

34 **In 1929, before the Bruins**: Springer and Arkush, *60 Years of USC-UCLA Football*, 41–43.

34 **The results the next year**: Cohane, *Great College Football Coaches*, 188.

34 **PCC schools pummeled the Bruins**: Springer and Arkush, *60 Years of USC-UCLA Football*, 43.

34 **Beginning in 1928 USC and UCLA**: http://en.wikipedia.org/wiki/Los_Angeles
_Memorial_Coliseum, accessed August 12, 2013.

35 **In 1931 UCLA played**: Springer and Arkush, *60 Years of USC-UCLA Football*, 45.

35 **In 1933 the Bruins' record was 6-4-1**: *Los Angeles Times*, October 22, 1933;
cited in Oriard, *King Football*, 298.

35 **In announcing his plans for Storey**: *Los Angeles Times*, September 19, 1933.

35 **Storey's grandson recalled**: https://thesouthernbranch.wordpress.
com/2014/02/26/uclas-football-immortals-a-new-series-on-this-blog/,
accessed February 11, 2015.

35 **By 1935 Spaulding's Bruins had improved enough**: Cohane, *Great College Football Coaches*, 184–85.

36 **Bill Ackerman noted**: Ackerman, *My Fifty Year Love-in at UCLA*, 5.

36 **As Jackie Robinson's biographer Arnold Rampersad pointed out**: Rampersad, *Jackie Robinson*, 67.

36 **Although Tom Bradley grew up**: James Robinson, *Tom Bradley*, 35.

36 **Bradley has said he knew Robinson**: James Robinson, *Tom Bradley*, 35.

36 **Robinson tended not to take part**: dailybruin.com/1997/04/23/a-bruin-for
-all-seasons/, accessed November 10, 2013.

37 **Blacks could not live in Westwood**: Rampersad, *Jackie Robinson*, 67–68.

37 **During the 1940s**: Ackerman, *My Fifty Year Love-in at UCLA*, 61.

37 **Bill Ackerman noted**: Ackerman, *My Fifty Year Love-in at UCLA*, 152–53.

5. Obstacles to Overcome

39 **"Somewhere behind the Sambo masks"**: Oriard, *King Football*, 299.

39 **In 1936 Edwin Bancroft Henderson**: Wiggins and Miller, *The Unlevel Playing Field*, 188.

40 **Virtually all of the black players**: Martin, *Benching Jim Crow*, 29.

40 **The gentleman's agreements**: Wiggins and Miller, *The Unlevel Playing Field*, 191–92.

40 **As Michael Oriard pointed out**: Oriard, *King Football*, 302.

41 **Henderson almost presciently saw**: Wiggins and Miller, *The Unlevel Playing Field*, 190.

41 **African American players**: Wiggins and Miller, *The Unlevel Playing Field*, 188–89.

41 **It was commonplace**: Wiggins and Miller, *The Unlevel Playing Field*, 189.

41 **USC's hostility**: McRae, *Heroes without a Country*, 15.

42 **The Hollywood League**: *Pasadena Post*, September 15, 1936.

42 **Unfortunately that was the pervasive thinking**: Cited in http://www
.americansc.org.uk/Online/walters.htm, accessed December 4, 2015.

6. A Sorry Season

43 **"Simply one of the most"**: http://www.imdb.com/name/nm0834754/bio, accessed, November 23, 2015.

43 **Woody Strode had followed**: Strode and Young, *Goal Dust*, 26, 27, 29.

43 **UCLA officials invited Strode**: Strode and Young, *Goal Dust*, 12.

43 **But he "took one look"**: Strode and Young, *Goal Dust*, 33–34.

44 **Strode almost flunked out**: Strode and Young, *Goal Dust*, 49.

44 **Looking back on his years**: Strode and Young, *Goal Dust*, 26.

44 **"We had the whole melting pot"**: Strode and Young, *Goal Dust*, 35.

45 **In those years freshmen weren't allowed**: Strode and Young, *Goal Dust*, 64–65.

45 **The next year**: Strode and Young, *Goal Dust*, 64–65

45 **Strode said that when he and Washington**: Strode and Young, *Goal Dust*, 253.

46 **Strode was nobody to fool with**: *Los Angeles Times*, March 26, 1991.

46 **Not long before**: Strode and Young, *Goal Dust*, 39.

46 **Once Strode was contacted**: Ackerman, *My Fifty Year Love-in at UCLA*, 155.

46 **They measured him**: Strode and Young, *Goal Dust*, 40.

46 ***Los Angeles Times* columnist Murray wondered**: *Los Angeles Times*, March 26, 1991.

46 **Strode was in training**: Strode and Young, *Goal Dust*, 40.

47 **Washington made his presence felt**: *Pasadena Post*, September 25, 1937; cited in Kaliss, *Everyone's All-Americans*, 103.

47 **The Bruins weren't so fortunate**: *Pasadena Post*, October 7, 1937; cited in Kaliss, *Everyone's All-Americans*, 103.

47 **In a game against the Oregon State University**: *Los Angeles Times*, October 17, 1937.

48 **Murray described Strode's toughness:** *Los Angeles Times*, August 8, 1963.

48 **Strode remembered that during a game:** Strode and Young, *Goal Dust*, 31.

48 **Strode recalled that "we ran into a few problems":** Strode and Young, *Goal Dust*, 65.

48 **But, Strode said:** Strode and Young, *Goal Dust*, 56.

48 **One of the biggest challenges UCLA faced:** Martin, *Benching Jim Crow*, 37.

49 **Bell would have none of that:** *Pittsburgh Courier*, October 29, 1938.

49 **"I don't know how Washington survived":** Springer and Arkush, *60 Years of USC-UCLA Football*, 52.

49 **"It made you sick":** Springer and Arkush, *60 Years of USC-UCLA Football*, 52.

49 **SMU players:** *Pasadena Post*, November 16, 1937; cited in Kaliss, *Everyone's All-Americans*, 100.

49 **Washington said years later:** *Los Angeles Times*, February 12, 1952.

49 **Washington and Strode received their due:** Cited in Smith, *Showdown*, 38.

49 **Several newspapers:** Martin, *Benching Jim Crow*, 38.

49 **The following year Wendell Smith:** *Pittsburgh Courier*, October 29. 1938; cited in Smith, *Showdown*, 38.

50 **On November 27 in a game:** *Los Angeles Times*, November 28, 1937.

50 **During the game:** *Pasadena Post*, November 28, 1937.

50 **Quarterback Ned Mathews:** www.today.ucla.edu/1997/970425teammates-Recall.html, accessed December 2, 2014.

50 **The *Los Angeles Examiner* noted:** *California Eagle*, December 16, 1937; cited in Kaliss, *Everyone's All-Americans*, 107.

50 **Going into the USC game:** Van Leuven, *Touchdown UCLA*, 48–49.

51 **In a preview of the USC game:** Cited in Strode and Young, *Goal Dust*, 67.

51 **Perhaps Washington's greatest game:** Strode and Young, *Goal Dust*, 56.

51 **Washington still found time:** *Los Angeles Times*, December 4, 1937.

51 **The Trojans had limited UCLA:** Cited in Strode and Young, *Goal Dust*, 68.

51 **Down three touchdowns:** *Los Angeles Times*, December 6, 1937.

52 **The distance was verified:** Van Leuven, *Touchdown UCLA*, 50.

52 **Hirshon ran in for the score:** Strode and Young, *Goal Dust*, 69.

52 **Washington had a bazooka:** Strode and Young, *Goal Dust*, 57.

52 **"In the winking of an eye":** *Los Angeles Times*, December 6, 1937.

52 **"I saw the ball coming":** Strode and Young, *Goal Dust*, 70.

52 **Coach Spaulding went to the USC locker room:** Van Leuven, *Touchdown UCLA*, 50–51.

52 **"Naked as a couple of chocolate cherubs":** Cited in Strode and Young, *Goal Dust*, 70.

53 **Rod Dedeaux, who coached USC:** http://www.si.com/nfl/2009/10/08/nfl-pioneers, accessed July 26, 2012.

53 **Strode said Robinson was faster:** Strode and Young, *Goal Dust*, 57.

53 **Washington hit a home run:** *Los Angeles Times*, December 4, 1939.

53 **"If a kid had [Washington's] ability today":** Strode and Young, *Goal Dust*, 56.

53 **"Next to me, Jackie"**: biography.jrank.org/pages/2533/Washington-Kenny
.html, accessed August 8, 2014.

53 **"Kenny's future"**: Strode and Young, *Goal Dust*, 56–57.

7. An Easy Choice

54 **"It just burns me up"**: Rowan with Robinson, *Wait Till Next Year*, 35.

54 **across town in Pasadena**: Rampersad, *Jackie Robinson*, 40–41.

55 **Mack almost didn't make the Olympics**: *Los Angeles Times*, June 12, 1968.

55 **When he returned to Pasadena**: *New York Times*, March 14, 2000.

55 **Mack couldn't find a decent job**: Rampersad, *Jackie Robinson*, 31.

56 **Jackie said that incident broke Mack's spirit**: *Washington Post*, August 21, 1949.

56 **Four years after the Olympics**: *California Eagle*, January 25, 1940; cited in Kaliss, *Everyone's All-Americans*, 152.

56 **After Jack broke the color barrier**: *Los Angeles Times*, June 12, 1968.

56 **While Mack was setting records**: Rampersad, *Jackie Robinson*, 42.

57 **That fall Robinson turned out for football**: Rampersad, *Jackie Robinson*, 45.

57 **At one point the players from Oklahoma refused**: http://cooperstown-
ersincanada.com/2013/04/04/jackie-robinson-couldve-been-a-football
-star/, accessed December 5, 2015.

57 **A boyhood friend of Jackie's**: Falkner, *Great Time Coming*, 44.

57 **When Robinson and Bartlett threatened to quit**: Rampersad, *Jackie Robinson*, 49.

57 **Robinson "was touchy"**: Allen, *Jackie Robinson*, 36.

57 **Bartlett, who also would earn**: http://www.pasadena.edu/about/history
/alumni/bartlett/bartlett1.cfm, accessed August 24, 2013.

58 **From that Robinson learned**: Rampersad, *Jackie Robinson*, 49.

58 **Robinson was clearly going to be**: Falkner, *Great Time Coming*, 45.

58 **At season's end**: Rampersad, *Jackie Robinson*, 46.

58 **While Robinson mixed freely**: Rampersad, *Jackie Robinson*, 48.

58 **Racism was no stranger to basketball**: Rampersad, *Jackie Robinson*, 50.

59 **In a game against the Vikings**: Jackie Robinson with Duckett, *Baseball Has Done It*, 44.

59 **When the final whistle blew**: Rowan with Robinson, *Wait Till Next Year*, 34–35.

59 **The Bulldogs finished third**: *Los Angeles Times*, September 12, 1939.

59 **Robinson and Bartlett almost hated to see**: Falkner, *Great Time Coming*, 51.

60 **Robinson's participation in track**: Rampersad, *Jackie Robinson*, 54.

60 **He had been given three jumps**: *Los Angeles Times*, March 31, 1997.

60 **Jack Gordon, a teammate**: Falkner, *Great Time Coming*, 43.

60 **In those early years**: *Los Angeles Times*, March 31, 1997; Snider, *The Duke of Flatbush*, 25; cited in Falkner, *Great Time Coming*, 43.

60 **In an exhibition game**: Rampersad, *Jackie Robinson*, 55.

61 **He said Robinson could play**: Jackie Robinson with Duckett, *Baseball Has Done It*, 46–47.

61 **Later Herman Hill**: Kahn, *Rickey & Robinson*, 59.

61 **Like Robinson, Bartlett**: http://www.pasadena.edu/about/history/alumni /bartlett/bartlett1.cfm, accessed August 24, 2013.

61 **In his junior college years**: Rampersad, *Jackie Robinson*, 55.

61 **For one game Pasadena traveled to Taft**: Rowan with Robinson, *Wait Till Next Year*, 40.

61 **Jackie had a superb season**: *Los Angeles Times*, February 17, 1939.

62 **Robinson had a sensational game**: *New York Daily News*, April 13, 1997.

62 **Hank Ives, who was called the nation's leading expert**: *New York Daily News*, April 13, 1997.

62 **"Jackie was really pigeon-toed"**: *New York Daily News*, April 13, 1997,

62 **For the season Robinson scored**: G. D. Johnson, *Profiles in Hue*, 277.

62 **Despite Jackie's acceptance**: Rampersad, *Jackie Robinson*, 61.

63 **When Robinson graduated**: Jackie Robinson with Duckett, *Baseball Has Done It*, 45–46.

63 **A Stanford alumnus purportedly offered**: *Ebony*, July 1957; cited in Falkner, *Great Time Coming*, 49.

63 **USC showed some interest**: Rampersad, *Jackie Robinson*, 58.

63 **Woody Strode said USC used its money**: Strode and Young, *Goal Dust*, 26, 28.

63 **Finally Jackie decided**: http://www.pasadena.edu/about/history/alumni /bartlett/bartlett1.cfm, accessed August 24, 2013.

64 **Bartlett joined Robinson**: *Los Angeles Times*, November 21, 1991.

64 **Robinson liked UCLA**: Jackie Robinson with Duckett, *I Never Had It Made*, 10.

64 **"I didn't want to see"**: Rampersad, *Jackie Robinson*, 59.

64 **Jackie liked the opportunity**: Rampersad, *Jackie Robinson*, 58–59.

64 **But first he had to make up classes**: *Los Angeles Times*, February 2, 1939.

64 **Bill Spaulding, now athletic director**: Mann, *The Jackie Robinson Story*, 52.

64 **In those days**: Strode and Young, *Goal Dust*, 77.

64 **Bartlett stayed at PJC**: *Los Angeles Times*, June 30, 1967.

8. Fitting in at UCLA

65 **"The new setting"**: Payne and Ratzan, *Tom Bradley*, 27.

65 **He recalled**: *Los Angeles Times*, April 24, 1998.

65 **He also worked summer jobs**: Bradley, "The Impossible Dream," 38.

65 **One of his best summer jobs**: tombradleylegacy.oprg/personal-biography .html, accessed July 20, 2012.

65 **Bradley wasn't the only athlete**: http://www.tcm.com/this-month /article/333896%7c0/woody-strode-8-5.html, accessed December 6, 2015.

66 **"I didn't take any persuasion"**: Bradley, "The Impossible Dream," 31.

66 **He was recruited**: LuValle, "Dr. James E. LuValle," 32.

66 **After talking with track coaches**: Payne and Ratzan, *Tom Bradley*, 25–26.

66 **Bradley said years later**: Bradley, "The Impossible Dream," 31.

66 **Bradley's long sought-after goal**: Payne and Ratzan, *Tom Bradley*, 27.

66 **Carl McBain, a white hurdler**: *Los Angeles Times*, September 9, 2007.

66 **Bradley commuted**: Payne and Ratzan, *Tom Bradley*, 27.

66 **"I don't know of any blacks"**: Bradley, "The Impossible Dream," 38.

66 **While minorities were accepted**: Morehouse, *Fighting in the Jim Crow Army*, 30.

67 **He became a firefighter**: *Los Angeles Times*, November 14, 2010.

67 **Bradley was convinced**: Bradley, "The Impossible Dream," 36-37.

67 **Bradley and Washington were close**: *Los Angeles Times*, June 28, 1973.

67 **Track was the perfect sport**: *Los Angeles Times*, June 28, 1973.

68 **Bradley joined Kappa Alpha Psi**: Payne and Ratzan, *Tom Bradley*, 28.

68 **Bradley also became a member**: Bradley, "The Impossible Dream," 38.

68 **Bradley and other black members**: Bradley, "The Impossible Dream," 36.

68 **On one trip to Arizona**: Payne and Ratzan, *Tom Bradley*, 29.

68 **Bradley recalled that his teammates**: Bradley, "The Impossible Dream," 36.

68 **When Bradley later became the mayor**: *Los Angeles Times*, June 28, 1973.

69 **Bradley ran track**: *Los Angeles Times*, April 23, 1939.

9. Under-the-Table Help

70 **"When they took me out to Westwood"**: Strode and Young, *Goal Dust*, 33.

70 **Strode revealed**: Strode and Young, *Goal Dust*, 32.

70 **Strode wrote**: Strode and Young, *Goal Dust*, 32.

71 **Strode noted that actor Joe E. Brown**: Strode and Young, *Goal Dust*, 33.

71 **Bradley received an athletic scholarship**: Bradley, "The Impossible Dream," 31.

71 **Alumni and boosters did most of the recruiting**: Rampersad, *Jackie Robinson*, 72, and Campbell and Campbell, "Town and Gown Booksellers Oral History," 211-12.

71 **Bob Campbell remembered Robinson**: Campbell and Campbell, "Town and Gown Booksellers Oral History," 68.

71 **Washington and Strode also worked for the Campbells**: Campbell and Campbell, "Town and Gown Booksellers Oral History," 67.

72 **The help still was forthcoming**: Rampersad, *Jackie Robinson*, 71.

72 **Bartlett believed**: Rampersad, *Jackie Robinson*, 72.

72 **Providing jobs for athletes**: Kemper, *College Football and American Culture in the Cold War Era*, 44.

72 **Because of such inducements**: *Los Angeles Times*, March 27, 1991.

72 **The PCC's Northwest members**: J. W. Johnson, *The Wow Boys*, 85-89.

73 **On January 5, 1940**: Associated Press in the *New York Times*, January 5, 1940.

73 **Atherton singled out UC Berkeley**: United Press in the *Los Angeles Times*, September 3, 1940.

73 **Atherton felt it was unfortunate**: *Los Angeles Times*, September 27, 1940.

73 **Campbell recalled**: Campbell and Campbell, "Town and Gown Booksellers Oral History," 67–69.

73 **As a result of the investigation**: Campbell and Campbell, "Town and Gown Booksellers Oral History," 67–69.

74 **Campbell said all UCLA players stayed in school**: Campbell and Campbell, "Town and Gown Booksellers Oral History," 68.

10. Filling the Coffers

75 **"They came to see Kenny and me play"**: Strode and Young, *Goal Dust*, 62.

75 **Woody Strode remembered**: Strode and Young, *Goal Dust*, 62.

75 **In 1933, partly because of the expenses**: Ackerman, *My Fifty Year Love-in at UCLA*, 282–83.

76 **UCLA fans received a scare**: *Los Angeles Times*, January 21, 1938.

76 **In the first game of the 1938 season**: *Los Angeles Times*, September 24, 1938.

77 **The Bruins traveled to Eugene**: *Los Angeles Times*, October 3, 1938.

77 ***Los Angeles Times* reporter Dyer wrote**: *Los Angeles Times*, October 13, 1938.

77 **Next the Bruins traveled north**: *Los Angeles Times*, October 16, 1938.

78 **In their next game**: *Los Angeles Times*, October 23, 1938.

78 **The Bruins beat Stanford**: *Los Angeles Times*, October 30, 1938.

78 **UCLA traveled to Pullman**: *Los Angeles Times*, November 6, 1938.

78 **UCLA went out of its conference**: *Los Angeles Times*, November 13, 1938.

79 **The two games in Hawaii**: *Honolulu Advertiser*, May 23, 2010.

79 **Spaulding took twenty-five of his favorite players**: Strode and Young, *Goal Dust*, 78.

79 **While attending a luau**: Strode and Young, *Goal Dust*, 78–79.

80 **The Wai brothers**: *Honolulu Advertiser*, May 23, 2010.

11. High Expectations

81 **"Take away the Negro stars"**: *Pasadena Star-News*, November 6, 1939; cited in Demas, *Integrating the Gridiron*, 39.

81 **While he was being hailed**: Rampersad, *Jackie Robinson*, 62–63.

81 **Robinson may have been limiting**: http://cooperstownersincanada.com/2013/04/04/jackie-robinson-couldve-been-a-football-star/, accessed January 31, 2015.

81 **When Robinson enrolled at UCLA**: Falkner, *Great Time Coming*, 51.

81 **Robinson concentrated on his studies**: *California Eagle*, March 9, 1939; cited in Rampersad, *Jackie Robinson*, 63.

81 **During the summer he found time**: *California Eagle*, July 6, 1939; cited in Rampersad, *Jackie Robinson*, 63.

82 **Brother Frank Robinson never got the chance**: Rampersad, *Jackie Robinson*, 64.

82 **Robinson kept busy**: *Los Angeles Times*, February 12, 1990.

82 **Ray Bartlett recalled**: Falkner, *Great Time Coming*, 29.

82 **Robinson found himself in trouble**: *Washington Post*, August 22, 1948.

83 **UCLA wasn't about to let that happen**: Rampersad, *Jackie Robinson*, 65–66.

83 **Newspapers used sports jargon**: Rowan with Robinson, *Wait Till Next Year*, 47–48.

83 **The event hung heavily**: *Washington Post*, August 22, 1949.

84 **The *Chicago Defender* printed**: *Chicago Defender*, September 9, 1939; cited in Kaliss, *Everyone's All-Americans*, 115.

84 **The *California Eagle* noted**: *California Eagle*, September 7, 1939; cited in Kaliss, *Everyone's All-Americans*, 115.

84 **The *Eagle* wrote**: *California Eagle*, September 28, 1939; cited in Kaliss, *Everyone's All-Americans*, 115–116.

84 **A great deal of the excitement**: *Los Angeles Times*, August 27, 1939.

84 **Robinson "was the first"**: Strode and Young, *Goal Dust*, 84.

84 **Coaches were singing**: *Los Angeles Times*, September 20, 1939.

84 **When Robinson joined Washington**: http://www.loumontgomerylegacy .com/whos-lou/university-defies-racial-segregation, accessed June 25, 2012.

85 **Just before the TCU game**: *Los Angeles Times*, September 28, 1939.

85 **Although the Horned Frogs were expected to win**: Rampersad, *Jackie Robinson*, 68.

85 **Robinson handed out some praise**: *California Eagle*, October 3, 1939.

85 **TCU's coach Dutch Meyer**: *Los Angeles Times*, September 30, 1939.

85 **For all the hoopla**: http://www.mocavo.com/California-Eagle-Volume -1941-Novolume-27-Dec-1942-Jan-Aug/633279/285, accessed December 12, 2014.

86 **As Charles H. Martin wrote**: Martin, *Benching Jim Crow*, 48.

12. Disappointing End to the Season

87 **"I guess you've got to have"**: Rowan with Robinson, *Wait Till Next Year*, 52.

87 **Their next opponent**: http://sportspressnw.com/2192490/2014/wayback -machine-history-at-husky-stadium, accessed December 4, 2014.

87 **The UCLA *Daily Bruin***: *Daily Bruin*, October 9, 1939; cited in Rampersad, *Jackie Robinson*, 68.

87 **A *Seattle Times* sportswriter**: http://sportspressnw.com/2192490/2014 /wayback-machine-history-at-husky-stadium, accessed December 4, 2014.

88 **Robinson also caught a 43-yard pass**: Rampersad, *Jackie Robinson*, 69.

88 **One sportswriter could not resist**: http://sportspressnw.com/2192490/2014 /wayback-machine-history-at-husky-stadium, accessed December 4, 2014.

88 **Local newspapers were finally acknowledging**: Strode and Young, *Goal Dust*, 253.

88 ***Los Angeles Times* sportswriter Paul Zimmerman**: *Los Angeles Times*, October 9, 1939.

88 **The *California Eagle***: *California Eagle*, November 2, 1939; cited in Kaliss, *Everyone's All-Americans*, 124–25.

89 **For example, the *Defender* proudly wrote**: *California Eagle*, October 7, 1939; cited in Kaliss, *Everyone's All-Americans*, 122.

89 **Robinson and Washington**: *Los Angeles Examiner*, September 30, 1939; cited in Kaliss, *Everyone's All-Americans*, 122.

89 **The *Daily Bruin* remarked**: *Daily Bruin*, October 9, 1939; cited in Demas, "On the Threshold," 31.

89 **The UCLA *Magazine* wrote**: UCLA *Magazine*, November 10, 1939; cited in Demas, "On the Threshold," 31.

89 **Next up for the Bruins**: *Los Angeles Times*, November 21, 1991.

89 **Said teammate Ned Mathews**: http://newsroom.ucla.edu/stories /970425teammatesRecall, accessed November 21, 2015.

89 **Before the game**: Smith, *Showdown*, 27.

90 **Stanford coach Tiny Thornhill**: Rowan with Robinson, *Wait Till Next Year*, 51.

90 **Robinson bristled**: Rampersad, *Jackie Robinson*, 69.

90 **Coach Horrell defended**: Rowan with Robinson, *Wait Till Next Year*, 49,

90 **One teammate, Buck Gilmore**: *Los Angeles Times*, August 21, 1988.

90 **One juxtaposition of a picture**: *Los Angeles Times*, November 16, 1948.

91 **Bob Hunter of the *Los Angeles Examiner***: Cited in Strode and Young, *Goal Dust*, 65.

91 **Tom Bradley did**: *California Eagle*, November 9, 1939; cited in Kaliss, *Everyone's All-Americans*, 102.

91 **Black players also were called**: *Los Angeles Times*, February 17, 1939.

91 **On at least two occasions**: *Los Angeles Times*, December 1, 1939.

91 **A black newspaper**: *Pittsburgh Courier*, September 9, 1939; cited in Smith, *Showdown*, 37.

91 **Braven Dyer**: *Los Angeles Times*, November 5, 1937; cited in Kaliss, *Everyone's All-Americans*, 103–4.

92 **The highlight of the game**: *Daily Bruin*, April 24, 1997.

92 **Then Robinson was injured**: *Daily Bruin*, November 2, 1939.

92 **Questions arose**: Rampersad, *Jackie Robinson*, 70–71.

92 **The *Los Angeles Examiner* reported**: *Los Angeles Examiner*, November 2, 1939; cited in Kaliss, *Everyone's All-Americans*, 126.

93 **While there were racial overtones**: Strode and Young, *Goal Dust*, 86–87.

93 **Because of Robinson's arrests**: Rampersad, *Jackie Robinson*, 66.

93 **Bill Ackerman, UCLA's athletic director**: Strode and Young, *Goal Dust*, 88–89.

93 **One rumor making the rounds**: Rowan with Robinson, *Wait Till Next Year*, 48.

93 **Robinson may have been upset**: Strode and Young, *Goal Dust*, 89.

94 **The *Chicago Defender* estimated**: *Chicago Defender*, November 11, 1939.

94 **Without Robinson Santa Clara ganged up on Washington**: *Los Angeles Times*, November 21, 1939.

94 Washington played the entire game: *Los Angeles Times*, November 19, 1939.

94 Robinson was back in the lineup: *Los Angeles Times*, November 26, 1939.

94 Robinson was back to full strength: *Daily Bruin*, December 1, 1939.

95 On a final TD drive: *California Eagle*, December 7, 1939.

95 To celebrate homecoming: *California Eagle*, November 30, 1939; cited in Kaliss, *Everyone's All-Americans*, 131, 134.

95 USC students burned the effigies: Strode and Young, *Goal Dust*, 97.

95 Alongside that controversy: *California Eagle*, December 7, 1939.

96 If the Bruins beat USC: *Pasadena Star-News*, November 6, 1939; cited in Demas, "On the Threshold," 94.

96 The *New York Times*'s esteemed sportswriter: *New York Times*, December 12, 1939; cited in Demas, "On the Threshold," 94.

96 There was no chance: *Pasadena Star-News*, November 11, 1939; cited in Demas, "On the Threshold," 94.

96 Danzig asked Tennessee coach Bob "Major" Neyland: *New York Times*, December 9, 1939; cited in Demas, "On the Threshold," 94.

96 Later Danzig, Neyland, and Tennessee supporters: *Knoxville News-Sentinel*, December 6, 1939; cited in Demas, "On the Threshold," 100.

96 The *California Eagle* saw: *California Eagle*, November 9, 1939; cited in Demas, "On the Threshold," 96.

97 The *Pasadena Star-News* wrote: *Pasadena Star-News*, November 6, 1939; cited in Kaliss, *Everyone's All-Americans*, 143.

97 A *Los Angeles Times* columnist speculated: *Los Angeles Times*, November 28, 1939; citied in Kaliss, *Everyone's All-Americans*, 143.

97 The 1939 USC-UCLA game: Wiki, http://en.wikipedia.org/wiki/Victory _Bell_(UCLA-USC), accessed January 11, 2016.

97 A record crowd of 103,303: *Chicago Defender*, December 12, 1939.

97 Sam Lacy, the sports editor: *Afro-American*, November 18, 1939; cited in Kaliss, *Everyone's All-Americans*, 86.

97 If it hadn't been for Robinson: Strode and Young, *Goal Dust*, 101.

98 Coach Horrell said after the game: *Chicago Defender*, November 23, 1939.

98 Horrell pulled Washington: Strode and Young, *Goal Dust*, 104.

98 "I have never been so moved emotionally: *Journal of Sport History* 15, no. 3 (Winter 1988); cited in Smith, *Outside the Pale: The Exclusion of Blacks from the National Football League, 1934–1946*.

98 After the game Horrell was asked: http://www.jewsinsports.org/profile .asp?sport=football&ID=353, accessed November 16, 2015.

98 The *Amsterdam News* of New York: *California Eagle*, November 21, 1939; cited in Kaliss, *Everyone's All-Americans*, 153–54.

99 The next day, when Tennessee was selected: *Amsterdam News*, November 16, 1939; cited in Demas, "On the Threshold," 101.

99 Toastmaster Paul R. Williams: *California Eagle*, November 16, 1939.

99 Coach Horrell attended the banquet: *California Eagle*, November 16, 1939

100 **Washington and Robinson were slighted**: biography.jrank.org/pages/2533 /Washington-Kenny.html, accessed August 22, 2014.

100 **Looking back over the season**: Demas, "On the Threshold," 92.

13. Decision Time

101 **"I guess we realized"**: Strode and Young, *Goal Dust*, 105.

101 **The team, loser of twenty-eight consecutive games**: Rampersad, *Jackie Robinson*, 73.

101 **Johns said Robinson was "a great player"**: *Los Angeles Times*, September 12, 1939.

102 **Robinson was unhappy with the pace**: Linge, *Jackie Robinson*, 25–26.

102 **The change put an end to the losing streak**: *Los Angeles Times*, March 2, 1940.

102 **But Price left Robinson off his all-conference team**: Rampersad, *Jackie Robinson*, 72

102 **Shav Glick, a reporter**: *New York Daily News*, April 13, 1997.

102 **About Luisetti, Robinson remarked**: Mann, "Say Jack Robinson."

102 **Coach Johns became Robinson's biggest booster**: Mann, *The Jackie Robinson Story*, 59.

103 **No sooner was basketball season over**: Rampersad, *Jackie Robinson*, 74.

103 **Booster Bob Campbell remembered**: Campbell and Campbell, "Town and Gown Booksellers Oral History," 213.

103 **Robinson told sportswriter Roger Kahn**: Kahn, *Rickey & Robinson*, 100.

103 **Despite his errors**: *Daily Bruin*, April 24, 1997.

103 **Nonetheless, the sports editor**: Tygiel, *Baseball's Great Experiment*, 60.

104 **Carl McBain, a hurdler**: *Los Angeles Times*, September 3, 2007.

104 ***Daily Bruin* sportswriter Milt Cohen**: *Daily Bruin*, May 15, 1940.

104 **The summer of 1940**: Bradley, "The Impossible Dream," 39.

104 **Bradley and his friends joked**: Bradley, "The Impossible Dream," 44.

105 **His trusted adviser at UCLA**: Bradley, "The Impossible Dream," 41.

105 **Bradley decided he needed a police job**: *Los Angeles Times*, June 3, 1974.

105 **Bradley was aware**: Bradley, "The Impossible Dream," 43.

105 **He was asked**: *Los Angeles Times*, October 21, 1982.

105 **The job at the Los Angeles Police Department**: Bradley, "The Impossible Dream," 40.

105 **Strode's last year at UCLA**: *Los Angeles Examiner*, December. 29, 1939; cited in Kaliss, *Everyone's All-Americans*, 153.

106 **After the season Strode realized**: Strode and Young, *Goal Dust*, 108.

14. Passed Over by the NFL

107 **"You know ... [Washington] would be the greatest sensation**: http://www .si.com/vault/2009/10/12/105865272/the-nfls-jackie-robinson, accessed November 16, 2015.

107 **The local media began stumping**: *Los Angeles Examiner*, November 11, 1939; cited in Kaliss, *Everyone's All-Americans*, 135.

107 **The *Los Angeles Times* wrote**: *Los Angeles Times*, November 13, 1939; cited in Kaliss, *Everyone's All-Americans*, 135.

107 **The press called the slight laughable**: *Los Angeles Examiner*, December 3, 1939; cited in Kaliss, *Everyone's All-Americans*, 137.

107 **Teammate Woody Strode said**: Strode and Young, *Goal Dust*, 96.

107 **"It's with a distinct sour taste"**: *Daily Bruin*, December 1, 1939; cited in Demas, "On the Threshold," 90.

108 **Washington had "put to shame those All-America pickers"**: *Los Angeles Times*, December 9, 1939.

108 **The *Pasadena Star-News* joined in**: *Pasadena Star-News*, December 7, 1939; cited in Demas, "On the Threshold," 93.

108 ***Crisis*, the NAACP magazine**: Wilkins, "Wrong Color," January 1940, 17.

108 **Washington also was passed over**: United Press article in the *Pasadena Post*, December 25, 1939; cited in Kaliss, *Everyone's All-Americans*, 149.

108 **His exclusion came**: http://biography.jrank.org/pages/2544/Washington -Kenny.html, accessed August 22, 2014.

108 **The mainstream and the black press**: *California Eagle*, December 21, 1939; cited in Kaliss, *Everyone's All-Americans*, 150.

108 **Even the lieutenant governor**: *Plaindealer* [Kansas City KS], January 5, 1940.

109 **Washington received some consolation**: *Chicago Tribune*, August 19, 1940.

109 **Charles "Buckets" Goldenberg**: *Chicago Tribune*, August 30, 1940.

109 **"He played on the same field"**: Wiggins and Miller, *The Unlevel Playing Field*, 200.

110 **What Bears coach George Halas saw of Washington**: http://www.nfl .com/news/story/09000d5d827061c3/printable/forgotten-hero-washington -broke-nfls-color-barrier-in-1946, accessed February 13, 2014.

110 **The prevailing thought**: *Chicago Defender*, September 7, 1940.

110 **NBC broadcaster Sam Balter**: Smith, *Showdown*, 39–40,

111 **"There are ten teams in the league"**: *Plaindealer* [Kansas City KS], December 22, 1939.

111 **In December 1940**: Wiggins and Miller, *The Unlevel Playing Field*, 200–201.

112 **Washington took a short venture**: *Chicago Defender*, January 6, 1940.

112 **Crosby sent Washington to a veteran manager**: *Chicago Defender*, January 6, 1940.

112 **He signed a contract**: http://www.museumca.org/picturethis/pictures /lobby-card-hollywood-film-iwhile-thousands-cheeri, accessed March 14, 2015.

112 **The sixty-four minute black-and-white film**: http://www.tcm.com/tcmdb /title/555587/While-ThousandsCheer/full-synopsis.html, accessed March 15, 2015.

112 **Washington invited the entire freshman team:** *Los Angeles Times*, November 19, 1940.

113 **In mid-September 1940 Washington played:** *Chicago Defender*, June 21, 1941.

113 **While Washington was earning his degree:** *Plaindealer* [Kansas City ҡѕ], November 29, 1940.

113 **Washington was "an inspiration":** *California Eagle*, December 31, 1940; cited in Demas, "On the Threshold," 98.

113 **After leaving UCLA Strode landed a job:** Strode and Young, *Goal Dust*, 108.

113 **But Strode was soon out of a job:** Strode and Young, *Goal Dust*, 110-11, 117.

114 **"That's all the money I needed":** *Los Angeles Examiner*, December 29, 1939; cited in Kaliss, *Everyone's All-Americans*, 153.

114 **Strode and Washington led the Bears:** Strode and Young, *Goal Dust*, 134.

114 **After graduation Washington looked:** *Arkansas State Press*, May 1, 1942.

115 **Washington's knees were so banged up:** Strode and Young, *Goal Dust*, 134.

115 **Mulling over the war:** Strode and Young, *Goal Dust*, 136.

15. The Indispensable Robinson

116 **"Jack was dedicated":** Allen, *Jackie Robinson*, 37.

116 **The 1940 football season:** *Daily Bruin*, September 30, 1940; cited in Rampersad, *Jackie Robinson*, 80.

116 **Robinson became a one-man show:** http://www.benzduck.com/the-program -project/, accessed December 4, 2014.

117 **"There were a number of games":** *Daily Bruin*, April 24, 1997.

117 **Ray Bartlett also figured prominently:** *Los Angeles Times*, September 4, 1940.

117 **In the season's opening game:** Martin, *Benching Jim Crow*, 38.

117 **Next the Bruins fell:** *Los Angeles Times*, October 5, 1940.

117 **Coach Horrell was upbeat:** *Los Angeles Times*, October 5, 1940.

118 *Los Angeles Times* **columnist:** *Los Angeles Times*, October 6, 1940.

118 **Despite Horrell's support:** Smith, *Showdown*, 38.

118 **The undefeated Stanford "Wow Boys":** J. W. Johnson, *The Wow Boys*, 48, 58.

119 **The Bruins were ready:** *San Francisco Chronicle*, November 2, 1940.

119 **The** *Stanford Daily* **"welcomed" Robinson:** J. W. Johnson, *The Wow Boys*, 100.

120 **Shaughnessy said about Robinson:** Covey, *The Wow Boys*, 124,

120 **The** *Los Angeles Times* **described Robinson:** *Los Angeles Times*, November 3, 1940.

120 **Coach Tex Oliver:** http://www.benzduck.com/the-program-project/, accessed November 4, 2014.

120 **Although the Ducks bottled up Robinson:** *The Oregonian*, November 10, 1940.

120 **As *Los Angeles Times* sportswriter Al Wolf put it:** *Los Angeles Times*, November 9, 1940.

121 **They had to come from behind:** *Los Angeles Times*, November 17, 1940.

121 **"They all wound up falling flat":** *Los Angeles Times*; cited in *Daily Bruin*, April 4, 1997.

121 **Coach Horrell had little to say:** *Los Angeles Times*, November 24, 1940.

122 **Robinson thought of dropping out:** Rampersad, *Jackie Robinson*, 81.

122 **It turned out to be another hapless year:** *Daily Bruin*, February 17, 1941; cited in Rampersad, *Jackie Robinson*, 81.

122 **Racial taunts from Berkeley fans:** Kaliss, *Everyone's All-Americans*, 121.

122 **Again Robinson was left off:** *Daily Bruin*, March 4, 1941; cited in Rampersad, *Jackie Robinson*, 81–22.

123 **"It's purely the case":** Tygiel, *Baseball's Great Experiment*, 61.

123 **Robinson decided he had had enough:** Jackie Robinson with Duckett, *I Never Had It Made*, 11.

123 **"My brothers, their friends and acquaintances":** Jackie Robinson with Duckett, *Baseball Has Done It*, 44.

123 **Robinson also realized:** Jackie Robinson with Duckett, *I Never Had It Made*, 11–12.

123 **The day Robinson departed UCLA:** dailybruin.com/1997/04/23/a-bruin -for(-all-seasons/, accessed November 10, 2013.

123 **In his senior year Robinson met his future wife:** *Los Angeles Times*, September 2, 1987.

123 **Rachel was shocked:** Rampersad, *Jackie Robinson*, 82.

124 **Jackie and Rachel's relationship and marriage:** Tygiel, *Extra Bases*, 4.

124 **One of Rachel's observations:** Rampersad, *Jackie Robinson*, 78.

124 **Newspaper sports pages effused over Robinson's career:** Rowan with Robinson, *Wait Till Next Year*, 65.

16. World War II Beckons

125 **"Things I had been doing all my life":** Strode and Young, *Goal Dust*, 125.

125 **It didn't take Robinson long:** Rampersad, *Jackie Robinson*, 83.

125 **The NYA saw a need:** Rampersad, *Jackie Robinson*, 84.

125 **While he was working at the NYA camp:** Rampersad, *Jackie Robinson*, 82.

125 **Only once during his time on the job:** Rampersad, *Jackie Robinson*, 84–85.

126 **Because of the war:** Jackie Robinson with Duckett, *I Never Had It Made*, 12.

126 **Robinson was having trouble:** Rowan with Robinson, *Wait Till Next Year*, 65.

126 **In one scrimmage:** *Chicago Tribune*, August 16, 1941.

126 **On August 28 the Bears:** *Chicago Tribune*, August 29, 1941.

126 **Robinson then sought a job:** Rampersad, *Jackie Robinson*, 86.

127 **"Jack didn't like to work":** Rampersad, *Jackie Robinson*, 86.

127 **Robinson continued to play football**: Tygiel, *Baseball's Great Experiment*, 61.

127 **Robinson headed home**: Jackie Robinson with Duckett, *I Never Had It Made*, 12.

127 **On December 7**: http://www.pasadena.edu/about/history/alumni/bartlett /bartlett1.cfm, accessed January 13, 2016.

128 **When Robinson returned**: http://thesportjournal.org/article/the-interrelated -back-stories-of-kenny-washington-reintegrating-the-nfl-in-1946-and-jackie -robinson-integrating-major-league-baseball-in-1947/, accessed November 11, 2015.

128 **Robinson took a job**: Rampersad, *Jackie Robinson*, 87–89.

128 **Robinson's bid for an exemption**: Rampersad, *Jackie Robinson*, 89.

129 **During the football offseason**: Strode and Young, *Goal Dust*, 121.

129 **Strode became the good guy**: Strode and Young, *Goal Dust*, 122.

129 **Then football season resumed**: Strode and Young, *Goal Dust*, 124.

129 **Segregation was in force**: Strode and Young, *Goal Dust*, 125.

129 **But being an athlete brought him privileges**: *Los Angeles Times*, March 26, 1991.

130 **"We started to have a good time"**: Strode and Young, *Goal Dust*, 126.

130 **The army football team**: Strode and Young, *Goal Dust*, 127.

130 **Strode played for three more years**: Strode and Young, *Goal Dust*, 128–29.

130 **Strode was sent to Guam**: Strode and Young, *Goal Dust*, 132.

130 **The Bears went on to win**: http://thesportjournal.org/article/the-interrelated -back-stories-of-kenny-washington-reintegrating-the-nfl-in-1946-and-jackie -robinson-integrating-major-league-baseball-in-1947/, accessed November 17, 2015.

17. Moving Up in the Ranks

131 **"When I followed [Bradley's] career"**: Payne and Ratzan, *Tom Bradley*, 43.

131 **Not long after Pearl Harbor**: *Los Angeles Times*, October 21, 1982.

131 **Soon thereafter he received his draft notice**: Payne and Ratzan, *Tom Bradley*, 37–38.

131 **Bradley knew it would be difficult**: Bradley, "The Impossible Dream," 42, 64.

132 **Bradley's first assignment**: Bradley, "The Impossible Dream," 64.

132 **That assignment lasted three months**: Payne and Ratzan, *Tom Bradley*, 36.

132 **Bradley's abilities as a track star**: Payne and Ratzan, *Tom Bradley*, 39.

132 **Bradley organized sports programs**: Payne and Ratzan, *Tom Bradley*, 37.

133 **After five years**: Payne and Ratzan, *Tom Bradley*, 43.

133 **Bradley became a mentor**: James Robinson, *Tom Bradley*, 61.

133 **After four years in vice**: Bradley, "The Impossible Dream," 61.

133 **After basic training**: Jackie Robinson with Duckett, *I Never Had It Made*, 13.

133 **Robinson was put in charge**: Jackie Robinson with Duckett, *I Never Had It Made*, 14–15.

134 **Robinson also was playing**: Jackie Robinson with Duckett, *I Never Had It Made*, 16–17.

134 **The army barred Robinson**: Rampersad, *Jackie Robinson*, 95.

134 **Robinson was soon transferred**: Jackie Robinson with Duckett, *I Never Had It Made*, 19–22.

135 **The upshot was**: Rampersad, *Jackie Robinson*, 110.

135 **Good fortune was about to come**: Rampersad, *Jackie Robinson*, 110.

135 **During the winter**: Rampersad, *Jackie Robinson*, 113–14.

136 **Southern humiliated outmanned Huston**: *New York Times*, May 23, 2015.

136 **In March Robinson headed off**: Rampersad, *Jackie Robinson*, 116–19.

136 **The Communist Party newspaper**: Rowan with Robinson, *Wait Till Next Year*, 96–100.

137 **Perhaps the most influential sportswriter**: http://sports.espn.go.com /espn/otl/news/story?id=4943434, accessed November 17, 2015.

137 **"You pay the prices"**: *Christian Science Monitor*, August 16, 2006.

137 **Rodney once told**: Kahn, *Rickey & Robinson*, 70.

137 **Rodney's "work"**: http://sports.espn.go.com/espn/otl/news/story ?id=4943434, accessed August 27, 2013.

137 **As early as 1934**: Kahn, *Rickey & Robinson*, 73–74.

138 **Outside of the black press**: *Christian Science Monitor*, August 18, 2006.

138 **"The conscience of American journalism"**: Dorinson and Warmund, *Jackie Robinson*, 74.

138 **Rodney and the *Daily Worker***: http://sports.espn.go.com/espn/otl/news /story?id=4943434, accessed August 27, 2013.

138 **Robinson always was appreciative**: Kahn, *Rickey & Robinson*, 83.

138 **Sports historian Larry Lester**: http://espn.go.com/espn/otl/news/story ?id=4943434, accessed January 13, 2016.

138 **Rodney said in 1996**: http://espn.go.com/espn/otl/news/story?id=4943434, accessed January 13, 2006.

138 **In his biography**: Silber, *Press Box Red*, 98.

139 **Life was not easy**: G. D. Johnson, *Profiles in Hue*, 280.

139 **"When I look back"**: Cottrell, *Two Pioneers*, no page number.

139 **Robinson questioned**: Jackie Robinson with Duckett, *I Never Had It Made*, 24–25.

139 **Robinson played in sixty-three games**: http://www.baseball-reference .com/nlb/team.cgi?id=993e3fb0, accessed February 22, 2014.

18. Making NFL History

140 **"From 1933 to 1946"**: Young, "Pro Football Discovers the Black College," 116.

140 **When the Chicago Bears' founder**: Levy, *Tackling Jim Crow*, 55.

140 **NFL owners never acknowledged**: Bishop, "A Nod from Destiny," 82.

141 **They wanted Coliseum officials to know**: http://www.si.com/vault /2009/10/12/105865272/the-nfls-jackie-robinson, accessed January 14, 2016.

142 **The Rams "didn't take Kenny":** "The NFL's Jackie Robinson," https://www
.si.com/vault/2009/10/12/105865272/the-nfls-jackie-robinson, accessed
March 31, 2017.

142 **"The people out there":** Strode and Young, *Goal Dust*, 142.

142 **Reeves also knew:** *Hartford Courier*, August 8, 1999.

142 **Head coach Bob Snyder also admitted:** Peterson, *Pigskin*, 186.

142 **Ironically while the Rams were forced to sign:** Smith, *Showdown*, 150–54.

143 **Washington's uncle, Rocky:** Ross, *Outside the Lines*, 82–83.

143 **The Rams decided:** Strode and Young, *Goal Dust*, 142.

143 **"My signing with the Rams":** Strode and Young, *Goal Dust*, 149–50.

143 **Strode said he had the ability:** http://www.biography.com/people
/woody-strode-40563#professional-sports-career, accessed January 14,
2016.

143 **Strode said he didn't realize:** Strode and Young, *Goal Dust*, 150.

143 **Dick Hyland, a sports columnist:** *Los Angeles Times*, March 22, 1946.

144 **Washington made the team:** *Los Angeles Times*, September 1, 1946.

144 **According to Strode:** Strode and Young, *Goal Dust*, 153.

144 **Gordon Macker:** Strode and Young, *Goal Dust*, 153.

144 **Although Strode played:** Strode and Young, *Goal Dust*, 154.

145 **Looking back on those days:** Strode and Young, *Goal Dust*, 154.

145 **Traveling with the Rams:** Strode and Young, *Goal Dust*, 150.

145 **On one trip to Chicago:** Strode and Young, *Goal Dust*, 152.

145 **"It was great":** *Los Angeles Times*, August 8, 1963.

145 **Strode wrote in his memoirs:** Strode and Young, *Goal Dust*, 152.

145 **At times white players hit Washington:** *Hartford Courier*, August 8, 1999.

145 **In a game against the Chicago Cardinals:** *Pittsburgh Courier*, October 19,
1946; cited in Levy, *Tackling Jim Crow*, 94.

145 **Bob Snyder noted:** biography.jrank.org/pages/2533/Washington-Kenny
.html, accessed August 22, 2014.

145 **Snyder recalled that Washington and Strode:** Peterson, *Pigskin*, 183.

146 **Strode played little that year:** http://www.si.com/vault/2009/10/12
/105865272/the-nfls-jackie-robinson, accessed January 14, 2016.

146 **Line coach George Trafton:** Strode and Young, *Goal Dust*, 154–55.

146 **It wasn't the first time:** Manchel, "The Man Who Made the Stars Shine
Brighter," 39

146 **On the field,:** http://www.stlouisrams.com/news-and-events/article
-1/The-Legacy-of-Kenny-Washington/d6ba4c71-fa7b-4fd4-8209
-fd44b84900b6, accessed January 14, 2016.

147 **But Strode's and Washington's mark:** *New York Times*, June 26, 1971.

147 **Washington left football:** *Los Angeles Times*, December 13, 1948.

147 **Strode's football career:** Strode and Young, *Goal Dust*, 161–67.

148 **"I loved football":** Strode and Young, *Goal Dust*, 170.

19. The Negro League Years

149 **"The plate is the same width"**: Mann, "Say Jack Robinson, Colliers, March 2, 1946, 66–67."

149 **Jackie Robinson was fed up**: Jackie Robinson with Duckett, *I Never Had It Made*, 24–25.

149 **The players often slept**: Rampersad, *Jackie Robinson*, 124.

149 **On August 24, 1945**: Jackie Robinson with Duckett, *I Never Had It Made*, 30.

150 **"I was thinking"**: Kahn, *Rickey & Robinson*, 103.

150 **Who was this Branch Rickey**: Kahn, *Rickey & Robinson*, 1.

150 **What transpired**: Rampersad, *Jackie Robinson*, 126.

150 **Rickey told Robinson**: Jackie Robinson with Duckett, *I Never Had It Made*, 34.

151 **"Mr. Rickey," Robinson asked**: Jackie Robinson with Duckett, *I Never Had It Made*, 32–33.

151 **"You've got to do this job"**: Dorinson and Warmund, *Jackie Robinson*, 110.

151 **Rickey drew on the New Testament**: Rampersad, *Jackie Robinson*, 127.

151 **Robinson withheld from Rickey**: Kahn, *Rickey & Robinson*, 105.

151 **He agreed to a contract**: Jackie Robinson with Duckett, *I Never Had It Made*, 34.

151 **Rickey recalled**: Denenberg, *Stealing Home*, 114.

151 **A childhood friend**: http://www.voanews.com/content/a-13-2007-03-28-voa71-66542467/554202.html, accessed November 21, 2015.

152 **On October 23, 1945**: Jackie Robinson with Duckett, *I Never Had It Made*, 34–35; Tygiel, *Baseball's Great Experiment*, 71.

152 **When Robinson spoke before the reporters**: Jackie Robinson with Duckett, *I Never Had It Made*, 35.

152 **The editor of a black New York weekly**: http://m.mlb.com/news/article/28518376/, accessed January 14, 2016.

153 **Future Hall of Fame pitcher Bob Feller**: Jackie Robinson with Duckett, *I Never Had It Made*, 35.

153 **Robinson replied that he wished**: Mann, "Say Jack Robinson."

153 **Sportswriters Dan Parker of the *New York Mirror* and Red Smith**: Jackie Robinson with Duckett, *I Never Had It Made*, 35–36.

153 **An editorial in the Bible of baseball**: http://sabr.org/bioproj/person/bb9e2490, accessed January 14, 2016.

153 ***Atlanta Journal* sports editor Ed Danforth**: https://www.gilderlehrman.org/history-by-era/civil-rights-movement/essays/before-jackie-how-strikeout-king-satchel-paige-struck-do, accessed January 10, 2016.

153 **Some supporters saw Rickey's and Robinson's efforts**: Tygiel, *Baseball's Great Experiment*, 74–76.

154 **It is interesting that black players were surprised**: Tygiel, *Baseball's Great Experiment*, 78.

154 **Even so, Paige was uncertain**: Eig, *Opening Day*, 18.

154 **Major League officials**: Tygiel, *Baseball's Great Experiment*, 79–80.

154 **Rickey traveled to Louisville:** Dorinson and Warmund, *Jackie Robinson*, 17.

155 **Before spring training began:** Jackie Robinson with Duckett, *I Never Had It Made*, 39–41; Rowan with Robinson, *Wait Till Next Year*, 131.

155 **At Daytona Beach:** Jackie Robinson with Duckett, *I Never Had It Made*, 42.

155 **The Robinsons faced discrimination:** Tygiel, *Baseball's Great Experiment*, 107.

155 **Robinson's manager at Montreal:** Tygiel, *Baseball's Great Experiment*, 103–4.

156 **Rickey had placed Hopper in this difficult situation:** Tygiel, *Baseball's Great Experiment*, 196.

156 **After Robinson's talents began to show:** Tygiel, *Baseball's Great Experiment*, 104.

156 **"They seemed to have little reaction":** Jackie Robinson with Duckett, *I Never Had It Made*, 43–44.

156 **Although Robinson's hitting was weak:** Rampersad, *Jackie Robinson*, 146.

157 **During spring training:** Rampersad, *Jackie Robinson*, 148.

157 **Toward the end:** Tygiel, *Baseball's Great Experiment*, 118.

157 **His turnaround:** *Baltimore Afro-American*, March 22, 1947.

157 **Along the way, Robinson's morale was stoked:** Jackie Robinson with Duckett, *I Never Had It Made*, 49.

157 **"He did everything":** *Los Angeles Times*, February 12, 1990; cited in http://sabr.org/bioproj/person/bb9e2490, accessed January 16, 2016.

158 **Montreal's early schedule:** Tygiel, *Baseball's Great Experiment*, 122.

158 **Although his manager tolerated Robinson:** Jackie Robinson with Duckett, *I Never Had It Made*, 48.

159 **A Montreal sportswriter:** *Montreal Gazette*, June 4, 1946; cited in Rampersad, *Jackie Robinson*, 152.

159 **The season was not without incidents:** *Montreal Gazette*, June 4, 1946; cited in Rampersad, *Jackie Robinson*, 154.

159 **Robinson was consistently the target:** Los *Angeles Times*, February 12, 1990.

159 **The Royals won:** Jackie Robinson with Duckett, *I Never Had It Made*, 50.

159 **The Royals lost two:** Jackie Robinson with Duckett, *I Never Had It Made*, 51.

160 **Robinson and his teammates:** Rampersad, *Jackie Robinson*, 157.

160 **After he showered:** Jackie Robinson with Duckett, *I Never Had It Made*, 51–52.

160 **Robinson finished the season:** Kahn, *Rickey & Robinson*, 108.

20. End of the Line at LAPD

161 **"The only thing that will stop you":** http://www.worldofquotes.com/author/Tom+Bradley/1/index.html, accessed January 14, 2016.

161 **If Tom Bradley encountered racial discrimination:** http://www.lausd.k12.ca.us/Tom_Bradley_EL/TBradBio.html, accessed February 18, 2015.

161 **When the Bradleys and their two children moved in:** *Los Angeles Times*, October 21, 1982.

161 **He refused to let such setbacks wear him down:** *Los Angeles Times*, July 27, 1974.

161 **On another occasion he remarked:** *Los Angeles Times*, October 21, 1982.

161 **When he was appointed as a lieutenant:** Bradley, "The Impossible Dream," 71.

162 **Until then blacks had been assigned to street duties:** Bradley, "The Impossible Dream," 68.

162 **After Bradley retired:** Bradley, "The Impossible Dream," 69.

162 **Off duty Bradley suffered the humiliation of discrimination:** *Los Angeles Times*, October 21, 1982.

162 **The rank of lieutenant:** *Los Angeles Times*, April 24, 2008.

163 **In 1974 Bradley revealed:** *Los Angeles Times*, June 3, 1974.

163 **Knowing that he could not move up any higher:** Bradley, "The Impossible Dream," 69, 72.

163 **While still on the force:** *Los Angeles Times*, October 21, 1982.

163 **He was hired:** Bradley, "The Impossible Dream," 84.

163 **Bradley joined the liberal California Democratic Council:** Payne and Ratzan, *Tom Bradley*, 57.

164 **Bradley agreed to seek the appointment:** Bradley, "The Impossible Dream," 74.

164 **It was a slap in the face:** Payne and Ratzan, *Tom Bradley*, 59.

164 **Two years into practicing law:** Payne and Ratzan, *Tom Bradley*, 61.

164 **Prejudice, however, followed him:** Payne and Ratzan, *Tom Bradley*, 66.

164 **This time the voters spoke:** Payne and Ratzan, *Tom Bradley*, 67.

164 **After Bradley won the election:** Bradley, "The Impossible Dream," 74.

165 **Bradley had said during the campaign:** http://www.tombradleylegacy.org/personal-biography.html, accessed May 20, 2015.

165 **Much of Bradley's term:** Payne and Ratzan, *Tom Bradley*, 73.

165 **At the same time Bradley tended to hide:** http://www.tombradleylegacy.org/personal-biography.html, accessed May 20, 2015.

165 **Bradley lacked charisma:** *Los Angeles Times*, September 30, 1998.

165 **Slowly but surely Bradley was making his mark:** Payne and Ratzan, *Tom Bradley*, 84.

165 **In 1969 Bradley decided:** Payne and Ratzan, *Tom Bradley*, 89–90.

166 **As election results came in:** Payne and Ratzan, *Tom Bradley*, 90.

166 **Weiner was right:** http://en.wikipedia.org/wiki/Tom_Bradley_(American_politician), accessed January 15, 2016.

166 **Bradley refused to lower himself:** Bradley, "The Impossible Dream," 159.

166 **"The voters have approved":** Payne and Ratzan, *Tom Bradley*, 108.

167 **No sooner was the race over:** Payne and Ratzan, *Tom Bradley*, 111.

167 **He was relentless:** Payne and Ratzan, *Tom Bradley*, 114.

167 **In formally announcing his intention:** Payne and Ratzan, *Tom Bradley*, 118.

167 **Bradley again finished on top:** Payne and Ratzan, *Tom Bradley*, 124.

167 **Little changed in Yorty's campaign:** Payne and Ratzan, *Tom Bradley*, 128–29.

168 **When Bradley moved into the mayor's office:** Payne and Ratzan, *Tom Bradley*, 136.

168 **Now it was time:** http://lanetwork.facinghistory.org/a-local-civil-rights -leader-mayor-tom-bradley/, accessed January 15, 2016.

21. Leaving Athletics

169 **"It would be a shame":** *Sun Reporter* (San Francisco), January 25, 1996.

169 **In 1950, when Kenny Washington was thirty-one years old:** *Los Angeles Times*, February 27, 1950.

169 **Washington said that if his batting was as good:** *Chicago Defender*, February 18, 1950.

169 **Giants manager Leo Durocher:** *Los Angeles Times*, March 24, 1950.

170 **The chance came too late:** *Los Angeles Times*, March 19, 1950.

170 **Five days later Durocher dropped the news:** *Los Angeles Times*, March 24, 1950.

170 **Washington did play:** http://www.baseball-reference.com/minors/player .cgi?id=washin002ken, accessed February 10, 2015.

171 **Between 1941 and 1950:** http://www.imdb.com/name/nm0913486/, accessed January 15, 2015.

171 **Washington became active:** Cited in https://en.wikipedia.org/wiki/Kenny _Washington_(American_football), accessed January 15, 2016.

171 **In 1956 UCLA retired Washington's No. 13 jersey:** http://www.biography. com/people/kenny-washington-40244#early-years, accessed January 15, 2016.

171 **In December 1970 Washington was honored:** *Los Angeles Times*, May 7, 1970.

172 **When Woody Strode heard:** Strode and Young, *Goal Dust*, 242–43.

172 **Bob Waterfield:** *Los Angeles Times*, June 25, 1971.

172 **When Robinson heard:** *Sun Reporter* (San Francisco), January 25, 1996.

172 **Strode wrote years later:** Strode and Young, *Goal Dust*, 243.

172 **A. S. "Doc" Young:** *Chicago Defender*, June 30, 1971.

172 **Many former teammates:** Strode and Young, *Goal Dust*, 243.

173 **After the war, Bartlett returned to Pasadena:** http://www.pasadena.edu /about/history/alumni/bartlett/bartlett1.cfm, accessed February 13, 2015.

173 **At the age of forty-seven:** *Pasadena City College Courier*, July 16, 2008.

173 **In 1999 Bartlett represented Jackie Robinson:** *Pasadena Star-News*, June 25, 2008.

174 **Bartlett was a past president:** http://file.lacounty.gov/bos/supdocs/32221 .pdf, accessed May 31, 2015.

174 **In 1987 Pasadena City College honored him:** http://collection.pasade- nadigitalhistory.com/cdm/singleitem/collection/p16237coll6/id/12830 /rec/6, accessed January 15, 2016.

174 **Said his son Bob:** *Los Angeles Times*, June 28, 2008.

22. Movie Star in the Making

175 **"I was strictly a mechanic"**: http://www.imdb.com/name/nm0834754 /bio, accessed January 15, 2016.

175 **When Woody Strode returned from Canada**: Strode and Young, *Goal Dust*, 171.

175 **Professional wrestling**: Strode and Young, *Goal Dust*, 173.

176 **When wrestling in Dallas, Texas, Strode remembered**: Strode and Young, *Goal Dust*, 176–79.

176 **On May 20, 1950**: *Chicago Defender*, May 5, 1950.

176 **Strode's fortunes soon changed again**: Strode and Young, *Goal Dust*, 179–83.

177 **Next came an offer**: Strode and Young, *Goal Dust*, 185–89.

177 **Another change was in the works**: Strode and Young, *Goal Dust*, 188–89.

177 **Strode's next big role**: Strode and Young, *Goal Dust*, 196–98.

178 **Peter Ustinov**: http://www.imdb.com/name/nm0834754/bio, accessed January 15, 2016.

178 **"For the first five or six years"**: Strode and Young, *Goal Dust*, 254.

178 **When Strode returned home**: Manchel, *The Man Who Made the Stars Shine Brighter*, 42.

178 **In the film, set in the 1860s**: http://tvtropes.org/pmwiki/pmwiki.php/Creator /JohnFord, accessed November 19, 2015; Strode and Young, *Goal Dust*, 199–207.

179 **But it was a disappointment**: *Boston Globe*, December 20, 1981.

179 **Ford told Strode**: Strode and Young, *Goal Dust*, 231.

179 *Ebony*, **a magazine predominantly for black readers**: Cited in Strode and Young, *Goal Dust*, 191.

179 *Sergeant Rutledge* **was the start**: *Boston Globe*, December 20, 1981.

179 **Ford's biographer**: McBride, *Searching for John Ford*, 652.

179 **It turned out Strode wasn't through with wrestling**: Strode and Young, *Goal Dust*, 213.

180 **In a movie with Charlton Heston**: Strode and Young, *Goal Dust*, 221.

180 **Strode said that after Peckinpah called him a mongrel**: Strode and Young, *Goal Dust*, 222–23.

180 **As Strode was obtaining better and better roles**: *Chicago Defender*, June 19, 1965.

180 **Strode decided in 1966**: *Boston Globe*, December 20, 1981.

180 **The recreated Tenth Cavalry unit**: *Los Angeles Times*, June 13, 1966.

181 **One of Strode's most popular movies**: *Chicago Defender*, June 4, 1966, and January 18, 1995.

181 **Once on the movie set**: http://www.imdb.com/name/nm0834754/bio, accessed November 11, 2015.

181 **Frank O'Rourke**: http://moviemorlocks.com/2010/08/06/ill-find-ya-woody -strode-in-the-professionals/, accessed January 15, 2016.

181 **Strode was feeling the heat:** Manchel, *The Man Who Made the Stars Shine Brighter*, 39.

182 **"Most of my life":** *Pittsburgh Press*, December 8, 1971.

182 **Frank Manchel in his book:** Manchel, *Every Step a Struggle*, 359.

182 **Strode's disenchantment:** *Boston Globe*, December 20, 1981.

182 **Said his nephew Tollie Strode Jr.:** http://www.ledger-enquirer.com/news /local/news-columns-blogs/article29329366.html, accessed January 15, 2016.

182 **From 1969 to 1971:** Strode and Young, *Goal Dust*, 241.

182 **"Race is not a factor":** *Boston Globe*, December 20, 1981.

182 **It was in Europe:** Strode and Young, *Goal Dust*, 240

183 **Strode next starred:** Manchel, *Every Step a Struggle*, 357.

183 **The *New York Times* wrote:** *New York Times*, August 26, 1971.

183 **Strode made one more Hollywood film:** Strode and Young, *Goal Dust*, 247.

183 **Strode returned to Italy:** Strode and Young, *Goal Dust*, 249.

184 **In 1980 Strode's wife Luana died:** *Boston Globe*, December 20, 1981.

184 **Age was catching up:** Strode and Young, *Goal Dust*, 254–55.

184 **In all Strode acted in fifty-seven movies:** *San Francisco Chronicle*, January 6, 1995.

184 **"You know what they saw in me":** Manchel, *The Man Who Made the Stars Shine Brighter*, 46.

23. A Promotion Earned

186 **[Robinson] was the only player:** Denenberg, *Stealing Home*, 104.

186 **Robinson's barnstorming trip:** Rampersad, *Jackie Robinson*, 158.

186 **Robinson averaged:** http://www.blackfives.org/jackie-robinson/, accessed January 16, 2016.

187 **Robinson's fate:** Rampersad, *Jackie Robinson*, 159–60.

187 **Even in Havana:** Eig, *Opening Day*, 36–37.

188 **Before Rickey made a decision:** Denenberg, *Stealing Home*, 77.

188 **After leaving Havana:** Denenberg, *Stealing Home*, 79.

188 **Rickey told Robinson:** Jackie Robinson with Duckett, *I Never Had It Made*, 56.

189 **If Robinson was anxious:** Eig, *Opening Day*, 38–39.

189 **Unbeknown to any:** Dorinson and Warmund, *Jackie Robinson*, 17.

189 **Reese's friends in Kentucky:** Denenberg, *Stealing Home*, 80.

189 **Apparently Higbe had had a few too many beers:** Jackie Robinson with Duckett, *I Never Had It Made*, 55.

189 **Said Reese: "You can hate":** G. D. Johnson, *Profiles in Hue*, 283.

190 **The team was in Panama:** Simon, *Jackie Robinson and the Integration of Baseball*, 106.

190 **Rickey also called the dissenting players:** Dorinson and Warmund, *Jackie Robinson*, 87.

190 **Durocher knew Robinson's value:** Kahn, *The Boys of Summer*, 358.

190 **While Rickey was preparing**: http://sabr.org/bioproj/person/bb9e2490, accessed January 16, 2016.

190 **The announcement about Robinson's promotion came**: *New York Times*, April 11, 1947.

190 **Still the move created a furor**: Dorinson and Warmund, *Jackie Robinson*, 18.

24. Blending In

191 **"When they start talking about me"**: Eig, *Opening Day*, 111.

191 **The Dodgers were facing a number of questions**: *New York Times*, April 9, 1947.

191 **The twenty-eight-year-old rookie**: *New York Times*, April 12, 1947.

191 **In his first game**: *New York Times*, April 14, 1947.

192 **Robinson was unsure what to expect**: http://sabr.org/bioproj/person /bb9e2490, accessed January 16, 2016.

192 **Rickey's charge**: Dorinson and Warmund, *Jackie Robinson*, 124–25.

192 **"I know where he is"**: Barber, *1947*, 146.

192 **As for Robinson's presence**: Barber, *1947*, 214.

192 **A less than capacity crowd**: Eig, *Opening Day*, 52.

192 **Brooklyn's total in National League attendance**: Dorinson and Warmund, *Jackie Robinson*, 185.

192 **In the dugout**: http://www.si.com/mlb/2015/04/15/jackie-robinson-day -william-nack-si-vault, accessed November 30, 2015.

193 **A teammate told a *New York Times* reporter**: Eig, *Opening Day*, 60.

193 **As Robinson took the field**: Eig, *Opening Day*, 57–58.

193 **Robinson called it "just another ball game"**: *The Sporting News*, April 23, 1947.

193 **Rickey kept an optimistic tone**: http://www.si.com/mlb/2015/04/15/jackie -robinson-day-william-nack-si-vault, accessed November 30, 2015.

193 **"He should be given a rest"**: Eig, *Opening Day*, 86.

193 **"Two of the notes"**: *The Breakthrough*, Sports Illustrated Vault, May 5, 1997, https://www.si.com/vault/1997/05/05/226554/, accessed April 1, 2017.

193 **Robinson wrote in the *Pittsburgh Courier***: *The Breakthrough*, Sports Illustrated Vault, May 5, 1997, https://www.si.com/vault/1997/05/05/226554/, accessed April 1, 2017.

194 **Then just as slumps come**: *The Breakthrough*, Sports Illustrated Vault, May 5, 1997, https://www.si.com/vault/1997/05/05/226554/, accessed April 1, 2017.

194 **One of the most vicious attacks**: Eig, *Opening Day*, 100.

194 **The Dodgers took a train**: Eig, *Opening Day*, 103.

195 **Ben Chapman and his players**: Jackie Robinson with Duckett, *I Never Had It Made*, 58.

195 **As a player, Chapman had been traded**: *New York Times*, July 27, 2008.

195 **"I have to admit"**: Jackie Robinson with Duckett, *I Never Had It Made*, 58–59.

195   **Yankee Hall of Famer Mickey Mantle**: Mantle and Creamer, *The Quality of Courage*, 50.

195   **The Brooklyn players**: Jackie Robinson with Duckett, *I Never Had It Made*, 60–61.

196   **Dan Parker, sports editor**: Quoted in Jackie Robinson with Duckett, *I Never Had It Made*, 60.

196   **Public reaction against Chapman**: Wilson, *Jackie Robinson and the American Dilemma*, 92.

196   **But together they held a bat up between them**: Jackie Robinson with Duckett, *I Never Had It Made*, 62.

196   **Dixie Walker**: Tygiel, *The Jackie Robinson Reader*, 144.

196   **Most of Walker's disdain**: Oliphant, *Praying for Gil Hodges*, 48.

196   **Howie Schultz, who was traded**: http://sabr.org/bioproj/person/44eeab12, accessed January 22, 2016.

196   **Chapman apparently had some regrets**: http://phillysportshistory.com/2011/04/15/jackie-robinson-and.-the-phillies/, accessed January 16, 2016.

197   **Robinson was greeted**: Long, *First Class Citizenship*, 10.

197   **When Robinson took the field**: Dorinson and Warmund, *Jackie Robinson*, 19.

197   **Robinson said he and Reese talked**: *Amsterdam News*, July 7, 1962; cited in Long, *Beyond Home Plate*, 27.

197   **Robinson also said**: Kahn, *Rickey & Robinson*, 272.

197   **Robinson's wife, Rachel**: Williams with Sielski, *How to Be like Jackie Robinson*, 154–55.

197   **Reese draped his arm around Robinson**: Oliphant, *Praying for Gil Hodges*, 40.

197   **Early in the season**: Jackie Robinson with Duckett, *I Never Had It Made*, 62.

197   **Dick Gephardt**: Oliphant, *Praying for Gil Hodges*, 36.

198   **Robinson still had trouble**: http://sabr.org/bioproj/person/bb9e2490, accessed January 16, 2016.

198   **Several of Robinson's teammates**: Jackie Robinson with Duckett, *I Never Had It Made*, 68.

198   **The next inning**: Falkner, *Great Time Coming*, 173.

198   **Musial was one**: Tygiel, *The Jackie Robinson Reader*, 217.

198   **Musial gave Robinson encouragement**: Tygiel, *The Jackie Robinson Reader*, 141.

198   **Vernon Jordan**: Oliphant, *Praying for Gil Hodges*, 52–53.

199   **African Americans loved Robinson**: S. Robinson, *Promises to Keep*, 40.

199   **Often when the Dodgers' train pulled into a city**: Oliphant, *Praying for Gil Hodges*, 42.

199   **Once at a game in Cincinnati**: http://www.si.com/mlb/2015/04/15/jackie-robinson-day-william-nack-si-vault, accessed November 30, 2015.

199   **Robinson was starting to relax**: http://www.si.com/vault/1997/05/05/226554/the-breakthrough-fifty-years-ago-over-fourteen-games

-in-may-jackie-robinson-erased-any-doubt-that-he-belonged-in-the-majors
-clearing-the-path-for-other-black-players, accessed November 19, 2015.

199 **In midseason:** http://www.si.com/mlb/2015/04/15/jackie-robinson-day
-william-nack-si-vault, accessed November 30, 2015.

199 **After Jackie won:** *Baseball Weekly*, February 26, 1997.

199 **In the World Series:** Allison and Gediman with Gregory and Merrick, *This
I Believe*, 197.

200 **Even one of Robinson's greatest critics:** http://sabr.org/bioproj/person
/bb9e2490, accessed January 16, 2016.

200 **Wendell Smith:** *Pittsburg Courier*, May 31, 1947; cited in Tygiel, *Baseball's
Great Experiment*, 189.

200 **According to a poll conducted in 1947:** Linge, *Jackie Robinson*, 71–72.

201 **Joining Robinson on the Dodgers' squad:** Dorinson and Warmund, *Jackie
Robinson*, 237.

201 **The year 1949 was a turning point:** Jackie Robinson with Duckett, *I Never
Had It Made*, 77–79.

202 **Now that Robinson was released:** http://sabr.org/research/memories-minor
-league-traveler, accessed November 17, 2015.

202 **Pitcher Don Newcombe:** Jackie Robinson with Duckett, *Baseball Has Done
It*, 85.

202 **Five years later:** Jackie Robinson with Duckett, *Baseball Has Done It*, 22.

203 **Yankee great Mickey Mantle once observed:** http://phillysportshistory.com
/2011/04/15/jackie-robinson-and-the-phillies/, accessed January 16, 2016.

203 **It was more than coincidental:** Jackie Robinson with Duckett, *I Never Had
It Made*, 86.

203 **Robinson was happy:** Jackie Robinson with Duckett, *I Never Had It Made*,
95–96; http://www.rottentomatoes.com/m/jackie_robinson_story/, accessed
January 16, 2016.

204 **In 1950 Robinson turned movie star:** http://www.rottentomatoes.com/m
/jackie_robinson_story/, accessed January 16, 2016.

204 **"I'm sure he felt":** R. Robinson with Daniels, *Jackie Robinson*, 115.

204 **In the middle of the season:** Jackie Robinson with Duckett, *I Never Had It
Made*, 81–85.

204 **Robinson was growing disenchanted:** Jackie Robinson with Duckett, *I
Never Had It Made*, 92, 95.

205 **Robinson wrote a letter:** Rampersad, *Jackie Robinson*, 231.

205 **Dodger center fielder Duke Snider:** Rudd and Fischler, *The Sporting Life*,
111–12.

206 **Five years had passed:** Simon, *Jackie Robinson and the Integration of Baseball*, 154.

206 **In 1952:** *New York Times*, June 26, 2008,

206 **For his good work:** Rudd and Fischler, *The Sporting Life*, 134.

207 **In 1954 the Robinson family decided:** Jackie Robinson, "Now I Know Why
They Boo Me"; cited in Long, *Beyond Home Plate*, 43.

207 **"It was not the best baseball strategy"**: Jackie Robinson with Duckett, *I Never Had It Made*, 120.

207 **During the offseason**: Long, *Beyond Home Plate*, 32.

208 **Not surprisingly as early as 1950**: Long, *First Class Citizenship*, 8.

208 **In 1960 Bill Veeck**: *New York Post*, September 2, 1960; cited in Long, *Beyond Home Plate*, 21.

208 **Robinson never let up**: Riordan, *The International Politics of Sport*, 170.

209 **Robinson knew he wasn't playing as well**: Dorinson and Warmund, *Jackie Robinson*, 198.

209 **Robinson had decided**: Jackie Robinson with Duckett, *I Never Had It Made*, 122.

209 **When Brooklyn general manager Buzzy Bavasi**: Jackie Robinson with Duckett, *I Never Had It Made*, 122.

209 **Besides, he wrote in *Look***: Jackie Robinson, "Why I'm Quitting Baseball."

210 **Robinson said he would miss the game**: Jackie Robinson, "Why I'm Quitting Baseball."

210 **"Baseball was just a part of my life"**: Rampersad, *Jackie Robinson*, 314.

25. Changing Los Angeles

211 **"As well as anybody"**: *Los Angeles Times*, October 21, 1982.

211 **"He came from the liberal reform section"**: http://www.tombradleylegacy.org/personal-biography.html, accessed January 17, 2016.

211 **As he had throughout most of his life**: *New York Times*, October 19, 2008.

212 **The *Los Angeles Times* wrote**: *Los Angeles Times*, September 30, 1998.

212 **One colleague remarked**: Payne and Ratzan, *Tom Bradley*, 137.

212 **He was a listener**: Payne and Ratzan, *Tom Bradley*, 162–63.

213 **Despite his high approval rating**: Payne and Ratzan, *Tom Bradley*, 229, 231.

213 **During the campaign**: Payne and Ratzan, *Tom Bradley*, 231–32.

214 **Bradley handily won the race**: Payne and Ratzan, *Tom Bradley*, 232.

214 **Bradley easily captured the Democratic nomination**: Payne and Ratzan, *Tom Bradley*, 235–40.

214 **A Bradley staff member**: Payne and Ratzan, *Tom Bradley*, 240–42.

215 **Bradley focused on the voters**: Payne and Ratzan, *Tom Bradley*, 249.

215 **About a month before the election**: *New York Times*, November 3, 1982.

215 **Once again race became the fodder of headlines**: Payne and Ratzan, *Tom Bradley*, 256.

215 **Bradley was stunned**: Payne and Ratzan, *Tom Bradley*, 256–57.

215 **Bradley had led the polls**: Allswang, "Tom Bradley of Los Angeles," 74–75.

216 **Bradley came close**: *Los Angeles Times*, September 30, 1998.

216 **Bradley never had the chance**: http://www.dailykos.com/story/2009/01/19/686138/-26-Years-Ago-Mayor-tom-Bradley-Ran-for-Governor-of-California-and-Making-the-Impossible-Dream-Poss#, accessed January 17, 2016.

216 **A disappointed Bradley**: http://www.spotlight.ucla.edu/alumni/tom-bradley_mayor/, accessed January 17, 2016.

216 **Bradley is credited:** http://www.tombradleylegacy.org/personal-biography
.html, accessed January 17, 2016.

217 **Bradley was not one to give up:** Payne and Ratzan, *Tom Bradley*, 348.

217 **In the 1986 election:** https://en.wikipedia.org/wiki/Tom_Bradley_
(American_politician), accessed January 17, 2016.

217 **Bradley may have been dejected:** *Los Angeles Times*, November 5, 1986.

217 **Bradley had the misfortune:** Stout, *Bringing Race Back In*, unpaged.

217 **In addition, no sitting governor had been defeated:** Allswang, "Tom Bradley of Los Angeles," 76–77.

217 **Bradley was back:** *Los Angeles Times*, November 6, 1986.

218 **One of Bradley's most difficult problems:** http://www.mayortombradley
.com/cch-article.html, accessed January 17, 2016.

218 **Five months later:** http://www.spotlight.ucla.edu/alumni/tom-bradley
_mayor/, accessed January 17, 2016.

218 **In 1993 Bradley stayed true to his promise:** *Los Angeles Times*, September 30, 1998.

219 **In a tribute to Bradley:** http://www.tombradleylegacy.org/personal-biography
.html, accessed January 17, 2016.

219 **In a eulogy:** http://clinton3.nara.gov/WH/EOP/OVP/speeches/bradley
.html, accessed January 17, 2016.

219 **Unemployed fifty-one-year-old Leon Cheatham:** *New York Times*, October 6, 1998.

26. The Civil Rights Years

220 **"He did us proud":** Angell, *This Old Man*, 215.

220 **Robinson wasn't about to fade into oblivion:** Rampersad, *Jackie Robinson*, 303.

220 **Robinson was amused:** Jackie Robinson with Duckett, *I Never Had It Made*, 126.

221 **A clincher was that Black gave full support:** Jackie Robinson with Duckett, *I Never Had It Made*, 126–27.

221 **He told Robinson:** S. Robinson, *Promises to Keep*, 52.

221 **Robinson was true to his word:** R. Robinson with Daniels, *Jackie Robinson*, 154.

221 **During his years at Chock Full O'Nuts:** http://espn.go.com/mlb/story
/_/id/7812986/jackie-robinson-everlasting-legacy, accessed January 17, 2016.

221 **Not long after Robinson retired:** Rampersad, *Jackie Robinson*, 319–20.

221 **The Robinsons were shocked:** R. Robinson with Daniels, *Jackie Robinson*, 143.

221 **Robinson may have been the first insulin-dependent diabetic:** http://
www.si.com/vault/1985/04/22/622389/the-diabetic-athlete-his-toughest
-opponent-is-his-own-metabolism, accessed January 17, 2016.

222 **In 1959 Robinson signed on:** Long, *Beyond Home Plate*, xxiv.

222 **Michael G. Long:** Long, *Beyond Home Plate*, xxv–xxvi.

222 **The columns lasted**: Rampersad, *Jackie Robinson*, 352.

222 **"No one will ever convince me"**: *Amsterdam News*, January 6, 1962; cited in Long, *Beyond Home Plate*, xxviii.

222 **Each of Robinson's ghostwriters**: Long, *First Class Citizenship*, xvii.

223 **Robinson wholeheartedly kept up his work**: Jackie Robinson with Duckett, *I Never Had It Made*, 130–31.

223 **Robinson continued to use**: Long, *Beyond Home Plate*, 37–40.

223 **For his contributions**: *New York Times*, February 4, 2015.

224 **Tiger Woods referred to Sifford**: *Los Angeles Times*, February 4, 2015.

224 **Although Robinson was active in politics**: Tygiel, *The Jackie Robinson Reader*, 223.

224 **Robinson supported several conservative issues**: Rampersad, *Jackie Robinson*, 341.

224 **He let his views on the candidates be known**: http://sabr.org/bioproj/person/bb9e2490, accessed January 15, 2016.

224 **Robinson later regretted**: Jackie Robinson with Duckett, *I Never Had It Made*, 135.

224 **The turning point**: Rampersad, *Jackie Robinson*, 350.

224 **Kennedy, however, intervened**: Long, *Beyond Home Plate*, xviii.

225 **Robinson was more in line**: Long, *Beyond Home Plate*, xix.

225 **In Robinson's autobiography**: Jackie Robinson with Duckett, *I Never Had It Made*, 169.

225 **In a column titled**: *Amsterdam News*, February 26, 1966; cited in Long, *Beyond Home Plate*, 149.

225 **"I admit freely"**: Tygiel, *The Jackie Robinson Reader*, 234.

225 **When Goldwater won the Republican nomination**: Long, *Beyond Home Plate*, xix.

225 **In the 1968 election**: *Amsterdam News*, August 17, 1968; cited in Long, *Beyond Home Plate*, 151.

225 **He warned that if Nixon was elected**: Rampersad, *Jackie Robinson*, 426.

225 **Robinson couldn't have been happy**: Long, *First Class Citizenship*, 295–96.

226 **In 1972 Robinson swung back**: Long, *Beyond Home Plate*, 152.

226 **Five years after he retired**: Long, *Beyond Home Plate*, 22.

226 **Sportswriters vote**: Rampersad, *Jackie Robinson*, 4–6.

226 **"I am so grateful"**: *New York Daily News*, January 14, 1962; cited in Rampersad, *Jackie Robinson*, 361.

226 **Among the crowd attending**: Tygiel, *The Jackie Robinson Reader*, 220.

226 **Robinson was selected**: *Boston Globe*, January 26, 1962.

227 **At the induction**: http://baseballhall.org/discover/remembering-jackie, accessed November 11, 2015.

227 **Not long after the induction**: Long, *First Class Citizenship*, 150.

227 **Robinson's Hall of Fame plaque**: http://baseballhall.org/discover/remembering-jackie, accessed November 12, 2015.

227 **The next year**: Jackie Robinson with Duckett, *Baseball Has Done It*, 26.

227 **Between 1965 and 1972:** Pederson, *Jackie Robinson*, 89.

228 **After he died:** Rampersad, *Jackie Robinson*, 462.

228 **Toward the end of his life:** G. D. Johnson, *Profiles in Hue*, 290.

228 **He became a drug counselor:** Jackie Robinson with Duckett, *I Never Had It Made*, 245.

228 **On June 17, 1971:** Falkner, *Great Time Coming*, 338.

228 **Robinson turned down requests:** *Los Angeles Times*, October 19, 1997.

228 **The Dodgers could honor him:** *Los Angeles Times*, October 19, 1997.

229 **Robinson made one final public appearance:** Kahn, *Rickey & Robinson*, 274–75.

229 **Irving Rudd, one-time publicist:** *Los Angeles Times*, October 24, 1999.

229 **In part he said:** Linge, *Jackie Robinson*, 149.

230 **In a tribute to Robinson:** Williams with Sielski, *How to Be like Jackie Robinson*, 194–95.

27. Their Legacy

231 **"A life is not important":** Pederson, *Jackie Robinson*, 94.

231 **As the *Los Angeles Times* put it:** *Los Angeles Times*, September 30, 1998.

231 **Dr. Martin Luther King:** https://kinginstitute.stanford.edu/our-god-marching, accessed January 18, 2015.

231 **Jim Murray:** *Los Angeles Times*, March 26, 1991.

232 **What would Robinson say:** *Los Angeles Times*, October 19, 1997.

232 **Robinson's efforts:** *Boston Globe*, March 2, 2005.

232 **According to historian Doris Kearns Goodwin:** Williams with Sielski, *How to Be like Jackie Robinson*, 212.

232 **Lester Rodney:** http://www.thisgreatgame.com/lester-rodney.html, accessed November 17, 2015.

232 **Robinson stressed:** Jackie Robinson with Duckett, *I Never Had It Made*, 95.

232 **Close friends like Dodgers teammate Don Newcombe:** http://m.mlb.com/news/article/28518376/, accessed January 18, 2016.

233 **Robinson changed issues:** Dorinson and Warmund, *Jackie Robinson*, 212.

233 **Perhaps a not so flattering legacy:** http://bleacherreport.com/articles/886332–50-most-hated-players-in-baseball-history, accessed November 21, 2015.

233 **After Robinson's death:** http://www.jackierobinson.org/impact/impact/, accessed November 7, 2015.

235 **A tribute to Robinson:** Email, Dr. Damion L. Thomas, museum curator of sports, Smithsonian National Museum of African-American History and Culture, November 16, 2015.

235 **Often described as a man of quiet determination:** http://www.tombradleylegacy.org/, accessed July 20, 2012.

235 **California state historian emeritus Kevin Starr:** *Los Angeles Times*, September 30, 1998.

235 **Although Bradley lost two races:** *Los Angeles Times*, June 13, 2015.

236 **In 2005 Antonio Villaraigosa**: http://www.tombradleylegacy.org/, accessed July 20, 2012.

236 **In 1993 Bradley participated**: http://www.tombradleylegacy.org/mission-accomplishment.html, accessed November 12, 2015.

236 **Here's how Strode saw his career**: Strode and Young, *Goal Dust*, 252.

237 **Author Terence Towles Canote**: http://mercurie.blogspot.com/2014/07/why-woody-strode-mattered.html, accessed November 15, 2015.

237 **Strode was inducted**: Strode and Young, *Goal Dust*, 254.

237 **Strode's son Kalai**: http://www.tcm.com/this-month/article/333896%7C0/Woody-Strode-8-5.html, accessed January 10, 2016.

238 **Kenny Washington could have been**: *Los Angeles Times*, October 11, 2011.

238 **Adam Rank, an NFL media writer**: http://www.nfl.com/halloffame/story/0ap2000000341520/article/kenny-washington-belongs-in-the-hall-of-fame, accessed January 18, 2016.

239 **"He was a very proud man"**: http://www.stlouisrams.com/news-and-events/article-1/The-Legacy-of-Kenny-Washington/d6ba4c71-fa7b-4fd4-8209-fd44b84900b6, accessed November 7, 2015.

240 **Ray Bartlett's legacy**: http://www.pasadena.edu/about/history/alumni/bartlett/bartlett.cfm, accessed November 21, 2015.

240 **In 2008 Los Angeles County Supervisor Michael Antonovich**: *Pasadena Star-News*, June 25, 2008.

BIBLIOGRAPHY

Oral Histories

Bradley, Thomas. "The Impossible Dream." Transcript of interview by Bernard Galm, July 18, 1978. Department of Special Collections, Charles E. Young Research Library, University of California, Los Angeles.

Campbell, Robert, and Blanche Campbell. "Town and Gown Booksellers Oral History." Interview by Joel Gardner, University of California, Los Angeles, Oral History Project, 1980.

LuValle, James E. "Dr. James E. LuValle, 1936 Olympic Games, Berlin, 400-Meters, Bronze Medalist." Transcript of interview by George A. Hodak. Amateur Athletic Foundation, June 1988.

Published Works

Ackerman, William C. *My Fifty Year Love-in at UCLA*. Los Angeles: Fashion Press, 1969.

Allen, Maury. *Jackie Robinson: A Life Remembered*. New York: Franklin Watts, 1987.

Allison, Jay, and Dan Gediman with John Gregory and Viki Merrick. *This I Believe: The Personal Philosophies of Remarkable Men and Women*. New York: Holt, 2006.

Allswang, John M. "Tom Bradley of Los Angeles." *Southern California Quarterly* 74, no. 1 (Spring 1992): 55–105.

Angell, Roger. *This Old Man: All in Pieces*. New York: Doubleday, 2015.

Barber, Red. *1947: When All Hell Broke Loose in Baseball*. Boston: Da Capo Press, 1984.

Bishop, Ronald. "A Nod from Destiny: How Sportswriters for White and African-American Newspapers Covered Kenny Washington's Entry into the National Football League." *American Journalism* 19, no. 1 (June 3, 2013): 81–106.

Bogle, Donald. *Bright Boulevards, Bold Dreams: The Story of Black Hollywood*. New York: One World Ballantine Books, 1995.

Cohane, Tim. *Great College Football Coaches of the Twenties and Thirties*. New Rochelle NY: Arlington House, 1973.

Cottrell, Robert C. *Two Pioneers: How Hank Greenberg and Jackie Robinson Transformed Baseball and America*. Washington DC: Potomac, 2012.

Covey, Cyclone. *The Wow Boys: The Story of Stanford's Historic 1940 Football Season, Game by Game*. New York: Exposition Press, 1957.

Demas, Lane: *Integrating the Gridiron: Black Civil Rights and American College Football*. New Brunswick NJ: Rutgers University Press, 2010.

———. "On the Threshold of Broad and Rich Football Pastures in Integrated College Football at UCLA, 1938–41." In *Horsehide, Pigskin, Oval Tracks and Apple Pie: Essays on Sports and American Culture*, ed. James A. Vlasich, 86–103. Jefferson NC: McFarland, 2005.

———. "Sports History, Race and the College Gridiron, a Southern California Turning Point." *Southern California Quarterly* 89, no. 2 (Summer 2007): 163–93.

Denenberg, Barry. *Stealing Home: The Story of Jackie Robinson*. New York: Scholastic, 1990.

Dorinson, Joseph, and Joram Warmund. *Jackie Robinson: Race, Sports, and the American Dream*. Armonk NY: Sharp, 1998.

Eig, Jonathan. *Opening Day: The Story of Jackie Robinson's First Season*. New York: Simon and Schuster, 2007.

Federal Writers Project of the Works Progress Administration. *Los Angeles in the 1930s: The WPA Guide to the City of Angels*. Berkeley: University of California Press, 2011.

Falkner, David. *Great Time Coming: The Life of Jackie Robinson from Baseball to Birmingham*. New York: Simon and Schuster, 1995.

Flamming, Douglas. *Bound for Freedom: Black Los Angeles in Jim Crow America*. Berkeley: University of California Press, 2005.

Gates, Henry Louis, and Evelyn Brooks Higginbotham, eds. *African American Lives*. New York: Oxford University Press, 2004.

Hamilton, Andrew, and John B. Jackson. *UCLA on the Move during Fifty Golden Years 1919–1969*. Los Angeles: Ward Ritchie Press, 1969.

Johnson, George D. *Profiles in Hue*. Bloomington IN: Xlibris, 2011.

Johnson, James W. *The Wow Boys: A Coach, a Team, and a Turning Point in College Football*. Lincoln: University of Nebraska Press, 2006.

Kahn, Roger. *The Boys of Summer*. New York: Harper Perennial Modern Classics, 2006.

———. *Rickey & Robinson: The True Untold Story of the Integration of Baseball*. New York, Rodale, 2014.

Kaliss, Gregory John. *Everyone's All-Americans: Race, Men's College Athletics, and the Ideal of Equal Opportunity*. Durham: University of North Carolina Press, 2008.

Kemper, Kurt Edward. *College Football and American Culture in the Cold War Era*. Urbana: University of Illinois Press, 2009.

Lamb, Chris. *Conspiracy of Silence: Sportswriters and the Long Campaign to Desegregate Baseball*. Lincoln: University of Nebraska Press, 2012.

Levy, Alan H. *Tackling Jim Crow: Racial Segregation in Professional Football*. Jefferson NC: McFarland, 2003.

Linge, Mary Kay. *Jackie Robinson: A Biography*. Westport CT: Greenwood, 2007.

Lomax, Michael. "Jackie Robinson: Racial Pioneer and Athlete Extraordinaire in an Era of Change." In *Out of the Shadows: A Biographical History of African*

American Athletes, ed. David K. Wiggins, 162–79. Fayetteville: University of Arkansas Press.

Long, Michael G., ed. *Beyond Home Plate: Jackie Robinson on Life after Baseball.* Syracuse NY: Syracuse University Press, 2013.

——, ed. *First Class Citizenship: The Civil Rights Letters of Jackie Robinson.* New York: Times Books, 2007.

Manchel, Frank. "The Man Who Made the Stars Shine Brighter: An Interview with Woody Strode." *Black Scholar* 25, no. 2 (Spring 1995): 37–46.

——. *Every Step a Struggle: Interviews with Seven Who Shaped the African-American Image in Movies.* Washington DC: New Academia Publishing, 2007

Mann, Arthur. *The Jackie Robinson Story.* New York: Grosset and Dunlap, 1950.

——. "Say Jack Robinson: Meet the Dodgers' New Recruit." *Colliers*, March 2, 1946, 67–68.

Mantle, Mickey, and Robert Creamer. *The Quality of Courage: Heroes in and out of Baseball.* Lincoln: University of Nebraska Press, Bison Books, 1999.

Martin, Charles. *Benching Jim Crow: The Rise and Fall of the Color Line in Southern College Sports, 1890-1980.* Champaign: University of Illinois Press, 2010.

McBride, Joseph. *Searching for John Ford: A Life.* New York: St. Martin's, Griffin, 2003.

McRae, Donald. *Heroes without a Country: America's Betrayal of Joe Louis and Jesse Owens.* New York: HarperCollins, 2002.

Moffi, Larry. *Crossing the Line: Black Major Leaguers, 1947-1959.* Lincoln: University of Nebraska Press, Bison Books, 2006.

Morehouse, M. Maggie. *Fighting in the Jim Crow Army: Black Men and Women Remember World War II.* Lanham MD: Rowman and Littlefield, 2006.

Neuberger, Richard L. "Purity League." *Collier's*, November 9, 1940, 18–63, 64–66.

Oliphant, Thomas. *Praying for Gil Hodges: A Memoir of the 1955 World Series and One Family's Love of the Brooklyn Dodgers.* New York: Thomas Dunn, 2005.

Oriard, Michael. *King Football, Sport and Spectacle in the Golden Age of Radio and Newsreels, Movies and Magazines, the Weekly and the Daily Press.* Chapel Hill: University of North Carolina Press, 2001.

Payne, J. Gregory, and Scott C. Ratzan, *Tom Bradley: The Impossible Dream.* Santa Monica CA: Roundtable Publishing, 1986.

Pederson, Charles E. *Jackie Robinson: Baseball Great and Civil Rights Activist.* Edina MN: Abdo, 2009.

Peterson, Robert. *Only the Ball Was White: A History of Legendary Black Players and All-Black Professional Teams.* New York: Gramercy Books, 1970.

——. *Pigskin: The Early Years of Pro Football,* New York: Oxford University Press, 1997.

Piascik, Andy. *Gridiron Gauntlet: The Story of the Men Who Integrated Pro Football in Their Own Words.* New York: Taylor Trade Publishing, 2009.

Rampersad, Arnold. *Jackie Robinson: A Biography.* New York: Ballantine Books, 1997.

Riordan, Jim. *The International Politics of Sport of the Twentieth Century.* New York: Routledge, 1999.

Roberts, Chris, and Bill Bennett. *UCLA Football Vault: The History of the Bruins.* Atlanta: Whitman Publishing, 2008.

Robinson, Jackie, with Alfred Duckett. *Baseball Has Done It*. Brooklyn: Ig Publishing, 2005.

———. *I Never Had It Made: An Autobiography of Jackie Robinson*. New York: HarperCollins Books, 1995.

———. "Now I Know Why They Boo Me." *Look*, January 25, 1955, 23–28.

———. "Why I'm Quitting Baseball." *Look*, January 9, 1957, 99–102.

Robinson, James Lee, Jr. *Tom Bradley: Los Angeles's First Black Mayor*. Los Angeles: University of California, 1976.

Robinson, Rachel, with Lee Daniels. *Jackie Robinson: An Intimate Portrait*. New York: Abrams Publishing, 1996.

Robinson, Sharon. *Promises to Keep: How Jackie Robinson Changed America*. New York: Scholastic Press, 2004.

Ross, Charles K. *Outside the Lines: African-Americans and the Integration of the National Football League*. New York: New York University Press, 2001.

Rowan, Carl T., with Jackie Robinson. *Wait Till Next Year*. New York: Random House, 1960.

Rudd, Irvin, and Stan Fischler. *The Sporting Life: The Duke and Jackie, Pee Wee, Razor Phil, Ali, Mushky Jackson and Me*. New York: St. Martin's Press, 1990.

Sides, Josh. *L.A. City Limits: African-American Los Angeles from the Great Depression to the Present*. Berkeley: University of California Press, 2003.

Silber, Irwin. *Press Box Red: The Story of Lester Rodney, the Communist Who Helped Break the Color Line in American Sports*. Philadelphia: Temple University Press, 2003.

Simon, Scott. *Jackie Robinson and the Integration of Baseball*. Hoboken NJ: Wiley and Sons, 2002.

Smith, Thomas G. *Showdown: JFK and the Integration of the Washington Redskins*. Boston: Beacon Press, 2011.

———. "Outside the Pale: The Exclusion of Blacks from the National Football League, 1934–1946." In *From Jack Johnson to LeBron James: Sports, Media, and the Color Line*, ed. Chris Lamb, 117–47. Lincoln: University of Nebraska Press, 2016. www.jstor.org/stable/j.ctt1d9nhwr.28.

Sonenshein, Raphael J. *Politics in Black and White: Race and Power in Los Angeles*. Princeton NJ: Princeton University Press, 1993.

Springer, Steve, and Michael Arkush. *60 Years of USC-UCLA Football*. Stamford CT: Longmeadow Publishing, 1991.

Starr, Kevin. *Coast of Dreams: California on the Edge, 1990–2003*. New York: Knopf, 2004.

———. *The Dream Endures: California Enters the 1940s*. New York: Oxford University Press, 1997.

———. *Embattled Dreams: California in War and Peace, 1940–1950*. New York: Oxford University Press, 2002.

Stout, Christopher T. *Bringing Race Back In: Black Politicians, Deracialization, and Voting Behavior in the Age of Obama*. Charlottesville VA: University of Virginia Press, 2005.

Strode, Woody, and Sam Young. *Goal Dust: The Warm and Candid Memoirs of a Pioneer Black Athlete and Actor.* New York: Madison Books, 1990.

Swain, Rick. *The Black Stars Who Made Baseball Whole: The Jackie Robinson Generation in the Major Leagues.* Jefferson NC: McFarland, 2006.

Thomas, Evan. *Being Nixon: A Man Divided.* New York: Random House, 2015.

Tygiel, Jules. *Baseball's Great Experiment: Jackie Robinson and His Legacy.* New York: Oxford University Press, 1983.

———. *Extra Bases: Reflections on Jackie Robinson, Race, and Baseball History.* Lincoln: University of Nebraska Press, 2002.

———, ed. *The Jackie Robinson Reader: Perspectives on an American Hero.* New York: Penguin Books, 1997.

Van Leuven, Hendrik. *Touchdown UCLA: The Complete Account of Bruin Football.* Huntsville AL: Strode Publishing, 1982.

Watterson, John Sayle. *College Football: History, Spectacle, Controversy.* Baltimore: Johns Hopkins University Press, 2000.

Wiggins, David K., and Patrick B. Miller. *The Unlevel Playing Field: A Documentary History of the African-American Experience in Sport.* Urbana: University of Illinois Press, 2003.

Wilkins, Roy. "Wrong Color." *Crisis*, January 1940, 17.

Williams, Pat, with Mike Sielski. *How to Be like Jackie Robinson: Life Lessons from Baseball's Greatest Hero.* Deerfield Beach FL: Health Communications, 2005.

Wilson, John R. M. *Jackie Robinson and the American Dilemma.* New York: Longman, 2010.

Young, A. S. (Doc). "Pro Football Discovers the Black College." *Ebony*, September 1970.

INDEX